AN INTRODUCTION TO FORD MADOX FORD

For students and readers new to the work of Ford Madox Ford, this volume provides a comprehensive introduction to one of the most complex, important and fascinating authors. Bringing together leading Ford scholars, the volume places Ford's work in the context of significant literary, artistic and historical events and movements. Individual essays consider Ford's theory of literary Impressionism and the impact of the First World War; illuminate *The Good Soldier* and *Parade's End*; engage with topics such as the city, gender, national identity and politics; discuss Ford as an autobiographer, poet, propagandist, sociologist, Edwardian and modernist; and show his importance as founding editor of the groundbreaking *English Review* and *transatlantic review*. The volume encourages detailed close reading of Ford's writing and illustrates the importance of engaging with secondary sources.

Ashley Chantler is Senior Lecturer in English at the University of Chester and Rob Hawkes is Senior Lecturer in English at Teesside University, UK.

T0331299

An Introduction to Ford Madox Ford

EDITED BY

ASHLEY CHANTLER
University of Chester, UK

&

ROB HAWKES
Teesside University, UK

Routledge
Taylor & Francis Group

LONDON AND NEW YORK

First published 2015 by Ashgate Publishing

2 Park Square, Milton Park, Abingdon, Oxfordshire OX14 4RN
52 Vanderbilt Avenue, New York, NY 10017

Routledge is an imprint of the Taylor & Francis Group, an informa business

First issued in paperback 2019

British Library Cataloguing in Publication Data
A catalogue record for this book is available from the British Library

The Library of Congress has cataloged the printed edition as follows:
An introduction to Ford Madox Ford / edited by Ashley Chantler and Rob Hawkes.
   pages cm
   Includes bibliographical references and index.
   ISBN 978-1-4724-6908-3 (hardcover) -- ISBN 978-1-4724-6909-0 (ebook) -- ISBN 978-1-4724-6910-6 (epub) 1. Ford, Ford Madox, 1873-1939--Criticism and interpretation. I. Chantler, Ashley, editor. II. Hawkes, Rob, editor.
   PR6011.O53Z69 2015
   823'.912--dc23

                                                                    2015015338

ISBN 13: 978-1-4724-6908-3 (hbk)
ISBN 13: 978-0-367-88121-4 (pbk)

Contents

Notes on Contributors

John Attridge is Senior Lecturer in English at the University of New South Wales, Sydney. His essays on modern literature include: '"I Don't Read Novels... I Know What's in 'em": Impersonality, Impressionism and Responsibility in *Parade's End*' (in *Impersonality and Emotion in Twentieth-Century British Literature*, Université Montpellier III, 2005); '"We Will Listen to None But Specialists": Ford, the Rise of Specialization, and the *English Review*' (in *Ford Madox Ford: Literary Networks and Cultural Transformations*, Rodopi, 2008); 'Steadily and Whole: Ford Madox Ford and Modernist Sociology' (in *Modernism/modernity*, 2008); 'Liberalism and Modernism in the Edwardian Era: New Liberals at Ford's *English Review* (in *Ford Madox Ford, Modernist Magazines and Editing*, Rodopi, 2010); "The Yellow-Dog Thing": Joseph Conrad, Verisimilitude and Professionalism' (in *ELH*, 2010); 'Nonsense, Ordinary Language Philosophy and Flann O'Brien's *The Third Policeman*' (in *Modern Fiction Studies*, 2014); and 'Taciturnity and Englishness in *Parade's End* and André Maurois' *Les Silence du Colonel Bramble* (in *Ford Madox Ford's Parade's End: The First World War, Culture, and Modernity*, Rodopi, 2014). He is co-editor of *Incredible Modernism: Literature, Trust and Deception* (Ashgate, 2013).

Christine Berberich is Senior Lecturer in Twentieth- and Twenty-First-Century Literature at the University of Portsmouth. She has published widely on Englishness and national identity formation, as well as authors as diverse as Ford, Barnes, Fleming, Hawes, Orwell, Sebald, Seiffert, and Waugh. She is author of *The Image of the English Gentleman in Twentieth-Century Literature: Englishness and Nostalgia* (Ashgate, 2007); editor of *The Bloomsbury Introduction to Popular Fiction* (Bloomsbury Continuum, 2014); and co-editor of *These Englands: A Conversation on National Identity* (Manchester University Press, 2011), *Land and Identity: Theory, Memory, and Practice* (Rodopi, 2012), and *Affective Landscapes in Literature, Art and Everyday Life* (Ashgate, 2015).

Isabelle Brasme is Senior Lecturer in British Literature and head of the English Undergraduate Program at the University of Nîmes, and a member of the EMMA research team at the University of Montpellier. She has published articles on Ford's novels in relation to war writing and musical modernism. Her essays include: 'Between Impressionism and Modernism: *Some Do Not . . .*, a Poetics of the *Entre-deux*' (in *Ford Madox Ford: Literary Networks and Cultural Transformations*, Rodopi, 2008); '"A caricature of his own voice": Ford and Self-Editing in *Parade's End*' (in *Ford Madox Ford, Modernist Magazines and Editing*, Rodopi, 2010); 'Towards an Ethics of Singularity: The Shattered Mirror of Identity in Ford

Madox Ford's *Parade's End'* (in *Ethics of Alterity in British Literature*, Present Perfect Publications, Universitaires de La Méditerranée, 2013); 'Articulations of Femininity in *Parade's End* (in *Ford Madox Ford's Parade's End: The First World War, Culture, and Modernity*, Rodopi, 2014); and 'Musicality in Ford Madox Ford's *Parade's End*: Towards Modernity' (in *Musical Modernism: Essays on Language and Music in Modernist Literature*, University of Notre Dame Press, forthcoming). She has recently completed a monograph on the aesthetics of crisis in *Parade's End* (forthcoming).

Ashley Chantler is Senior Lecturer in English at the University of Chester. He is the series editor of *Character Studies* (Continuum); author of *Heart of Darkness: Character Studies* (Continuum, 2008); and co-editor of *Translation Practices: Through Language to Culture* (Rodopi, 2009), *Studying English Literature* (Continuum 2010), and *Literature and Authenticity, 1780–1900* (Ashgate, 2011). His essays include: 'Ford's Pre-War Poetry and the "Rotting City"' (in *Ford Madox Ford and the City*, Rodopi, 2005); 'Ford and the Impressionist Lyric' (in *Ford Madox Ford and Visual Culture*, Rodopi, 2009); 'Editing Ford's Poetry' (in *Ford Madox Ford, Modernist Magazines and Editing*, Rodopi, 2010); 'Ford Madox Ford and the Troubadours' (in *Ford Madox Ford, France and Provence*, Rodopi, 2011); and '"In This Dead-Dawning Century": Ford Madox Ford's Edwardian Poetry' (in *The Edwardian Ford Madox Ford*, Rodopi, 2013). With Rob Hawkes, he is co-editor of *Ford Madox Ford's Parade's End: The First World War, Culture, and Modernity* (Rodopi, 2014) and *War and the Mind: Ford Madox Ford's Parade's End, Modernism, and Psychology* (Edinburgh University Press, 2015).

Laura Colombino is Associate Professor in English at the University of Genova, Italy. Her major research interests are in post-1900 and contemporary fiction and culture, with a longstanding focus on the inter-art analogy and transdisciplinary studies. She is author of *Ford Madox Ford: Vision, Visuality and Writing* (Peter Lang, 2008) and *Spatial Politics in Contemporary London Literature: Writing Architecture and the Body* (Routledge, 2013); editor of *Ford Madox Ford and Visual Culture* (Rodopi, 2009); and co-editor of *The Edwardian Ford Madox Ford* (Rodopi, 2013). Further publications include chapters and articles on Robert Byron, Hardy, Huxley, and the urban imaginary and spatial metaphors in twentieth-century British literature. Her essays on this topic include 'The Imagination of Space: Ford Madox Ford and France' (in *Franco-British Cultural Exchanges, 1880–1940: Channel Packets*, Palgrave Macmillan, 2012).

Andrew Frayn is Lecturer in English at Edinburgh Napier University. He is author of *Writing Disenchantment: British First World War Prose, 1914–1930* (Manchester University Press, 2014) and has previously published on *Parade's End* and the war in *Ford Madox Ford: Literary Networks and Cultural Transformations* (Rodopi, 2008). He also edits the *New Canterbury Literary Society Newsletter*, which gives information about Richard Aldington; he has published several pieces on Aldington, including an article in *Modernist Cultures* on his Imagist poetry and ideas of 'the masses'. A chapter on C.E. Montague is in *The Silent Morning: Culture and Memory After the Armistice* (Manchester University Press, 2013), and he has written on memory and the First World War for the *Guardian*. He is secretary of the Ford Madox Ford Society.

Andrzej Gąsiorek is Professor and Head of the English Department at the University of Birmingham. He has published numerous articles and chapters on modernist writers, and is author of *Post-War British Fiction* (Edward Arnold, 1995), *Wyndham Lewis* (Northcote House, 2003), and *J.G. Ballard* (Manchester University Press, 2005). He is also co-editor of *T.E. Hulme and the Question of Modernism* (Ashgate, 2006), *Ford Madox Ford: Literary Networks and Cultural Transformations* (Rodopi, 2008), *The Oxford Handbook of Modernisms* (Oxford University Press, 2010), *The Oxford History of the Novel in English – Vol. 4: The Reinvention of the British Novel 1880–1940* (Oxford University Press, 2011), and *Wyndham Lewis and the Cultures of Modernity* (Ashgate, 2011). He is editor of the *Journal of Wyndham Lewis Studies*.

Sara Haslam is Senior Lecturer in English at the Open University. She is author of *Fragmenting Modernism: Ford Madox Ford, the Novel and the Great War* (Manchester University Press, 2002); editor of Ford's *The Good Soldier* (Wordsworth Classics, 2010) and *England and the English* (Carcanet Press, 2003), as well as *Ford Madox Ford and the City* (Rodopi, 2005); and co-editor of *Ford Madox Ford and America* (Rodopi, 2012). Her annotated critical edition of Ford's *A Man Could Stand Up –* was published in 2010 (Carcanet Press). Further publications include *Life Writing* (Routledge, 2009, with Derek Neale), and chapters and articles on the Brontës, Hardy, James, modernism, and the literature of the First World War, most recently 'From Conversation to Humiliation: *Parade's End* and the Eighteenth Century' (in *Ford Madox Ford's Parade's End: The First World War, Culture, and Modernity*, Rodopi, 2014). She is chair of the Ford Madox Ford Society.

Rob Hawkes is Senior Lecturer in English at Teesside University. He is author of *Ford Madox Ford and the Misfit Moderns: Edwardian Fiction and the First World War* (Palgrave Macmillan, 2012). His essays include: 'Personalities of Paper: Characterisation in *A Call* and *The Good Soldier*' (in *Ford Madox Ford: Literary Networks and Cultural Transformations*, Rodopi, 2008); 'Visuality vs. Temporality: Plotting and Depiction in *The Fifth Queen* and *Ladies Whose Bright Eyes*' (in *Ford Madox Ford and Visual Culture*, Rodopi, 2009); and 'Trusting in Provence: Financial Crisis in *The Rash Act* and *Henry for Hugh*' (in *Ford Madox Ford, France and Provence*, Rodopi, 2011). With Ashley Chantler, he is co-editor of *Ford Madox Ford's Parade's End: The First World War, Culture, and Modernity* (Rodopi, 2014) and *War and the Mind: Ford Madox Ford's Parade's End, Modernism, and Psychology* (Edinburgh University Press, 2015).

Seamus O'Malley is English Lecturer at Stern College for Women, Yeshiva University. He is author of *Making History New: Modernism and Historical Narrative* (Oxford University Press, 2014) and co-editor of *Ford Madox Ford and America* (Rodopi, 2012). He has published articles on D.H. Lawrence, Frank McGuinness, Alan Moore, Stevenson, Rebecca West, Edmund Wilson, and Yeats. His essays on Ford include: '*The Return of the Soldier* and *Parade's End*: Ford's Reworking of West's Pastoral' (in *Ford Madox Ford's Literary Contacts*, Rodopi, 2007); 'The Ferociously Odd, Mutually Beneficial Editorial Relationship of Ford Madox Ford and Wyndham Lewis' (in *Ford Madox Ford, Modernist Magazines and Editing*, Rodopi, 2010); 'America's Ford: Glenway Wescott, Katherine Anne Porter, and Knopf's *Parade's End*' (in *Ford Madox Ford and America*, Rodopi, 2012); 'Nostalgia and Its Discontents: Ford Madox Ford's *The Fifth Queen*' (in *The Edwardian Ford Madox Ford*, Rodopi, 2013); 'Listening for Class in Ford Madox Ford's *Parade's End*' (in *Modernism/modernity*, 2014); and 'How Much Mud Does a Man Need? Land and Liquidity in *Parade's End*' (in *Ford Madox Ford's Parade's End: The First World War, Culture, and Modernity*, Rodopi, 2014).

Stephen Rogers was Research Fellow for the Modernist Magazines Project. He has published a number of essays on modernist periodicals, including: 'Nostalgia and Reaction' (in *Oxford Critical and Cultural History of Modernist Magazines: Britain and Ireland, 1880–1955*, Oxford University Press, 2009, 2013); and on 'Bruno's Bohemia' and 'Village Voices' (in *Oxford Critical and Cultural History of Modernist Magazines: North America, 1894–1960* (Oxford University Press, 2012). He has also published on Laura Riding Jackson in *Revues modernistes, revues engages (1900–1939)* (Rennes, 2011). His essays on Ford include: '*A Royal Personage in Disguise*: A Meeting Between Ford Madox Ford and John Cowper Powys' (in *Ford Madox Ford's Literary Contacts*, Rodopi, 2007); 'The *transatlantic review*' (in *Ford Madox Ford, Modernist Magazines and Editing*, Rodopi, 2010); 'North and South: Ford Madox Ford's American Journalism During the Depression' (in *Ford Madox Ford and America*, Rodopi, 2012); and 'Ford Madox Ford's *English Review* and the Launching of Modernism' (in *Letteratura e Letterature*, 2014).

Max Saunders is Director of the Arts and Humanities Research Institute, Professor of English and Co-Director of the Centre for Life-Writing Research at King's College London. He is author of *Ford Madox Ford: A Dual Life*, 2 vols (Oxford University Press, 1996) and *Self Impression: Life-Writing, Autobiografiction, and the Forms of Modern Literature* (Oxford University Press, 2010); the editor of Ford's *Selected Poems, War Prose, Some Do Not . . .*, and (with Richard Stang) *Critical Essays* (Carcanet Press, 1997, 1999, 2010, 2002), and of the Oxford World's Classics edition of *The Good Soldier* (2012). He has published essays on life writing, Impressionism, Ford, Aldington, Burgess, Conrad, Eliot, Forster, Freud, James, Joyce, Lawrence, Lehmann, Pound, Ruskin, Sinclair, and others. He is general editor of International Ford Madox Ford Studies.

Paul Skinner edited Ford Madox Ford's *No Enemy* for Carcanet Press (2002) and *Ford Madox Ford's Literary Contacts* (Rodopi, 2007). His annotated critical edition of Ford's *Last Post* was published by Carcanet Press in 2011. He has published essays on Ezra Pound and Rudyard Kipling; and essays on Ford in several volumes of International Ford Madox Ford Studies, the latest being 'Tietjens Walking, Ford Talking' (in *Ford Madox Ford's Parade's End: The First World War, Culture, and Modernity*, Rodopi, 2014). He is treasurer of the Ford Madox Ford Society.

Martin Stannard is Professor of Modern English Literature at the University of Leicester. He has published extensively on Evelyn Waugh, following *The Critical Heritage* (1984) with a major biography in two volumes (1986 and 1992). His Norton Critical Edition of Ford's *The Good Soldier* (1995, revised 2012) is an experiment in textual editing which includes material engaging with the challenge of literary theory to traditional editorial practice, and with the phenomenon of literary Impressionism. He edited a 37-volume Ashgate series with Professor Greg Walker, *Studies in European Cultural Transition* (2000–2007). *Muriel Spark: The Biography* followed in 2009. Since 2011, he has been Co-Executive Editor with Professor David Bradshaw of OUP's *The Complete Works of Evelyn Waugh* (42 volumes). He has also published essays and review-essays on Kingsley Amis, Arlen, Dickens, David Garnett, Greene, Gerhardie, Isherwood, and Larkin, and on the subjects of textual criticism, biography, autobiography, and letters.

Angus Wrenn teaches English and Comparative Literature at the London School of Economics (University of London). His books include *Henry James and the Second Empire* (Legenda, 2009) and (with Olga Soboleva) *The Only Hope of the World: George Bernard Shaw and Russia* (Peter Lang, 2012). He contributed the chapter on Paul Bourget and Marcel Proust in *The Reception of Henry James in Europe* (Continuum, 2006) and has published a recent chapter, 'Some Allusions in the Early Stories', in *Henry James's Europe* (Openbook, 2011) as well as the chapter on Henry James in *The Cambridge Companion to the European Novel* (Cambridge University Press, 2012). His publications on Ford include: 'Henry, Hueffer, Holbein, History and Representation' (in *History and Representation in Ford Madox Ford's Writings*, Rodopi, 2004); 'Angle of Elevation: Social Class, Transport and Perception of the City' (in *Ford Madox Ford and the City*, Rodopi, 2005); '"Long Letters about Ford Madox Ford": Ford's Afterlife in the Work of Harold Pinter' (in *Ford Madox Ford's Literary Contacts*, Rodopi, 2007); and 'Wagner's *Ring* Cycle and *Parade's End*' (in *Ford Madox Ford's Parade's End: The First World War, Culture, and Modernity*, Rodopi, 2014).

Acknowledgements

We would first like to thank our brilliant contributors, mainly for their excellent chapters, which realised our aims for this volume, but also for their patience. All at Ashgate involved in getting the book to press were a pleasure to work with; Ann Donahue's perfect support, ideas and guidance were invaluable. Thank you, thank you. We are sincerely grateful to Jason Andrew, the estate of Janice Biala and Tibor de Nagy Gallery, New York, for permission to reproduce the cover image, *Portrait of a Writer (Ford Madox Ford)* (1938). Biala was Ford's late-in-life love and it seemed right to use one of her many great works on a volume about a writer of many great works. We are grateful to our universities for supporting the book; thanks in particular are due to Chris Walsh (University of Chester) and Gerda Roper (Teesside University). Finally, many thanks to Nanette and Ruth for, well, so much – and to Charlie and Rose for welcome interruptions, big and small.

Introduction:
The Brilliant Ford Madox Ford

Ashley Chantler and Rob Hawkes

Ford – Then

Ford Madox Ford (1873–1939) ignored his father's advice to 'never write a book'[1] and went on to become one of the most engaging, important and influential authors of the twentieth century. From 1891 to 1939, he published over eighty books, including novels, poetry collections, art and literary criticism, historical and sociological surveys, war 'propaganda', biographies, reminiscences and illustrated children's stories; he also wrote introductions and prefaces for younger authors, including Ernest Hemingway and Jean Rhys, short stories for a wide range of literary periodicals, and significant articles and reviews, among them 'A Literary Causerie: On Some Tendencies of Modern Verse' (1905), 'On Impressionism' (1914), 'Les Jeunes and *Des Imagistes*' (1914) and '*Ulysses* and the Handling of Indecencies' (1922).[2] In response to *Ulysses* and perhaps T.S. Eliot's *The Waste Land* (both 1922), Ford wrote the wonderful *Mister Bosphorus and the Muses: Or a Short History of Poetry in Britain: Variety Entertainment in Four Acts: Words By Ford Madox Ford: Music By Several Popular Composers: With Harlequinade, Transformation Scene, Cinematograph Effects, and Many Other Novelties, As Well As Old and Tried Favourites* (1923). Ford's most widely-known works, *The Good Soldier* (1915) and *Parade's End* (1924–28), are acknowledged as modernist masterpieces, and the importance of his other writing and roles as an editor and mentor are increasingly receiving the recognition they deserve (see below).

Ford's grandfather was the Victorian painter Ford Madox Brown, about whom Ford wrote a biography and study in 1896, and he grew up in London surrounded by the Pre-Raphaelite Brotherhood, on which he wrote a critical monograph. In Kent at the turn of the century, Ford became friends with Stephen Crane, Henry James and H.G. Wells. He collaborated with Joseph Conrad on three novels, and later wrote *Joseph Conrad: A Personal Remembrance* (1924), which contains an elaboration of the writers' thoughts on literary Impressionism. In 1908, he founded

---

[1] Ford Madox Ford, *Ancient Lights and Certain New Reflections: Being the Memories of a Young Man* (London: Chapman and Hall, 1911), p. 156.

[2] See Ford Madox Ford, *Critical Writings of Ford Madox Ford*, ed. Frank MacShane (Lincoln: University of Nebraska Press, 1964) and *Critical Essays*, ed. Max Saunders and Richard Stang (Manchester: Carcanet Press, 2002).

the *English Review* and published Arnold Bennett, Rupert Brooke, Conrad, John Galsworthy, Thomas Hardy, James, Wells and W.B. Yeats, and several of the group Ford called '*les jeunes*': F.S. Flint, D.H. Lawrence, Wyndham Lewis (who later published Ford in *Blast* in 1914 and 1915 and illustrated the pamphlet of Ford's poem *Antwerp* in 1915) and Ezra Pound, who became a lifelong friend and published him in *Des Imagistes* (1914). Later, in Paris in 1924, Ford founded the *transatlantic review* and published Djuna Barnes, Jean Cocteau, e.e. cummings, H.D. (Hilda Doolittle), Flint, Hemingway, James Joyce (Ford coined the title 'Work in Progress' for the work-in-progress *Finnegans Wake*), John Dos Passos, Man Ray, Rhys, Gertrude Stein and Paul Valéry. In America in the 1930s, Ford was good friends with Allen Tate, Caroline Gordon and John Crowe Ransom, and he founded the Society of the Friends of William Carlos Williams, in order to help get Williams's poetry published. Members included Sherwood Anderson, W.H. Auden, cummings, Christopher Isherwood, Henry Miller, Marianne Moore, Charles Olson, Katherine Anne Porter and Ford's partner, the painter Janice Biala. In Boston in 1937, towards the end of his life, Ford met a twenty-year-old aspiring poet, Robert Lowell, who followed Ford to Tate and Gordon's house in Clarksville, then to Olivet College, Michigan, and finally to the University of Colorado, where Ford gave a lecture on 'The Literary Life'. Lowell later wrote the highly influential *Life Studies* (1959), in which Ford appears.

Ford – Now

Ford's posthumous appearance in *Life Studies* is not surprising: he was an important figure for Lowell. What is surprising is that it was not until the end of the twentieth century that Ford (beyond *The Good Soldier* and *Parade's End*) began to receive the critical attention he warranted. True, articles, chapters and monographs on Ford were written before then; several biographies were published, including Arthur Mizener's *The Saddest Story: A Biography of Ford Madox Ford* (1971), and several volumes of letters, among them *Pound/Ford: The Story of a Literary Friendship* (1982); Frank MacShane edited *Ford Madox Ford: The Critical Heritage* (1972) and Sondra J. Stang edited *The Presence of Ford Madox Ford* (1981) and *The Ford Madox Ford Reader* (1986). But, for whatever reason, these didn't radically change the landscape of early twentieth-century English literary studies.

An important stage in the history of Ford's critical reception came in 1995, when *The Good Soldier*, edited by Martin Stannard, was published as a Norton Critical Edition. This gave scholars a better understanding of literary Impressionism (about which many had previously been silent or sceptical) and showed how Ford's fiction and theory linked to James's and Conrad's. But the main person we have to thank for Ford's current standing as a major figure in twentieth-century literature and culture is Max Saunders. In 1996, Saunders published his two-volume biography, *Ford Madox Ford: A Dual Life*, with

Oxford University Press. This set the agenda for the scholarly work on Ford that has followed in the (almost) two decades since its publication, as well as paving the way for the wider appreciation of Ford and his writing in the world beyond academia. While the critical landscape, especially in modernist studies, has shifted markedly since 1996 – with a plurality of modernisms and the roles of gender, geography, national identity, politics and little magazines increasingly recognised – Saunders's seminal work remains an indispensable reference point for Ford studies and, indeed, continues to resonate with the concerns that have come to the fore in twentieth-century literary studies since it first appeared. The following year, Saunders founded the Ford Madox Ford Society and, soon after, the International Ford Madox Ford Studies series (IFMFS; published by Rodopi to 2014, now by Brill / Rodopi): the Society's annual conferences (which have been held in Britain, France, Germany, Italy and the United States) have laid the groundwork and inspired many of the topics for subsequent IFMFS volumes. The first volume in the series is the aptly titled *Ford Madox Ford: A Reappraisal* (2002); to date, fourteen volumes have been published (see 'Guide to Further Reading'). Saunders was also important in the founding of Carcanet Press's Millennium Ford series, which has reprinted several key works by Ford, including *England and the English* (1907), *No Enemy: A Tale of Reconstruction* (1929), *Return to Yesterday* (1931), *The Rash Act* (1933), *It Was the Nightingale* (1934) and *Provence: From Minstrels to the Machine* (1935). In the series is also *Selected Poems* (1997) and collections of Ford's *War Prose* (1999) and *Critical Essays* (2002). In 2010–11, *Parade's End* was published by Carcanet as a four-volume critical edition, providing for the first time reliable texts, detailed annotations and discussions of the textual histories.

Today, Ford is known by an audience beyond colleges and universities. In August–September 2012, the BBC screened a five-part television adaptation of *Parade's End*, scripted by Tom Stoppard, directed by Susanna White, and starring Benedict Cumberbatch, Rebecca Hall, Adelaide Clemens, Rupert Everett and Miranda Richardson. It has now been screened, or is due to be screened, in over thirty-five countries around the world, including Australia, Bulgaria, Canada, China, France, Germany, Hungary, Iceland, Ireland, Italy, Japan, Poland, Portugal, Russia, South Africa, Spain, Sweden, Turkey and the USA. A DVD has been released, the soundtrack is available and the script has been published by Faber and Faber. To coincide with the adaptation, the BBC also screened *Who On Earth Was Ford Madox Ford? A Culture Show Special*, written, produced and directed by Rupert Edwards, and featuring, among others, scholar and Ford Society Chair Sara Haslam, biographers Alan Judd and Hermione Lee, chef Rowley Leigh (who cooked one of Ford's recipes) and Booker Prize-winning novelist Ben Okri, along with Max Saunders and Tom Stoppard.

As a reader of Ford's endlessly fascinating writing, you are now part of the growing international Fordian community. Welcome.

An Introduction to Ford Madox Ford

The key aim of this volume is to provide those encountering Ford for the first time – or, perhaps, returning to Ford, interested to find out more – with a comprehensive introduction to the life and work of one of the most complex and rewarding (yet, at times, baffling) modern authors. The fourteen chapters are written by Ford experts and they explore his diverse body of work (though of course not all of it!), consider his links to other authors and position his writing in various contexts. Also illuminated are Ford's thoughts on gender, politics, the urban experience, national identity, art and literature, all from a range of perspectives, notably his theory of literary Impressionism, and his roles as a critic, social commentator, editor and mentor during a time of major social, political and cultural change.

As well as helping you get a better understanding of Ford, we hope that the volume also encourages you to be a slow reader: to take your time with Ford's words. He, like all great writers, demands close attention to every sentence, every paragraph, and a critical pondering, a wondering about, a questioning. Look, for example, at the very end of *The Good Soldier*. Given what Dowell has repeatedly said about Ashburnham throughout the course of the novel, his use of 'trotted' – 'so I trotted off'[3] – is surely rather unexpected? But perhaps it isn't. Either way, one word demands critical engagement; one word might complicate much that precedes it. We also hope that the volume inspires you to make connections, between words, sentences, paragraphs; between Ford's novels, poetry and non-fiction; between his texts and those of his contemporaries; and between them and their cultural and historical contexts. A writer of the time, E.M. Forster, famously wrote: 'Only connect'.[4] Don't only do that, but do do that.

An Introduction to Ford Madox Ford can be read consecutively, from Chapter 1 to Chapter 14, but it does not have to be. You might find it beneficial to 'do a Dowell' and abandon linearity ('when one discusses an affair – a long, sad affair – one goes back, one goes forward'[5]). The earlier chapters focus on aspects of Ford's life and work, and his connections to various literary, artistic and historical events, 'movements' and periods. There are multiple ways in which connections might be made between these chapters. For example, Max Saunders's chapter on 'Ford's Lives', which deals with Ford's fascinating life through the medium of his memoirs, reminiscences and other life writing, might be thought about in connection with John Attridge's discussion of Ford's collaboration with Joseph Conrad and also with Stephen Rogers's chapter on Ford's involvement in and relationship to a number of modernist 'Movements, Magazines and Manifestos', which might also be read in connection with Seamus O'Malley's chapter on Ford's modernism, which, in turn, can be considered with Rob Hawkes's chapter on Ford's Edwardian

---

[3]   Ford Madox Ford, *The Good Soldier*, second edition, ed. Martin Stannard (New York: Norton, 2012), p. 169.

[4]   E.M. Forster, *Howards End* (London: Penguin, 2000), p. 159.

[5]   Ford, *The Good Soldier*, pp. 124–5.

fiction and its development towards the modernism of *The Good Soldier* and Paul Skinner's examination of Ford's modern poetry. Given their importance in Ford and early twentieth-century literary studies, there are chapters devoted to *The Good Soldier*, *Parade's End*, literary Impressionism and the First World War. The final four chapters – 'Ford and the City', 'Ford and Gender', 'Ford and National Identity', 'Ford and Politics' – take a broader, thematic approach, designed to give you other ways of thinking about Ford's work.

One thing not to forget about *An Introduction* is that it is an introduction. Much else has been written on Ford that you will find useful when researching: see 'Guide to Further Reading', then look at the bibliography. Don't feel overwhelmed: it will quickly become apparent which texts are most relevant to you.

We hope you find this volume a useful guide and companion, but also that it helps you come to admire the brilliant Ford Madox Ford as much as we do.

Chapter 1

Ford's Lives

Max Saunders

He began to tell me about himself, filling me with pride by confiding all his troubles and weaknesses. The most monumental of authors – the fountain, apparently of all wisdom, who appeared already to have lived a dozen lives . . .[1]

Writing about Ford's life and his life-writings presents a set of challenges. Ford wrote copiously – even compulsively – about his memories, often producing some of his best writing. But its brilliance can eclipse a more objective biographical narrative. Then there is the problem presented by his insouciance about fact. His playful exaggerations sometimes provoked accusations that he was a fantasist or a liar. A biographer thus has to try not only to sort fact from imagination, but also to try to understand the significance of any fabrications. A striking feature of these is the number of different versions Ford would spin of essentially the same story, some appearing in memoirs and some in fictions. Such issues affect not only his autobiographical works, but also his biographical writing. He explicitly described books such as his memoir of *Joseph Conrad* (1924) or his reminiscences *It Was the Nightingale* (1933) as novels. Such a strategy was again provocative, but enables us to see now how precisely he situated so much of his work on the borderline between auto/biography and fiction. It is only recently that such work has been re-described as a mould-breaking experiment in metafiction.[2] Finally, Ford had an extensive network, or set of networks, of literary friendships and contacts. A striking, often captivating or exasperating figure, he frequently incited his writer-friends and acquaintances to write about him. His shadow-selves thus haunt a range of texts by other writers: memoirs with anecdotes of his conduct and conversation; or poems and novels with Fordian characters – notably by Joseph Conrad, H.G. Wells, Richard Aldington, Wyndham Lewis, Ezra Pound, Ernest Hemingway, Gertrude Stein, and Anthony Burgess.[3] As with his own multiple versions of experiences, the multiple accounts of Ford's character are bafflingly

---

[1] Stella Bowen, *Drawn from Life* (London: Virago, 1984), p. 63.

[2] See, for example, Joseph Wiesenfarth, 'Ford's *Joseph Conrad: A Personal Remembrance* as Metafiction: Or, How Conrad Became an Elizabethan Poet', *Renascence*, 53.1 (2000), 43–60.

[3] See David D. Harvey, *Ford Madox Ford: 1873–1939: A Bibliography of Works and Criticism* (Princeton: Princeton University Press, 1962); and for further details Max Saunders, 'Ford Madox Ford: Further Bibliographies', *English Literature in Transition*, 43.2 (2000), 131–205.

diverse and sometimes contradictory. He seemed extraordinarily able to inspire love, loyalty, and admiration on the one hand, as well as anger, betrayal, ridicule and condemnation on the other. Such conflicting accounts have inevitably affected the biographies of him: from the hagiographical early studies by his younger contemporary Douglas Goldring and the appreciative novelist's portrait by our contemporary Alan Judd to the more psychoanalytically-inflected books by Arthur Mizener and Thomas Moser. My own critical biography emphasises the ways in which Ford's writing about others (whether in fiction or memoir) expresses aspects of himself.[4]

The present chapter will seek to tessellate these kaleidoscopic views of Ford so as to present his life through his own and others' life-writings. The emphasis here will be on what he writes about his own life. The main aim is to demonstrate how much of his *oeuvre* can be seen as constituting an extended autobiographical project, comparable to the work of other Impressionists and modernists such as Proust, George Moore, Dorothy Richardson, Frank Harris, and James Joyce. Though his later reminiscences are as richly time-shifted as his best novels, there is an essential logic whereby he works systematically through his life-stories – though, as the biographies of him have shown, autobiographical elements also play across his fiction.

Ford was born into an intensely bohemian milieu. His father was the German musicologist and champion of Wagner, Franz Hüffer, who emigrated to London, anglicised his name to Francis Hueffer, and became music critic of *The Times*. He married Catherine, herself a painter and the daughter of the English artist Ford Madox Brown. Ford Madox Ford, as he became known after the First World War, was born in 1873 and christened Ford Hermann Hueffer. He was to alter his name in stages, adopting the 'Madox' and dropping the 'Hermann' to publish as Ford Madox Hueffer until 1923, though he had changed his surname to Ford in 1919. Ford Madox Brown's other daughter, Lucy, married William Michael Rossetti, the brother of Dante Gabriel and Christina Rossetti, who were thus Ford's uncle and aunt by marriage. Ford described his upbringing in this cosmopolitan Pre-Raphaelite hothouse as a process of being 'trained for genius', and duly published

---

4   There have been six biographies of Ford: Douglas Goldring, *The Last Pre-Raphaelite: A Record of the Life and Writings of Ford Madox Ford* (London: Macdonald, 1948), published in the USA as *Trained for Genius* (New York: Dutton, 1949); Frank MacShane, *The Life and Work of Ford Madox Ford* (London: Routledge and Kegan Paul, 1965); Arthur Mizener, *The Saddest Story: A Biography of Ford Madox Ford* (New York: Harper and Row, 1971; London: Bodley Head, 1972); Thomas C. Moser, *The Life in the Fiction of Ford Madox Ford* (Princeton: Princeton University Press, 1980); Alan Judd, *Ford Madox Ford* (London: Collins, 1990); and Max Saunders, *Ford Madox Ford: A Dual Life*, 2 vols (Oxford: Oxford University Press, 1996). Goldring's *South Lodge: Reminiscences of Violet Hunt, Ford Madox Ford and the English Review Circle* (London: Constable, 1943) includes valuable biographical material on Ford, as does Violet Hunt's *The Flurried Years* (London: Hurst and Blackett, 1926), published in the US as *I Have This to Say* (New York: Boni and Liveright, 1926).

his first book, a fairy tale called *The Brown Owl* (1891), written for his sister Juliet, at the precociously early age of seventeen. By his twentieth birthday he had added a second fairy story, a volume of verse, and his first novel, *The Shifting of the Fire* (1892). A career as an author may have appeared inevitable, though Ford had also considered music, having demonstrated skill as a composer. He was to write in increasingly fluid and genre-defying forms, which are perhaps best thought of as exercises in the techniques Ford was to come to call Impressionism, played across the different keys of fiction, poetry, life-writing, criticism, and writing about topography and travel.

Until his mid-thirties, he was arguably best known as an authority on the Pre-Rapahelites. His first book of life-writing was his biography of his grandfather, *Ford Madox Brown* (1896). Though written impersonally, with almost no reference to himself, the entire work is a testimony to his love for his grandfather, and to how Ford came by many of his deepest aesthetic and ethical principles. The Pre-Raphaelite milieu is also where biographies of him tend to begin. Ford later wrote little books on *Rossetti* (1902) and *The Pre-Raphaelite Brotherhood* (1907). But most of his reminiscences of his grandfather's circle appeared in his first major autobiographical work, *Ancient Lights* (1911), which thus contains the bulk of his memories of his early childhood in London, first with his parents in Hammersmith, then, after the premature death of his father, living in his grandfather's studio at St Edmund's Terrace in Primrose Hill. (His later book *Provence* (1935) adds important material about how his London childhood fostered a love of Provence, poetry, and romantic fabulation.)

Ancient Lights was written in 1910 when Ford was living in Germany while trying to obtain German nationality. It was thus, in a sense, the first of his several farewells to England and London and his English roots. The chapters focus on different arts, different artists and different topics. Several were published first in periodicals; and if read there, or by dipping into the book, they might appear as separate critical essays on the atmosphere of late-nineteenth-century literary London ('Gloom and the Poets'), Anarchists, the press, musicians, or eminent individual Victorian painters or writers such as Holman Hunt, Madox Brown or Christina Rossetti. But Ford prefaced the book with a ten-page 'Dedication' to his daughters, which makes something strikingly different of it. First, by arguing that he had discovered he had only 'grown up' recently, when he realised he was forgetting his childhood, he frames his reminiscences as being as much about that childhood as their ostensible subjects. This duality, whereby Ford's writing about others reflects qualities of himself, and vice-versa, was fundamental to most of his writing. As he puts it here, he has always been interested in 'the subject, not so much of myself, as in how far the rest of humanity seem to *themselves* to resemble me'.[5] The book's full title – *Ancient Lights and Certain New Reflections: Being*

------

⁵   Ford Madox Ford, *Ancients Lights and Certain New Reflections: Being the Memories of a Young Man* (London: Chapman and Hall, 1911), p. 253. All further references are to this edition.

the Memories of a Young Man – captures the duality precisely. 'Ancient lights'
are windows protected by law from being obstructed by new buildings. Ford's
are thus the towering artistic luminaries – 'those terrible and forbidding things –
the Victorian great figures' (p. xi) whose example he describes as oppressive and
impossible to emulate. The 'New Reflections' are his thoughts about them, his
memories. That image of reflections on a window was one Ford was to use in his
crucial essay 'On Impressionism' (1914), in which he says:

> I suppose that Impressionism exists to render those queer effects of real life that
> are like so many views seen through bright glass – through glass so bright that
> whilst you perceive through it a landscape or a backyard, you are aware that, on
> its surface, it reflects a face of a person behind you.[6]

Like that essay, the Dedication to *Ancient Lights* is also a manifesto for literary
Impressionism; and this is the second way in which the frame alters the picture.
Ford includes a long 'P.S.' 'to make plain the actual nature of this book', saying
that 'It consists of impressions' (p. xiii); and – controversially – that:

> This book, in short, is full of inaccuracies as to facts, but its accuracy as to
> impressions is absolute. [...] I don't really deal in facts, I have for facts a most
> profound contempt. I try to give you what I see to be the spirit of an age, of a
> town, of a movement. (pp. xv–xvi)

By way of example, he writes that when he says 'the Pre-Raphaelite poets carried
on their work amidst the glooms of Bloomsbury', if he were to give meteorological
statistics about the number of days of fog as opposed to sunshine it 'would not
seriously help the impression' (p. xvi). This explanation is offered as part of a
humorous defence against pedants inclined to complain about inaccuracy (as Ford's
uncle William, the least poetical of the three Rossetti siblings, did indeed write to
the papers to complain). But when we read *Ancient Lights* in the light of Ford's
definition of Impressionism, it becomes clear that Impressionism too is one of its
reflected subjects as much as its technique.[7] Because Ford's veracity is frequently
impugned, it is important to be clear about exactly how he handles questions of
accuracy or truth. Though the Dedication might sound as if he simply distorts or
exaggerates tacitly in the rest of the text, and only attaches the defensive label of
Impressionism pre-emptively in the opening pages, in fact what he does is much
more subtle; and characteristic of his method in any genre or form. Essentially,
he gives an episode of some extremity, but then immediately complicates it by
juxtaposing something contradictory, or which raises questions about veracity.

Thus *Ancient Lights* recounts how Robert Louis Stevenson's cousin, 'Bob'
(R.A.M.) Stevenson, publicly delivered a hyperbolic assessment of Madox Brown,
as: 'the only real English painter since Hogarth – the only national one, the only one

---

[6]   Ford Madox Ford, 'On Impressionism', *Poetry and Drama*, 2 (June 1914), 174. On
Ford and Impressionism, see Chapter 5 in this volume.

[7]   The US edition was titled *Memories and Impressions* (New York: Harper, 1911).

who could paint'; and pausing before the painting *The Pretty Baa-Lambs* (1851) exclaimed: 'By God! the whole history of modern art begins with that picture. Corot, Manet, the Marises, all the Fontainebleau School, all the Impressionists, never did anything but imitate that picture' (p. 207).[8] Of course, such claims are far more sweeping than anything in academic art history. (Though the view of Madox Brown as a pioneer, especially in this picture, of traits popularly associated with the Impressionists, such as painting *en plein air* or giving haystacks purple shadows, is shared by his most recent biographer, Angela Thirlwell.[9]) Ford was perhaps exaggerating Stevenson's praise, wanting him to make the case about Madox Brown, that Ford may have felt it unbecoming to make himself about his grandfather. But he complicates it by preceding it with its opposite: Stevenson lecturing him the day before on how Madox Brown 'could not paint for nuts' and 'ought never to have been a painter at all' (p. 207). A cynic might say Ford only mentions this attack to counterbalance the accolade, which is what he really wants said about Madox Brown, but wants to look objective even while reporting it. Yet behind Ford's presentation of himself as perplexed – as he often portrays himself in the proximity of Victorian great figures – by this contradiction might lie a psychological subtlety: perhaps Stevenson exaggerated his praise the following day because he felt he had hurt Ford's family feelings. At another level, though, Stevenson's conflicting exaggerations are characteristic of the milieu Ford is trying to represent; and, indeed, of Madox Brown himself, who, Ford says, 'had anecdotes more lavish and more picturesque than any man I ever knew' (p. 223). And that, ultimately, is the style Ford cultivates in his own memoirs. Not just the lavishness and exaggeration which he sees as the atmosphere of Pre-Raphaelism, but also the awareness he sees the Pre-Raphaelites as cultivating of their lavish exaggeration. As Ford says of another writer, the editor, critic and poet W.E. Henley: 'You had the man before you, you were much better able to appreciate from his tone of voice where he exaggerated and where he meant you to know that he exaggerated' (p. 196). The placing of these words as the ending of chapter 10, on the literary and critical worlds, makes them echo through the rest of the book, indicating that Ford means us to be aware of how his artists, as well as himself, have exaggerated. In the context, he is saying that it was better to hear Henley's talk than read his prose because such ironies were easier to detect; but the challenge Ford poses himself in his life-writing is to use prose to put exaggeration continually in question.

---

[8]   By 'Fontainebleau School', Stevenson (or possibly Ford) means not the sixteenth-century mannerists of that name, but the nineteenth-century artists now known as the Barbizon group, who painted the forests of Fontainebleau.

[9]   See Angela Thirlwell, 'Ford's Provence: A Pre-Raphaelite Vision', in Dominique Lemarchal and Claire Davison-Pégon (eds), *Ford Madox Ford, France and Provence*, International Ford Madox Ford Studies 10 (Amsterdam: Rodopi, 2011), p. 199: and 'From Paint To Print – Grandfather's Legacy', in *Ford Madox Ford and Visual Culture*, ed. Laura Colombino, International Ford Madox Ford Studies 8 (Amsterdam: Rodopi, 2009), p. 33.

In the chapter 'Deaths and Departures', occasioned by reading in 1910 of the death of Holman Hunt, which appeared to bring the era of Pre-Raphaelism – and thus also the era that included his childhood – to a close, Ford writes of Hunt:

> The 'I' that is so eternal in his autobiography is not the 'I' that was William Holman Hunt. It was all that he stood for – the principles, the hard life, the bitter endurance, the splendid record of young friendship, the aims, the achievement. It was this that Mr. Hunt desired to have acknowledged. (p. 220)

That claim – that what in an autobiography might appear egotism should be read as dedication to art – is what Ford desired to have acknowledged in his own reminiscential books.

I have discussed *Ancient Lights* in some detail because it is a pivotal text: the first in which Ford elaborates the Impressionist method that was to underpin the rest of his work and the one which enables him to exorcise the intimidating ghosts of what he called the 'Middle Victorian, tumultuously bearded Great',[10] reinvent himself as a novelist of modernity and go on to write *The Good Soldier* (1915). His mode of enacting Impressionism in the way he discusses it was to characterise all his later life-writing, dispersed through his memoirs, books about other writers, and books about culture and place. But *Ancient Lights* does more than explore the nature of his Impressionism. It also investigates its genealogy. Ford is not just recreating what he calls the 'romantic home of my childhood' (p. 214), he is showing how that element of romance, of romancing, of heightening and transforming, was part of the texture of his childhood and his aesthetic heredity. Insofar as *Ancient Lights* is autobiographical, its story is of what made Ford Impressionist.

Before the First World War, the focal points of Ford's life – and thus of *Return to Yesterday* (1931), the later autobiographical volume that takes up the story of his young manhood – were London, where he was born, and the south coast, where he had been sent to a boarding school (in Folkestone, Kent, run by an émigré German couple who knew Madox Brown). Ford was fifteen when his father died suddenly in 1889. That was when Ford and his brother Oliver had to go and live with Madox Brown, their sister Juliet staying with their widowed mother. Back in London, Ford attended University College School in Gower Street as a day-boy. And he got to know the Garnetts, Madox Brown's old friends and neighbours, whose son Edward and daughter Olive became close friends. When Richard Garnett became Keeper of Printed Books at the British Museum they moved into an official residence on the museum site, and W.M. Rossetti and his family took

---

[10]   Ford Madox Ford, *Mightier Than the Sword* (London: Allen and Unwin, 1938), p. 264; published in the US as *Portraits from Life* (Boston: Houghton Mifflin, 1937). The book consists of reminiscential sketches of 11 writers, from those Ford had known well (James, Crane, Conrad, Galsworthy, Lawrence, Wells) to those whose influence was strong even if their biographical connection with Ford was more tenuous (Hudson, Swinburne, Dreiser).

over their house in St Edmund's Terrace. The young Rossettis and Garnetts were passionately interested in Anarchism, and got to know radical Russian émigrés such as Prince Kropotkin and the assassin known as Stepniak. Edward Garnett later became a prominent publisher's reader and critic, discovering Conrad and introducing him to Ford; his wife, Constance, became the leading translator of Russian literature. Part II of *Return to Yesterday*, 'The Left', gives a vivid account of Ford's encounters with this political underworld of Anarchist London, his knowledge of which enabled him to tell Conrad details of the story that inspired *The Secret Agent* (1907).

In 1894, Ford married his girlfriend from his first school, Elsie Martindale, the daughter of a prosperous pharmacologist who thought Ford an unsuitable suitor. The couple eloped, leaving London to settle back by the south coast, on the Romney Marsh. Ford was always reticent about his private, domestic life in his writing, and says virtually nothing about the marriage and little about their married life, except as occasional background to his ruminative trilogy of books about *England and the English* (1905–07). In these volumes, impressionistic and sometimes about impressions, though not yet addressing 'Impressionism', he gives glimpses of his life at this time especially in *The Heart of the Country* (1906), where he writes about the Kentish peasants he befriended, some of whom – particularly the resilient 'Meary' Walker – would recur throughout his writing. Ford was leading the 'simple life' of a 'small-producer'. He was later to describe this period as one in which he'd 'buried' himself in the countryside (as perhaps he wanted to bury his by then failed marriage);[11] yet he was still an aspiring man of letters. It was his friendships in Kent and Sussex with Henry James, Stephen Crane and H.G. Wells, and his friendship with, and then decade of collaboration with, Joseph Conrad, that turned him into a major novelist. The central Part III of *Return to Yesterday*, also called 'The Heart of the Country', begins with what he calls the 'peasant biographies' of his Romney Marsh neighbours, but moves on to three chapters about his literary apprenticeship: 'Pure Letters'; 'Working with Conrad'; and 'Rye Road' (Rye being where James lived). Where *Ancient Lights* mapped the origins of Ford's Impressionism, *Return to Yesterday* recounts his experiences of living amongst the three major literary Impressionists writing in English: James, Crane and Conrad. They did not organise into a group like the Pre-Raphaelite Brotherhood or the French Impressionists, nor did they have a shared programme. (James and Conrad were, initially at least, too ambivalent about Impressionism for that.) But for Ford, their aesthetic solidarity, and pervasive discussions about art and technique, not only defined his own manifesto as an Impressionist but provided a model of artistic community that echoed his experience of the Pre-Raphaelites, and which he would henceforth seek to re-establish. This aspiration provides the logic of *Return to Yesterday*, which moves from describing this circle of Impressionist writers – jokingly described by Wells (according to Ford) as 'a ring

---

[11]   Ford Madox Ford, *Return to Yesterday*, ed. Bill Hutchings (Manchester: Carcanet Press, 1999), p. 109.

of foreign conspirators plotting against British letters'[12] – to recounting how Ford set up the *English Review* to propagate his vision and theoretical justification of the movement, and to recreate it in London; and it goes on to record the modernist challenges to it that arose partly as a result of his own editorial activities.

Collaboration with Conrad had seemed a good idea for both men. Conrad hoped to rely on Ford's fluency to alleviate anxieties about his command of English. Ford had been working on a story about Cuban pirates, but lacked Conrad's experience of ships and colonies. Ford's insubstantial 185-leaf draft was completely rewritten and elaborated into the 460-page novel *Romance* (1903). But it fell between the two stools of existential psychological drama and Stevensonian adventure story, and the poor reviews and sales were disappointing compensation for five years' toil. Each had meanwhile continued with his own work, Conrad producing some of his finest fiction – *Heart of Darkness* (1899) and *Lord Jim* (1900) – Ford writing most of *The Inheritors* (1901), which Conrad revised and was published as another collaboration. Neither book is nearly as good as either man's best work. But the experiment had two more important results for Ford.

First, almost daily discussion with Conrad about style, structure, handling, plot, language, techniques, taught him the meaning for writers of 'the principles, the hard life, the bitter endurance' and 'the aims' that the Pre-Raphaelites had shown him for painters. Conrad was sixteen years the senior, so 'the splendid record of young friendship'[13] in this case was somewhat one-sided. But they did sustain a splendid friendship based on their dedication to the craft of writing, and continued the collaboration on and off in different forms for a further five years, Ford taking dictation for some of Conrad's reminiscences and both reworking another of Ford's stories into an intriguing psychological novella, *The Nature of a Crime* (1924). If 'the achievement' of their joint work did not match what Conrad had already achieved alone, and Ford would go on to achieve, Conrad provided Ford with an intimate example of what it meant to be a serious artist in literature. Ford never lost his belief in James and Conrad as the greatest writers of their age or his sense of privilege in knowing them both well, and Conrad exceptionally well. But the connections damaged Ford's reputation in the long term. His relations with both men ran into difficulties when Ford left his wife for the risqué socialite and novelist Violet Hunt in 1908–09, after which James tended to refer to him ambivalently, and Conrad negatively.[14] Both were much older than Ford (James by thirty years). He was in awe of their styles and in his early fiction imitated their mannerisms excessively. They did not live to know much of his best work, and by the time it began to appear, they did not want to know – an attitude which was

---

12   Ford, *Return to Yesterday*, p. 21.
13   Ford, *Ancient Lights*, p. 220.
14   It is also possible that James might have been offended by Ford's use of some of his characteristics for Robert Grimshaw, the renunciatory protagonist of *A Call* (1910); and Conrad by the caricature of him as Simeon Brandetski in *The Simple Life Limited* (1911); though there is no evidence that either man read either book; and anyway the latter was published under the pseudonym 'Daniel Chaucer'.

taken up until relatively recently by influential scholars of both writers, irritated by Ford's fictionalising reminiscences, which they saw as exaggerating his intimacy with his masters and aggrandising himself.[15]

The other main after-effect of the protracted strain of the collaboration was Ford's severe agoraphobic breakdown in 1904, the year after the publication of *Romance*. We cannot be sure of the precise cause, though guilt from a possible affair with his sister-in-law may have been the major factor. He does not describe the experience directly – for that, one needs to read the sympathetic account in Olive Garnett's diary.[16] But it does colour much of his subsequent fiction and reminiscences. Thomas Moser, for example, sees agoraphobia as shaping Ford's Impressionist aesthetic of bewildered receptivity.[17] *Return to Yesterday* is remarkably frank about his subsequent depression, and his experiences in Germany where he went first for a 'nerve cure' in a spa sanatorium, then to stay with his wealthy Hüffer relations, especially an aunt who lived at Boppard on the Rhine.

The cloud of melancholy hangs over *The Soul of London* (1905), the first book of his *England and the English* trilogy. But it was a surprise success, causing Ford to be 'boomed' in the press, as he put it.[18] His spirits lifted, he was able to complete that trilogy and write another, this time of historical novels dealing with Henry VIII and his fifth wife, Katharine Howard. *The Fifth Queen* trilogy (1906–08) was well-received too; and Ford was writing regularly for the papers and attending literary gatherings, especially after he separated finally from Elsie and returned to live in London. By now he was in the first of three phases of especially intense literary-critical activity (the others being in the mid-1920s and the late 1930s), producing frequent reviews as well as substantial essays and critical books. But his criticism often proceeds via reminiscence, just as his reminiscences often proceed via literary criticism.

In 1908, with help from Conrad and another mutual friend from Kent, Arthur Marwood (Ford was to base the character of Christopher Tietjens, the protagonist of *Parade's End* (1924–28), on a fusion of Marwood and himself), Ford launched a literary monthly, the *English Review*. Ford has been seen as one of the great literary editors of the period. Though his tenure as editor lasted little over a year, the *English Review* had a powerful effect, redefining modern English literature and criticism by assembling an extraordinary range of talent, publishing established figures like James, Hardy and Conrad alongside successful and up-and-coming younger writers such as Wells and Bennett, but also including Ford's discoveries, who would prove amongst the most influential figures in modernism: Ezra Pound, D.H. Lawrence and Wyndham Lewis. The final section of *Return to Yesterday* – titled 'The Last of London' in one of Ford's many allusions to Madox Brown's

---

[15] For more on Ford and Conrad, see Chapter 2 in this volume.

[16] See Saunders, *Ford Madox Ford*, I, p. 171.

[17] Moser, *The Life in the Fiction of Ford Madox Ford*, Chapter 4.

[18] Ford, *Return to Yesterday*, p. 179. See Saunders, *Ford Madox Ford*, I, p. 197 on Edward Garnett and John Galsworthy using the same term about Ford at this time.

fictionalised self-portrait as an emigrant in *The Last of England* (1852–55) – covers this editorial adventure and Ford's increasing involvement with the writers he called *les jeunes* in the frenetic, revolutionary days of British modernism on the eve of the war.

This period of literary apprenticeship, first successes, and editing of the *English Review*, was first treated in the reminiscences he published just after the war, *Thus to Revisit* (1921). That title alludes to Hamlet's question to the ghost: 'What may this mean, / That thou, dead corpse, again in complete steel, / Revisitst thus the glimpses of the moon[?][19] The allusion conflates several meanings. Who is revisiting what or whom? Memoir summons – or seeks to lay to rest – the ghosts of friends and ancestors. That the ghost is in armour, however, perhaps suggests that it is Ford, just out of the army, who is paying the revisitations, feeling a ghost himself as he returns to the past of pre-war literary London. There is also a sense that the corpse is that pre-war world, utterly dead and gone; killed by the war. Ford said in the Dedicatory Letter he wrote for a second edition of *The Good Soldier* in 1927 that he had taken 'a formal farewell of Literature' in a little magazine before enlisting in 1915.[20] If he expected not to survive the war, when he did come back he would describe himself as if he had died, as if one motive for his change of name was a feeling that the pre-war Ford Madox Hueffer no longer existed. *Thus to Revisit* is structured so as to represent the literary scene as itself warlike: with Ford and Conrad struggling to find a 'New Form' (pp. 44–5) for the novel in the first of the two major sections, 'Prosateurs'; and with the fight for 'free verse' in the second, titled 'The Battle of the Poets'. But whereas Ford presents his childhood self, in *Ancients Lights* and later in *Mightier Than the Sword* (1938), as transfixed by terrifying giant elders, he presents his modernist self as already overrun by the younger avant-gardists he helped to drill. In one of the stories he re-imagined at least six times with increasingly Impressionist flair, he recalls Wyndham Lewis (sometimes with Pound) frog-marching him down Holland Street during the period of the Vorticist magazine *Blast* in the months just before the outbreak of war, denouncing Ford and Impressionism as 'Finished! Exploded! Done for! Blasted in fact'.[21] Lewis's verbal violence prefigures the war; and *Return to Yesterday* ends on the day war was declared: 4 August 1914.

Return to Yesterday is also an attempt to portray the society that allowed itself to be drawn into the catastrophe of the First World War (it was written in 1930–31,

---

[19]   Ford Madox Ford, *Thus to Revisit: Some Reminiscences* (London: Chapman and Hall, 1921), p. 25. All further references are to this edition. William Shakespeare, *The Tragedy of Hamlet, Prince of Denmark, Complete Works*, ed. Stanley Wells and Gary Taylor (Oxford: Clarendon Press, 1986), 1.4.32–34. Ford felt ghostly before the war had ended. Back in England after two spells in France, he wrote to Lucy Masterman on 8 September 1917: 'I haven't had any news of you for a long time – or indeed from anybody: it is like being a ghost, rather': *Letters of Ford Madox Ford,* ed. Richard M. Ludwig (Princeton: Princeton University Press, 1965), p. 84.

[20]   Ford, *The Good Soldier*, p. 4.

[21]   Ford, *Return to Yesterday*, p. 311.

just as the spectre of a return to war began to menace Europe). At the outbreak of the war, and before he enlisted, Ford wrote cultural propaganda for the War Propaganda Bureau, run by his friend C.F.G. Masterman, who had been a Liberal Cabinet minister. Ford's two propaganda books are not autobiography, but they are intensely personal – especially in the way their triangulation of English, French and German life, art and thought mirrors Ford's own complex cultural heritage (his progressive Folkestone school, for example, had lessons in all three languages). Like many participants in the war, Ford came to feel it as a fracture between past and present.

His relationship with Violet Hunt had come under strain before the war. Elsie Hueffer had refused a divorce, so a plan was devised for Ford to use his German heritage to acquire German nationality in order to obtain a German divorce. It was a risky venture. Ford would still not have been divorced under English law, and if a German marriage had been recognised he might have been tried for bigamy if he had returned. Yet Hunt craved the respectability of marriage, and they found a lawyer who encouraged the scheme. Ford lived in Germany again from 1910–11, and experiences from this period, as well as from his 1904 nerve cure, went into his first fictional masterpiece, *The Good Soldier*. (When Ezra Pound visited Ford and acted as his secretary in Giessen in 1911, Ford and Hunt took him to see the spa town of Nauheim, where much of the action of *The Good Soldier* is set.) But Ford did not write directly about his relationship with Hunt, or their attempt at marriage, or even much about this German episode. For that, one has to read Hunt's vivid but self-justifying memoir *The Flurried Years* (1926) for one of the most detailed intimate biographical portraits of Ford. Having recently made his name in Britain, Ford did not want to fade into oblivion in a provincial continental town, so when the application for German nationality failed, he returned to London and they claimed to have married on the continent. When Hunt was referred to in the *Throne* magazine as Mrs Hueffer, Elsie sued for libel and won. The court case was socially devastating to Ford and Hunt, and the major source of their reputation as liars. Ford had already made enemies in the literary world due to his haughty judgments of much conventional English fiction. In England, it took almost a century for his literary reputation to recover from the sexual scandal and from his condemnation as a 'cad' – though his motive for lying about their marriage should perhaps rather be seen as a chivalrous attempt, however doomed, to protect Hunt's name whatever the damage to his own. They travelled in France to weather the worst of the storm, then returned to London to brave out the rest. But by 1915 they were both miserable, and the Army offered Ford a way out.

Ford was literally 'blasted' when a shell exploded near him during the Battle of the Somme, and he suffered concussion and near-total temporary amnesia. He must indeed have felt 'Done for' for several years. It was not until 1923, when he had finished *Some Do Not . . .* (1924), the first volume of his great tetralogy covering the years of the First World War, *Parade's End*, that he told H.G. Wells he felt he had got over the 'nerve tangle of the war'.[22] Unlike so many combatants, Ford did not write a war memoir. Many of his war experiences of being shell-shocked in the Battle of the Somme went into *Parade's End*. But he did also write a strange book, *No Enemy* (1929): a semi-fictionalised reminiscence, akin to Sassoon's *Memoirs of an Infantry Officer* (1930) in the use of its persona George Sherston, though unlike it because it deals with the psychological and aesthetic side-effects of the war rather than treating his war experiences directly.[23]

Ford continued to appear socially as Violet's husband, and it was during one of these visits that in 1917 she introduced him to a young Australian painter, Stella Bowen, whom Pound had met as his neighbour in Kensington. If, like Leonora Ashburnham, Violet thought she could manage her man's infidelities, she was wrong. Soon after Ford was demobilized in 1919 he set up a new home, and a new life, with Stella, his new love, and with a new name: Ford Madox Ford. He felt he needed the sanctuary of a rural retreat to recover from the traumatic experiences of the war. With Stella, he returned to the South-East of England, living in the Sussex countryside as a small producer once more. Their daughter, Julie, was born in 1920. Again, Ford characteristically does not describe their family life directly in his memoirs. But he does draw on it in the long poem *A House* (1921) and in *No Enemy* (written immediately after the war, though not published for a decade), in which he divides himself into an anonymous 'Compiler' who interviews and takes dictation from a poet, Gringoire, whose wartime reminiscences form the core of the book, and who is now living with a French woman, Madame Sélysette, in a simple home not unlike 'Red Ford', the auspiciously named Sussex cottage Bowen found for herself and Ford.

But after three years of muddy winters they were tempted to winter in Provence, where Ford's friend Harold Monro, who ran the Poetry Bookshop in London, rented them his villa on the ridge of Cap Ferrat with breathtaking views over the Mediterranean in both directions. When they had to leave in the summer of 1923 they travelled slowly through France up to Paris, where a chance meeting with Ford's brother Oliver Madox Hueffer provided them with a studio on the Boulevard Arago, and the prospect of starting another literary magazine. They decided to stay in Paris. And in 1924 Ford was once again editor of a pioneering literary magazine, the *transatlantic review*, and again publishing established figures alongside Ford's latest batch of discoveries.

It Was the Nightingale, Ford's second major instalment of autobiography, takes up the story with his demobilisation in 1919, and, like *No Enemy*, recounts something of his process of reconstruction in rural Sussex, but continues it with his life in France, first in Provence, and later Paris. Where *Return* is essentially an account of how he came to start the *English Review* and write *The Good Soldier*,

---

[22]   Ford to Wells (14 Oct. 1923), *Letters of Ford Madox Ford*, p. 154.

[23]   For further discussion of the comparison between *No Enemy* and the Sherston memoirs, see Rob Hawkes, *Ford Madox Ford and the Misfit Moderns: Edwardian Fiction and the First World War* (Basingstoke: Palgrave Macmillan, 2012), pp. 99–136.

Nightingale explains how he was able to reinvent himself as a man, as well as a novelist; that is, how he was able to recover enough from the war to write *Parade's End* and to launch the *transatlantic*. Its coruscating account of post-war Paris describes a new network of artists: including Pound again, whom he had known in London, but now also James Joyce, Gertrude Stein, Ernest Hemingway, Jean Rhys, and Basil Bunting, all of whom he published in the *transatlantic*. Ford ends *Nightingale* with the Wall Street Crash, so again he presents a world of freedoms and energies and experiment on the verge of disaster. Thus, it too is an elegiac book, one which this time actually describes his departure from England for good: a decision he also allegorised in the extraordinary experimental pastiche poem *Mister Bosphorus and the Muses* (1923). Ford wrote widely about France, and the more autobiographical parts of *A Mirror to France* (1926) and his preface to Jean Rhys's *The Left Bank* (1927) date from the period described in *Nightingale*.

Ford told his publisher: 'The world before the war is one thing and must be written about in one manner; the after-war world is quite another and calls for quite different treatment'.[24] The treatment in *It Was the Nightingale* is certainly different from that of his earlier reminiscences. It uses the interior monologue and stream-of-consciousness techniques of *Parade's End*, elaborating complex, convoluted structures of association and interconnection. It deals with dark, painful subjects: the psychological scarring of the war; his suicidal state after leaving the army with only his kit-bag to his name. But its story of regeneration is told with brio and a theatrical panache.

Also in 1924, as soon as Ford heard of Conrad's death, he began writing his elegiac book *Joseph Conrad: A Personal Remembrance*, one of his finest examples of critical reminiscence. Though he relates Conrad's stories from his earlier life, the focus is inevitably on the decade when they were closest, and on their collaborative discussions. One entire section, titled (with a Conradian echo) 'It Is Above All to Make You See. . . .', is devoted to an analysis of the Impressionist techniques they evolved, and reads like a composition manual, with headings such as 'General Effect', 'Impressionism', 'Conversations', 'Style' and 'Structure'. Ford refers to himself throughout as 'the writer', which sounds a rather formal, laborious way of avoiding too many 'I's, until you realise that what brought the two men together was the craft of writing; and that just as what he says about Conrad can be read as displaced autobiography, so what he says about himself can be read as displaced biography. In other words, the book – like most of Ford's memoirs of other writers – is also about what it means to be a writer. Composed soon after Ford's decision to settle in France, while editing the *transatlantic* and mixing largely with expatriate American writers, *Joseph Conrad* is also another form of farewell to England.

The novels of *Parade's End*, appearing from 1924 to 1928, brought Ford his greatest success, especially in the USA, and he started dividing his time between

---

[24] Ford to T.R. Smith (27 July 1931): quoted in Saunders, *Ford Madox Ford*, II, p. 382.

New York, Paris and Provence from the mid-1920s. His increasing involvement with American writers in Paris, and then with America itself, from the late 1920s through the 1930s, led him to begin to define himself as an American or even a Franco-American writer. Some of his visits to the US, living in New York and making lecture tours, are described in *New York Is Not America* (1927). He made these visits alone. Ford and Bowen had taken Jean Rhys in to live with them in 1925 when her husband had been sent to prison. Ford and Rhys began an affair over the next two years which marked the beginning of the end of his liaison with Bowen. It was at this point that he named her in print – as 'Stella Ford' – as the dedicatee of a new edition of *The Good Soldier* in 1927; but, as with Elsie Hueffer and Violet Hunt, he did not feel he should write about her in his memoirs.[25] On his US trips in the late 1920s Ford had another two affairs: first with a wealthy divorcee, Rene Wright, then with a younger woman he met on the ship to New York, Elizabeth Cheatham. He again tried to obtain a divorce from Elsie Hueffer, but was again refused. Cheatham was persuaded by her family to break off relations with a married man, and Ford was left disconsolate. *No Enemy* – described by one review as 'the book of himself'[26] – was published in November 1929. It was intended to capitalise on the success of *Parade's End*. But the Wall Street Crash had intervened three weeks earlier, and the bottom fell out of Ford's sales, and of his publishing prospects.

Ford had meanwhile turned to a new kind of project: a work called *A History of Our Own Times* (published posthumously in 1988), which was to give a personal account of the public events of the period of his own life. '[O]ur own times are our own property in a sense that nothing else is or can be', he wrote: 'for our own times are made up of the most intimate and most inviolable portion of a man – of his memories'.[27] He had begun it in mid-1929 – after Cheatham had married her local beau in April. Perhaps the panoramic scale of *Parade's End* had left him wanting to write more about the origins of the war. Perhaps, especially after the Crash of October 1929, he hoped history would be easier to sell than fiction. And perhaps the coincidence of personal despair and economic disaster had the effect less of turning him morbidly inwards, and more of looking outwards, at how the personal and the historical seemed intertwined.

Then, back in Paris in 1930, Ford was introduced to the young Polish-American painter Janice Biala. She was not quite half his age – twenty-seven to his fifty-six – but was entranced and impressed, and they began a relationship which was to last for the rest of Ford's life. Her energy gave him new life and hope; and her Jewishness and left-wing politics gave him a new perspective on

---

[25]   Joseph Wiesenfarth's *Ford Madox Ford and the Regiment of Women* (Madison: University of Wisconsin Press, 2005) covers Ford's relationships with Hunt, Bowen, Rhys and Janice Biala.

[26]   Herbert Gorman, [Untitled], *New York Herald Tribune Books* (29 Dec. 1929), 5.

[27]   Ford Madox Ford, *A History of Our Own Times*, ed. Solon Beinfeld and Sondra J. Stang (Manchester: Carcanet Press, 1989), p. 15.

the rise of Fascism and the imminence of another war. Her arrival also had an effect on his work, which illuminates his recursive life-writing practices. It was now he produced *Return to Yesterday*, turning back to his pre-war literary life by turning back to his previous writings about the period: extracting the more personal passages from the *History*; and revisiting *Thus to Revisit*, incorporating its more personal sections about his reminiscences of James, Conrad and Crane, and his Romney Marsh peasant friends. The resultant book is entirely different: the first volume that might be called an instalment of Ford's autobiography; and these episodes that had earlier functioned as illustrations of the literary or historical scene now formed part of a much more personal narrative.

In a sense, *Return to Yesterday* was written for Biala. The book feels like a man wanting to tell himself to someone too young to know the milieu that shaped him. It was also written during the Depression, which Ford referred to as the 'Crisis'. He and Biala needed to spend more time in New York to earn a living, and they saw how the world was sliding towards another apocalypse. *Return* thus also, and characteristically, constitutes a farewell to the European civilisation of Ford's youth, and perhaps anticipates a farewell to Europe altogether.

Ford's increasingly peripatetic life in the 1930s, moving between Provence, Paris and America, is represented by two major generically protean books: *Provence* (1935) and *Great Trade Route* (1937). While these take on cultural history and cultural geography, and elaborate a theory of the flow of culture through the routes of itinerant traders, they are also works of psychogeography, exploring the relation of mind – Ford's mind – to places and to travel.[28] They also introduce a new form of candour about his private life, introducing Biala, not only as their illustrator, but as a character in the text, incorporating her responses and conversation (though cunningly dividing the real-life Biala into two figures in the books: 'Biala' and 'the patient New Yorker', a purportedly male figure who acts as spectral chaperone). These last books – together with his reminiscences of writer-friends and acquaintances in *Portraits from Life* (1937) and his titanic last book, the literary history *The March of Literature* (1938) – constitute his final development of his idea of Impressionism, which arguably made him such a controversial and intriguing personality, as well as such a significant modern writer.

The fictionality inherent in all narratives, including auto/biography, is a truism of postmodern criticism. This was the seam Ford worked presciently in his life-writing, which is perhaps best understood as a version of what another writer of the period, Stephen Reynolds (who had worked for Ford on the *English Review*), defined as 'autobiografiction'.[29] However, Ford's pioneering frank novelizations

---

[28]   See Max Saunders, 'Ford Madox Ford and Nomadic Modernism', in Giovanni Cianci, Caroline Patey and Sara Sullam (eds), *Transits: The Nomadic Geographies of Anglo-American Modernism* (Bern: Peter Lang, 2010), pp. 77–100; and 'Ford's Thought-Experiments: Impressionism, Place, History, and "the frame of mind that is Provence"', in *Ford Madox Ford, France and Provence*, pp. 259–76.

[29]   Stephen Reynolds, 'Autobiografiction', *Speaker*, new series, 15.366 (6 Oct. 1906), 28, 30. See also Max Saunders, *Self Impression: Life-Writing, Autobiografiction and the*

of auto/biography have proved enduringly controversial. Other writers and critics have been drawn towards his characterisations of his friends, while censuring him as unreliable. H.G. Wells's view was that 'The pre-war F. M. H. was tortuous but understandable, the post-war F. M. H. was incurably *crazy*'.[30] But Wells saw little of Ford after the war, and that little was just after it, before Ford moved to France in 1922, and while he was still recovering from shell shock. In his own *Experiment in Autobiography* (1934), Wells wrote of Ford: 'What he is really or if he is really, nobody knows now and he least of all; he has become a great system of assumed personas and dramatized selves'.[31] But Wells's argument is that we all assume personas and writers all dramatise selves. His comment should perhaps be read as his own oblique autobiography. But his view of Ford as incurably damaged by the war, which he had elaborated cruelly in the portrayal of a hopeless egotistical fantasist in his novel *The Bulpington of Blup* (1932), influenced Arthur Mizener's biography of 1971, except that Mizener reduced all Ford's fictionalising to a putative psychological flaw which he saw as already present long before the war:

> The pain of living with his own divided nature was unendurable to Ford, and he spent much of his life and his imaginative energy inventing an alternative and more flattering image of himself that he could endure; the major source of the romancing Ford did all his life lies here.[32]

Such a diagnosis ignores the force of Ford's achievement (in his novels as well as his reminiscences), ignores the pleasure of art and the pleasure *in* art everywhere evinced by his writing. Of course those who felt travestied by Ford's reinventions were resentful. But reading his life-writing freed from the pressures of such grievances, we can see that the crucial point is the continuity and coherence of his methods whether he was writing poetry, criticism, biography, autobiography or fiction. What matters, in his life-writing as in all his work, is the telling of a good story.

Forms of Modern Literature (Oxford: Oxford University Press, 2010).

[30] Wells to Douglas Goldring (30 May 1945): quoted in Goldring, *The Last Pre-Raphaelite*, pp. 89–90.

[31] Wells, *Experiment in Autobiography*, 2 vols (London: Victor Gollancz and Cresset Press, 1934), II, p. 617.

[32] Mizener, *The Saddest Story*, p. xv.

Chapter 2

Ford and Conrad

John Attridge

Ford Madox Ford and Joseph Conrad met in September 1898, while Conrad was staying with their mutual friend Edward Garnett at The Cearne, near Limpsfield in Surrey. Garnett took Conrad to meet Ford at his nearby home, Grace's Cottage, where Ford, busy 'doing something at the open fireplace in the house-end', was mistaken by Conrad for the gardener.[1] 'You had always a love for Mother Earth', Conrad would recall some twenty-three years later: 'The first time I set eyes on you was in your potato-patch'.[2] Sixteen years Ford's senior, Conrad was an émigré who had left partitioned Poland in 1874 to become a seaman. Much of his nautical career was spent on voyages to Australia and the Far East in the British Merchant Marine, as ordinary seaman, mate and finally captain, but he also commanded a Congo River steamer for a Belgian company in 1890 and sailed to the Caribbean while still a teenager. Conrad's first novel, begun in 1889, was accepted by the publisher T. Fisher Unwin in 1894, and he retired from the sea the same year, settling in England. By the spring of 1898 he had published two full-length novels and a novella, as well as the five short stories collected in *Tales of Unrest* (1898) and a handful of essays. The twenty-five-year-old Ford had published three fairy stories, a volume of poetry, some essays of art criticism, a biography of his grandfather Ford Madox Brown and his first novel. Both writers were thus near the beginning of their literary careers, and faced uncertain futures, although Conrad at this stage had done more to make his mark in the genre of narrative fiction.

There followed from this meeting a remarkable instance of literary friendship and collaboration, lasting until the two authors fell out in 1909. Apart from the artistic advantages of close communion with a sympathetic fellow practitioner, the relationship was also a morally sustaining one for both authors, vulnerable as they were to melancholia and self-doubt.[3] Three co-authored texts resulted from the association, but there was also what Cedric Watts calls 'the covert part of their arrangement', in which Ford assisted with several of Conrad's works, in a variety

---

[1]   Ford Madox Ford, *Return to Yesterday*, ed. Bill Hutchings (Manchester: Carcanet Press, 1999), p. 44.

[2]   Joseph Conrad, *The Collected Letters of Joseph Conrad: Volume 7, 1929–1922*, ed. Laurence Davies and J.H. Stape (Cambridge: Cambridge University Press, 2005), p. 395.

[3]   Zdzisław Najder describes the 'moral support' Conrad derived from working with Ford: *Joseph Conrad: A Life* (Rochester, NY: Camden House, 2007), p. 320.

of ways.[4] Ford's elegiac 1924 memoir *Joseph Conrad: A Personal Remembrance* incensed some members of Conrad's circle – notably Garnett and Conrad's wife Jessie – with its account of Ford's contributions to Conrad's books, and Ford has sometimes been suspected of exaggerating their intimacy and the degree of his involvement with certain of Conrad's works. In response to the memoir's claim that Ford had supplied Conrad with story ideas, Jessie Conrad protested indignantly in a letter to the *Times Literary Supplement* that her husband never 'poached on Mr. Hueffer's vast stock of plots'.[5] But, as Watts says, this early, virulent scepticism has mellowed over the years, and scholars now tend to accept that Ford was intimately involved with Conrad's literary production in a variety of ways during the decade of their friendship. Moreover, as Max Saunders points out, it takes a very partial reading of Ford's memoir to find, as Jessie Conrad did, that Ford built himself up at Conrad's expense. 'I do not mean to claim any special creative part in these works', Ford wrote, 'but in such matters as providing good working conditions, trying passages from dictation, suggesting words, listening to reading and the endless supplying of the moral support [...] I certainly bothered more over Conrad's work than over my own'.[6]

Perhaps Ford's most controversial claim about helping Conrad was his assertion, made publicly in *Return to Yesterday* (1931), that he had written parts of *Nostromo* (1904) when Conrad was ill and under deadline pressure. In a 1960 PhD dissertation on Ford and Conrad's collaboration, John Hope Morey argued that analysis of the fifteen pages of the manuscript in Ford's hand supported this claim, and Arthur Mizener echoed this conclusion in his 1971 biography.[7] More recently, however, Xavier Brice has challenged this view, basing his case on a cogent reassessment of the textual evidence and a careful account of surrounding

---

[4]   Cedric Watts, *Joseph Conrad: A Literary Life* (Basingstoke: Macmillan, 1989), p. 90. These included: coaxing Conrad through the writing of *The Mirror of the Sea* (1906) and taking it down from dictation; supplying ideas for the stories 'Amy Foster' (1901) and 'To-morrow' (1902); letting drop information about the Greenwich observatory bombing that inspired the plot of *The Secret Agent* (1907); and encouraging Conrad to write 'Some Reminiscences' (later *A Personal Record*), which Ford published in the *English Review*. Ford probably also assisted with rewriting sections of 'The End of the Tether' that were destroyed by an exploding table-lamp (1902), and gave Conrad advice about the structure of *The Rescue* (1920). See Max Saunders, *Ford Madox Ford: A Dual Life*, 2 vols (Oxford: Oxford University Press, 1996), I, p. 150. On Ford's contributions to 'Amy Foster', see Arthur Mizener, *The Saddest Story: A Biography of Ford Madox Ford* (London: Bodley Head, 1972), p. 69.

[5]   Jessie Conrad, 'Correspondence', *Times Literary Supplement* (4 Dec. 1924), 826. Edward Garnett reviewed the books twice, the second time more mildly: 'Review of *Joseph Conrad: A Personal Remembrance*', *Nation and Athenaeum*, 36 (6 Dec. 1924), 366, 368; 'Review of *Joseph Conrad: A Personal Remembrance*', *Weekly Westminster* (14 Feb. 1925), 473.

[6]   Quoted in Saunders, *Ford Madox Ford*, I, p. 150. For more on Ford's memoir, see Chapter 1 in this volume.

[7]   Mizener, *The Saddest Story*, pp. 89–90.

circumstances. Brice makes a strong case that Ford's particular claim about the pages from *Nostromo* was false. Nonetheless, on the broader question of the importance of Ford's contribution to Conrad's work, he affirms that Ford's role was critical: 'Ford was invaluable to the novel's writing, providing moral support and practical assistance to a friend as well as the professional support and advice of a fellow writer.'[8]

The idea of working together originated with Conrad. Writing to the poet W.E. Henley on 18 October 1898, Conrad explained that Ford 'had some good stuff to use' which might be more easily publishable with his name attached, and also that working with Ford might dispel 'the particular devil that spoils my work for me as quick as I turn it out', enabling him to work faster. Ford, he concluded, was an 'honest workman', and the product of their collaboration would likely be 'tolerable'.[9] This letter does not mention Conrad's desire to refine his mastery of English, his third language after Polish and French, but this was undoubtedly an important motive for collaborating. As Conrad's biographer Zdzisław Najder writes: 'the most important argument in favour of the arrangement must have been the opportunity to perfect his English by acquiring a keener sense of the shades of meaning and emotional associations linked with words, expressions, and rhythms'.[10] This is the reason given by Ford himself in his memoir, although Najder rejects Ford's story that Conrad claimed to have been referred to him by Henley as 'the finest stylist in the English language of to-day'.[11] Whether Conrad employed precisely this piece of flattery or not – Ford is quite clear he didn't believe Henley ever said it – the story plainly contains grains of truth: Conrad did hope to benefit from Ford's stylistic fluency, and some such form of ornate *politesse* would not have been untypical of Conrad's courtly manner.

The two novels that Ford and Conrad co-authored attempt to couple literary artistry with the stock materials of a popular genre. *The Inheritors: An Extravagant Tale* (1901), with its story of invaders from the Fourth Dimension, drew on the tropes of the emergent science fiction novel, and also bore comparison with the popular Edwardian cycle of foreign invasion stories. *Romance: A Novel* (1903), which might have been subtitled 'Pirates of the Caribbean', superficially resembled the late-nineteenth-century neo-romance novels of Henry Rider Haggard, G.A. Henty, Rudyard Kipling, and Robert Louis Stevenson.[12] Ford and Conrad's self-conscious technical artistry was to ring the changes on this generic material,

---

[8]   Xavier Brice, 'Ford Madox Ford and the Composition of *Nostromo*', *Conradian*, 29.2 (2004), 93.

[9]   Joseph Conrad, *The Collected Letters of Joseph Conrad: Volume 2, 1898–1902*, ed. Frederick R. Karl and Laurence Davies (Cambridge: Cambridge University Press, 1986), p. 107.

[10]   Najder, *Joseph Conrad*, p. 275.

[11]   Ford Madox Ford, *Joseph Conrad: A Personal Remembrance* (London: Duckworth, 1924), p. 37.

[12]   On *Romance* and the romance tradition, see Katherine Isobel Baxter, *Joseph Conrad and the Swan Song of Romance* (Aldershot: Ashgate, 2010), pp. 53–63.

however: *Romance* was, Conrad told his agent J.B. Pinker, 'the old thing (if you like) done in a way that is new only through the artistic care of the execution';[13] according to Ford, Conrad expected to be collaborating on a cross between Stevenson's *Treasure Island* (1883) and Gustave Flaubert's *Salammbô* (1862).[14] Ford postulated in *A Personal Remembrance* that Conrad saw *The Inheritors* as 'another unexplored creek with possible gold in its shallows or its huts', and Conrad acknowledged a commercial motive behind both novels in letters: *The Inheritors* (1901) was an 'experiment', intended to 'extract shekels' from the 'Bsh Public's pocket', *Romance* (1903) an excursion into 'the genre that is currently very much in vogue with the public'.[15] Nonetheless, what Conrad called the 'artistic care of the execution' is apparent on every page of the collaborations – for better or for worse – and both *The Inheritors* and *Romance* also bear some marks of heavy-handed thematic seriousness, making them fairly cumbersome vehicles for their cargo of popular tropes.

Although the plot device of invaders from the Fourth Dimension locates *The Inheritors* in the nascent popular genre of science fiction, the novel's real energy is concentrated in a knockabout satire of Edwardian politics, mass culture and commercial imperialism. A *roman à clef*, it recounts the conflict between a sympathetic Tory based on Arthur Balfour – confusingly named Churchill – and an unscrupulous champion of Empire called Gurnard, based on the Unionist politician Joseph Chamberlain. King Leopold II of Belgium (the duc de Mersch) also features, as do the newspaper magnate Lord Northcliffe (Fox) and the popular novelist Hall Caine (Callan). One of the inspirations for the Fourth Dimensionists – 'a race clear-sighted, eminently practical, incredible; with no ideals, prejudices, or remorse; with no feeling for art and no reverence for life; free from any ethical tradition; callous to pain, weakness, suffering and death'[16] – was the National Efficiency movement, an eclectic turn-of-the-century ideology whose various subscribers (Joseph Chamberlain among them) were united by a belief in scientific methods and utilitarian ends. The depiction of a Fourth Dimensionist plot to undermine 'the traditional ideals of honour, glory, conscience' (p. 282) resembles Ford's actual beliefs about the ills of contemporary politics; it is continuous, for example, with his *English Review* essays lamenting the hegemony of utilitarian argument and the death of ideals in political discourse.[17] As Ford recalls in *A*

---

13   Conrad, *The Collected Letters of Joseph Conrad: Volume 2, 1898–1902*, p. 366.

14   Ford, *Joseph Conrad*, p. 28.

15   Ford, *Joseph Conrad*, p. 146. Conrad, *The Collected Letters of Joseph Conrad: Volume 2, 1898–1902*, pp. 261, 335; *The Collected Letters of Joseph Conrad: Volume 3, 1903–1907*, ed. Frederick R. Karl and Laurence Davies (Cambridge: Cambridge University Press, 1988), p. 76.

16   Joseph Conrad and Ford Madox Ford, *The Inheritors: An Extravagant Story* (Garden City: Doubleday, Page, 1920), pp. 11–12. All further references are to this edition.

17   See, for example, Ford Madox Ford, 'The Critical Attitude: Women's Suffrage – The Circulating Libraries – The Drama – Fine Arts, Etc.', *English Review*, 4 (1910), 329–46. For more on Ford's politics, see Chapter 14 in this volume.

Personal Remembrance, Conrad's role in the actual writing of *The Inheritors* was limited: of its 75,000 words, Ford estimated, no more than 2,000 were written by Conrad.[18]

Conrad's contribution to *Romance* was more significant. His recollection in 1924 was that the novel's first, second and fifth parts were written almost entirely by Ford, while he wrote the fourth part and 'about 60%' of the third; Ford concurred with this distribution in *A Personal Remembrance*, and it is corroborated in Raymond Brebach's study of the manuscript documents.[19] Ford's early draft of the novel was entitled 'Seraphina', after the Cuban planter's daughter with whom the hero John Kemp falls in love. The source for this story was an essay in Charles Dickens's magazine *All the Year Round* relating the trial for piracy of Aaron Smith in 1823. *Romance* begins with Kemp's flight from Kent to Jamaica with a pair of Spanish smugglers, Carlos Riego and Tomas Castro, his one-armed henchman. Although Kemp initially declines to team up with these two romantic desperadoes, the whirligig of plantation politics in the turbulent Abolition era soon throws them together again; Kemp absconds to Cuba, where he falls in love with Seraphina (Riego's cousin), and incurs the enmity of a powerful Irish nationalist called O'Brien, Seraphina's would-be suitor. Amphibious swashbuckling on and off the Cuban coast ensues, and after a series of narrow escapes Kemp is captured by O'Brien and framed as a pirate. The story ends with his trial in England.

Apart from occasional references to ironic fate, it is difficult to discern obvious continuities between *The Inheritors* and Conrad's other novels, but *Romance*, as Katherine Baxter notes, 'proved a testing ground for characters and writing that appear elsewhere in fiction he was working on at the time, notably *The Rescue, Lord Jim*, and *Nostromo*'.[20] There is a clear parallel between the dreams of exotic adventure that animate the title character of Conrad's *Lord Jim* (1900) and the longing for 'Romance' (with a capital 'R') that whets John Kemp's appetite for adventure in the first place. The novel, as Baxter points out, also allowed Conrad to explore the possibilities of a transatlantic setting, perhaps preparing the way for *Nostromo* (1904), and the convoluted political situation and depictions of Spanish Creole society are also reminiscent of that novel. *Romance* also illustrates more clearly than *The Inheritors* the aesthetic theory that Ford later codified as Impressionism, and which was, he said, propounded by Conrad as well. It contains, for example, instances of what Ian Watt called 'delayed decoding' – the device of temporarily occluding the real cause of incoherent sensory experiences.[21] Riding alone at night, for example, Kemp sees:

---

[18] Ford, *Joseph Conrad*, p. 134.

[19] Joseph Conrad, *The Collected Letters of Joseph Conrad: Volume 8, 1923–1924*, ed. Laurence Davies and Gene M. Moore (Cambridge: Cambridge University Press, 2008), p. 216; Raymond Brebach, *Joseph Conrad, Ford Madox Ford, and the Making of Romance* (Ann Arbor: UMI Research Press, 1985).

[20] Baxter, *Joseph Conrad and the Swan Song of Romance*, p. 49.

[21] Ian Watt, *Conrad in the Nineteenth Century* (Berkeley: University of California Press, 1979), pp. 176, 179.

a mass of objects, picked out with white globes [...] in the high window of
the inn, standing motionless. They resolved themselves into a barouche, with
four horses steaming a great deal and an army of negresses with bandboxes on
their heads.[22]

Although Watt coined this term in a critical study of Conrad, Ford identified the
device as a tenet of Impressionist theory in a 1935 essay, taking Stephen Crane as
an example, and he used it in his own fiction.[23] The novel's last section, meanwhile,
in which John Kemp relates his adventures to the court that is trying him for piracy,
provides a *mise en abyme* of Impressionist narration: Kemp's satisfaction that 'I
had made them see things' (p. 456) evokes Conrad's dictum from the preface to
The Nigger of the 'Narcissus' (1897): 'before all, to make you *see!*'[24]

Ford and Conrad's third collaboration, *The Nature of a Crime*, appeared
first in two issues of the *English Review* in 1909, under the pseudonym Baron
Ignatz von Aschendrof. As with *The Inheritors* and *Romance*, the story originated
with Ford and already existed in draft form when Conrad's help was enlisted,
probably in May 1906.[25] Ford republished the story under the authors' names in
the *transatlantic review* in 1924, and it appeared in book form the same year.
Both authors provided prefaces for the book publication, and Ford was moved by
Conrad's nostalgic evocation of the founding of the *English Review*, using it as an
epigraph in his memoir. The negative reviews of the 1924 book, some of which
expressed annoyance at the whimsicality of its premise and the preciousness of
its execution, are understandable.[26] The epistolary story is narrated as a suicide
note from an embezzling estate lawyer to his mistress, who is informed that
the narrator's risky financial speculations are about to be exposed by the heir's
marriage. The piece is slight, but does contain an interesting foretaste of *The Good
Soldier* (1915) both in the narrator's reflections on how outward respectability can
conceal double-dealing for long periods of time, and in the heir Edward Burden's
complex feelings of guilt about having bestowed his 'protection' on a mistress for
two years prior to his marriage. The macabre, sensational premise fits the pattern
established by the two earlier collaborations of applying artistic treatment to a
potentially popular subject.

An indispensable foundation for Ford and Conrad's relationship was their
shared interest in the form of the novel, especially as it had developed in France.
They both revered the French writers Guy de Maupassant and Gustave Flaubert,
whom they associated with an aesthetics of the sentence and a sophisticated grasp

---

[22]   Joseph Conrad and Ford Madox Ford, *Romance: A Novel* (London: Smith, Elder,
1903), p. 55. All further references are to this edition.

[23]   Ford Madox Ford, 'Techniques', *Southern Review*, 1 (1935), 20–35.

[24]   Joseph Conrad, Preface, *The Nigger of the 'Narcissus'*, ed. Robert Kimbrough
(New York: Norton, 1979), p. 147.

[25]   Saunders, *Ford Madox Ford*, I, p. 221.

[26]   See David Dow Harvey, *Ford Madox Ford: 1873–1939: A Bibliography of Works
and Criticism* (Princeton: Princeton University Press, 1962), pp. 346 –7.

of narrative technique. Recommending Maupassant's novel *Bel-Ami* (1885) to Edward Garnett in 1898, Conrad wrote: 'The technique of that work gives to one acute pleasure. It is simply enchanting to see how it's done'.[27] Camping up his improbable persona of country gentleman aesthete, Ford later recalled that he and Conrad set out to blend the influence of these two French authors in about the proportion of 'a sensible man's whiskey and soda'.[28] Conrad's letters to Ford suggest that these names were touchstones in their relationship.[29]

This shared interest in technique is reflected in Ford's memoir by its enumeration of 'formulae for the writing of the novel at which Conrad and the writer had arrived, say in 1902 or so'.[30] This part of the memoir has also excited controversy. Some readers have felt that Conrad would not have endorsed all of these principles, and that Ford, again, exaggerates his influence on Conrad by claiming to have helped to define the latter's literary theory.[31] But it is incidental to Ford's account whether these ideas originated in their discussions or whether, on the other hand, either or both authors had arrived at them independently. What is important in Ford's memoir is that he and Conrad did earnestly discuss them over a prolonged period, reinforcing one another's belief that such technical questions were worthy of serious, meticulous attention. It is this story of mutual, ardent, sociable engagement in the craft of the novel – 'solidarity of the craft',[32] Conrad might have called it – that is at the core of Ford's book, evoked in vividly remembered scenes like this one:

> For the days have been innumerable upon which, behind the amiable mare of Conrad's or a far less amiable Exmoor pony of the writer's, we drove – say between 1898 and 1905 – over a country of commonplace downlands and asked ourselves how we should render a field of ripe corn, a ten-acre patch of blue-purple cabbage. We would try the words in French: *sillonné, bleu foncé, bleu-du-roi*; we would try back into English; cast around in the back of our minds for other French words to which to assimilate our English and thus continue for quiet hours.[33]

'Both Conrad and Ford were aware that loneliness increases depression', writes Najder; we should read Ford's memories of intense debate over verbal niceties that

---

[27]   Conrad, *The Collected Letters of Joseph Conrad: Volume 2, 1898–1902*, p. 62.

[28]   Ford, *Joseph Conrad*, p. 195.

[29]   Conrad casually quotes *L'Education sentimentale* in one 1902 letter, and observes that, happily for their collaboration, the Maupassant translation being done by Ford's wife Elsie Hueffer meant that 'we shall all *think* Maupassant': *The Collected Letters of Joseph Conrad: Volume 2, 1898–1902*, pp. 388–9, 436.

[30]   Ford, *Joseph Conrad*, p. 179.

[31]   Garnett wrote that Conrad would have been 'bemused' by these guidelines. Garnett, 'Review of *Joseph Conrad*', p. 141. On the question of Ford's part in originating the theories set down in the memoir, see Saunders, *Ford Madox Ford*, I, pp. 150–51.

[32]   Joseph Conrad, *Lord Jim: A Tale* (London: Penguin, 1989), p. 139.

[33]   Ford, *Joseph Conrad*, p. 31.

few would take seriously in light of the epigraph to Conrad's *Lord Jim*, taken from Novalis: 'It is certain that my Conviction gains infinitely, the moment another soul will believe in it.'[34]

It is also relevant that Ford's emphasis on these theoretical confabulations is consistent with his oft-expressed belief in the importance of literary solidarity. The Pre-Raphaelite Brotherhood with which his grandfather was closely associated provided an early model of this ideal. Its values of 'solidarity' and 'self-sacrifice', Ford wrote in 1911, were a rare exception to the tendency for 'Anglo-Saxon writers' to sit 'each on his little hill surrounded each by his satellites'.[35] Proclaiming his former intimacy with Conrad may have been gratifying to Ford's ego, but this image of literary fellowship was not merely a flattering fancy; rather, it expressed Ford's established credo that, as he later put it in relation to the *transatlantic review*, the 'young writer may find himself without being actually published, but he cannot do so without contacts with ardent fellows in his art'.[36]

Raymond Brebach finds that 'Ford certainly over-emphasizes the two men's agreement on the techniques described in this portion of his book',[37] and a reader familiar only with *A Personal Remembrance* would perhaps expect Ford's and Conrad's novels to be more similar than they are. In particular, one might gather from the memoir that Ford and Conrad were self-declared members of a literary school called Impressionism: 'we accepted without much protest the stigma "Impressionist" that was thrown at us'.[38] This may seem to overstate the case: Conrad probably would not have assented publicly to the appellation 'Impressionist' – at least not without qualification. He distanced himself from Ford's 'theories' in a letter to William Blackwood (although praising Ford himself), and told a critic of *The Nigger of the 'Narcissus'* that 'Formulas and theories are dead things, and I wrote straight from the heart'.[39] And when Conrad characterises Stephen Crane as 'the *only* impressionist and *only* an impressionist' in a letter to Garnett, the implication is that Conrad's own aesthetic philosophy went beyond what was commonly referred to as 'impressionism'.[40] Nonetheless, 'Impressionist' certainly was an epithet that contemporary readers applied to Conrad's work. Arnold Bennett, for example, proclaimed in 1908 that 'the opening paragraph of "The Return," [is] perhaps the most dazzling feat of impressionism

---

[34]   Najder, *Joseph Conrad*, p. 277.

[35]   Ford Madox Ford, *Ancient Lights and Certain New Reflections: Being the Memories of a Young Man* (London: Chapman and Hall, 1911), pp. 231, 23.

[36]   Ford Madox Ford, *It Was the Nightingale*, ed. John Coyle (Manchester: Carcanet Press, 2007), p. 317.

[37]   Raymond Brebach, 'Ford's *Joseph Conrad: A Personal Remembrance*: A Reappraisal', *Conradian*, 12.2 (1987), 171.

[38]   Ford, *Joseph Conrad*, p. 182.

[39]   Joseph Conrad, *The Collected Letters of Joseph Conrad: Volume 1, 1861–1897*, ed. Frederick R. Karl and Laurence Davies (Cambridge: Cambridge University Press, 1983), pp. 420–21; *The Collected Letters of Joseph Conrad: Volume 2, 1898–1902*, p. 301.

[40]   Conrad, *The Collected Letters of Joseph Conrad: Volume 1, 1861–1897*, p. 416.

in modern English'.[41] Moreover, many of Conrad's signature aesthetic devices – the prevalence of vivid description, the adroit management of point of view, the technique of 'delayed decoding' mentioned above – are generally agreed to be hallmarks of Impressionist writing.[42] One should conclude from Ford's remark that he and Conrad recognised 'Impressionist' as a roughly accurate description of their work, but not that they were seen or saw themselves as card-carrying members of the same group. Ford, of course, did publicly assume this mantle, although usually not without a certain amount of equivocation.

In the rest of this chapter, I will consider some of Ford's other remarks about Conrad's literary theory and practice, both in *A Personal Remembrance* and in other appreciations written closer to the time of their collaboration. The aim here is to read Ford as one of Conrad's most perceptive early critics, and also to point to some similarities, and also some differences, between their respective *oeuvres*. Notwithstanding Conrad's misgivings, Ford's theory of Impressionism does aptly capture some important features of his fictional theory and practice. The essence of Impressionism as Ford describes it in his memoir is the recognition that 'Life did not narrate, but made impressions on our brains', and that novelists should seek to emulate this process.[43] The aim of communicating raw experiences rather than orderly, reflected accounts was a consistent feature in Ford's appraisals of Conrad. In a 1907 appreciation written for the *Tribune*, Ford praised his ability 'to give the unprovincial man the impression of having had a real experience';[44] in 1909, he commented on the reader's sense that 'we are experiencing [...] the actual scenes that he describes for us';[45] and in 1911, 'The self-appointed work of an artist of Conrad's type is to make each of his stories an experience for his reader'.[46] The title of the chapter of *A Personal Remembrance* in which Ford summarises their aesthetic dicta is 'It Is Above All to Make You See. . . .', a slight misquotation of Conrad's 'before all, to make you *see*'. In reaching his 1907 judgement that Conrad was in the business of providing experiences rather than narratives, and in reiterating this judgement seventeen years later in the memoir, Ford doubtless had this statement in mind. Conrad's pledge of 'fidelity to the truth of my own sensations'[47] is also consistent with Impressionism in this sense, as is the device of delayed decoding I have mentioned, practiced by both Conrad and Ford.

When he says that life does not narrate, Ford is also thinking of the erratic operations of memory: 'Life does not say to you: In 1914 my next-door neighbour,

---

[41] Jacob Tonson [Arnold Bennett], 'Books and Persons', *New Age*, 3.21 (1908), 412.

[42] For a persuasive account of Conrad as an Impressionist, see John G. Peters, *Conrad and Impressionism* (Cambridge: Cambridge University Press, 2001).

[43] Ford, *Joseph Conrad*, p. 182.

[44] Ford Madox Ford, 'Mr Joseph Conrad', *Critical Essays*, ed. Max Saunders and Richard Stang (Manchester: Carcanet Press, 2002), p. 39.

[45] Ford Madox Ford, 'The Critical Attitude: English Literature of To-day II', *English Review*, 3.12 (Nov. 1909), 661.

[46] Ford Madox Ford, 'Joseph Conrad', *English Review*, 10 (1911), 76.

[47] Joseph Conrad, *Within the Tides* (London: Penguin, 1978), p. 10.

Mr. Slack, erected a greenhouse and painted it with Cox's green aluminium paint. . . . If you think about the matter you will remember, in various unordered pictures, how one day Mr. Slack appeared in his garden and contemplated the wall of his house'.[48] There is an equivocation in Ford's theory here, since he seems concerned both with the serial temporal structure of experience in general and with the way experiences are later recalled as 'unordered pictures'. This is a point at which Ford's account hews to his own writing more closely than to Conrad's. Ford's interest in mimicking the movement of memory is most fully developed in *The Good Soldier*, which explicitly posits the vicissitudes of a remembering mind as a sign of verisimilitude:

> when one discusses an affair – a long, sad affair – one goes back, one goes forward. One remembers points that one has forgotten and one explains them all the more minutely since one recognizes that one has forgotten to mention them in their proper places and that one may have given, by omitting them, a false impression.[49]

Conrad never foregrounded the processes of memory as a narrative principle to the same extent. The time-shifts and ellipses of his novels – even those with first-person narrators such as *Lord Jim* (1900), *Under Western Eyes* (1911) and *Chance* (1914) – are rarely explained as quirks of the narrator's memory, but tend rather to be caused by the architecture of the frame tale. Thus, the narrator of *Chance* explains, 'the story of Flora de Barral was imparted to me in stages. At this stage I did not see Marlow for some time'.[50] This differs from the method that Ford perfected in *The Good Soldier*, whose time-shifts and loops are often determined by the zigzags of Dowell's mind and memory as he gradually works towards a coherent account of the events of the story. Perhaps the narrator of Conrad's *Under Western Eyes* comes close to Dowell's manner when he breaks off Razumov's story at the end of Part I with a confession of 'artlessness'.[51] However, it is clear that this 'artlessness' is not the result of a disordered or fluctuating recollection, but is a deliberate decision, motivated, perhaps, by a reluctance to narrate the more damning parts of Razumov's story. Ford made the workings of memory and understanding an object of representation to a greater extent than Conrad, and it seems to be his own technique that he has primarily in mind when he describes remembering Mr Slack's greenhouse.[52]

Ford's remarks about the importance of 'justification' and conveying a sense of 'inevitability'[53] in *A Personal Remembrance* communicate an astute understanding

---

[48]   Ford, *Joseph Conrad*, p. 181.

[49]   Ford Madox Ford, *The Good Soldier*, second edition, ed. Martin Stannard (New York: Norton, 2012), pp. 124–5. All further references are to this edition.

[50]   Joseph Conrad, *Chance: A Tale in Two Parts* (London: Penguin, 1974), p. 217.

[51]   Joseph Conrad, *Under Western Eyes* (New York: Random House, 2001), p. 77.

[52]   For more on Ford and Impressionism, see Chapter 5 in this volume.

[53]   Ford, *Joseph Conrad*, p. 204.

of Conrad's literary practice. This idea of justification is another leitmotif of Ford's criticism on Conrad, appearing in the 1911 *English Review* appraisal and also, in a slightly parodic form, in his earlier 1909 article for the same journal. In 1911, Ford wrote:

> And that is the great faculty of this author – that he can make an end seem inevitable, in every instance the only possible end. He does this by every means – by the explanations of heredity, of temperament, of the nature of sea and sky, by the sound of a song, by the straws in the street.[54]

Ford's comments on this quality of Conrad's fiction in the 1909 article seem to have *The Secret Agent* as an unnamed referent, explaining humorously that Conrad, when plotting a murder, would find it necessary to explain why the 'man who sold the murderer the knife [...] was predisposed to the selling of lethal instruments to men of wild appearance'.[55] The reason why Ford associated Conrad's concern with 'inevitableness' particularly with *The Secret Agent* is explained in his memoir, in which he recalls Conrad elaborating the need for 'justification' during a discussion of the plot of that novel.[56] This recollection was surely accurate: *The Secret Agent* establishes the psychological verisimilitude of the thoughts and actions leading to Verloc's murder with meticulous care. The penultimate chapter, in particular, which narrates the murder, carefully reminds the reader of the intensity of Winnie Verloc's love for her brother, born of their shared experience of paternal brutality, and Verloc's fatal ignorance of this key to his wife's character, which leads him to underestimate Winnie's sorrow and anger on learning of his role in her brother's death. Moreover, Conrad extensively revised this scene between the novel's serial publication and its appearance as a single volume, bolstering the psychological 'justification' for Verloc's stabbing, suggesting that this question was indeed on his mind during composition.[57]

Ford's observation that not only 'heredity' and 'temperament' but also vivid physical description were among the devices used by Conrad to attain the end of 'inevitableness' was also perceptive. 'The note of truth', Conrad wrote to T. Fisher Unwin in 1896, 'is not in the possibility of things but in their inevitableness. Inevitableness is the only certitude; it is the very essence of life – as it is of dreams. A picture of life is saved from failure by the merciless vividness of detail'.[58] This

---

54   Ford Madox Ford, 'Joseph Conrad', *Critical Essays*, p. 82.

55   Ford Madox Ford, 'The Critical Attitude: English Literature of To-Day II', 660–61.

56   Ford, *Joseph Conrad*, pp. 206–7.

57   In comparison with the expanded 1907 version, the 1906 periodical publication is a mere synopsis, compressing the last three chapters of the book version – Verloc's murder, Ossipon's betrayal of Winnie, and his final, guilt-ridden meeting with the Professor at the Silenus Restaurant – into a single brisk instalment. The serial version is reproduced in *The Secret Agent*, ed. Bruce Harkness and S.W. Reid (Cambridge: Cambridge University Press, 1990).

58   Conrad, *The Collected Letters of Joseph Conrad: Volume 1, 1861–1897*, p. 302.

is one of the points made in Ford's 1911 essay: vivid description is conceived as a means of producing 'inevitableness'. Ford was an acute reader of Conrad, and, of course, underlying the perceptiveness of many of his critical judgements was the intimate understanding of Conrad's working methods he had picked up during their discussions of literary technique.

Another technical maxim detailed in *A Personal Remembrance* is the diffracted presentation of character, in which an initial 'strong impression' is supplemented and, often, contradicted by subsequent discoveries.[59] This is supposed to imitate the empirical experience of getting to know people: 'an English gentleman at your golf club' who seems 'beefy, full of health, the moral of the boy from an English Public School of the finest type' will only subsequently reveal himself to be a neurasthenic, dishonest in petty matters, self-sacrificing, a liar, a lepidopterist, a bigamist and a dangerous financial speculator.[60] Readers of *The Good Soldier* will recognise this schema as the same one that organises Ford's presentation of Edward Ashburnham, likewise an English gentleman whose hyperconventional exterior is bafflingly inconsistent with his personal behaviour: 'You would have said that he was just exactly the sort of chap that you could have trusted your wife with. And I trusted mine – and it was madness' (p. 14). With regard to Conrad's fiction, the text that was foremost in Ford's mind when he set out this principle of characterisation was probably *Lord Jim*. This is the novel of Conrad's that conforms most closely to what Ford says in his memoir about diffracted characterisation: Jim is, indeed, introduced on the first page of the novel with a 'strong impression', and the narrative's epistemological drama centres on Marlow's subsequent efforts to resolve his various impressions of Jim into a knowable character: to penetrate, as he says, the 'fog'[61] swirling around his essential nature.

Ford's comments about characterisation signal not only a formal, but also a thematic similarity connecting his work to Conrad's. Jim, like Edward Ashburnham, appears to embody a conventional idea of English national identity. He may not have attended an 'English Public School of the finest type', but the naval training ship where he learns the 'craft of the sea' (probably based on the HMS Conway) is a functional equivalent: Jim speaks in the slang of a public-school novel – 'What a bally ass I've been [...]. You are a brick!' – and is, as he insists, a 'gentleman'.[62] Englishness is one of the shared categories evoked by the phrase 'one of us', which Marlow uses to describe Jim, and the consternation Marlow feels when this outward appearance is contradicted by Jim's behaviour is reminiscent of Dowell in *The Good Soldier*: 'I would have trusted the deck to that youngster on the strength of a single glance, and gone to sleep with both eyes – and, by Jove! it wouldn't have been safe'.[63] Ford was deeply marked by reading *Lord Jim* – 'it is a part of my soul,

[59]   Ford, *Joseph Conrad*, p. 130.
[60]   Ford, *Joseph Conrad*, p. 129.
[61]   Conrad, *Lord Jim*, p. 99.
[62]   Conrad, *Lord Jim*, pp. 139, 178.
[63]   Conrad, *Lord Jim*, p. 76.

of my life. It has entered into me like the blood in my veins'[64] – and Conrad's story of the subtle untrustworthiness of the English gentleman is an important intertext for *The Good Soldier*. Neither Ford nor Conrad was altogether at home with the cultural norms of Englishness, and both subjected the increasingly precarious image of the English gentleman to probing analysis in several of their novels: Ford in characters such as George Moffat in *The Benefactor* (1905), Mr Blood in *Mr. Fleight* (1913), Edward Ashburnham in *The Good Soldier* and, above all, Christopher Tietjens in *Parade's End* (1924–28); Conrad most notably in Jim and Charles Gould in *Nostromo*, but also in such crypto-Englishmen as Axel Heyst, the 'last gentleman' of *Victory* (1915) and Razumov, the taciturn student-cum-secret-agent of *Under Western Eyes*. Ford's designation of the deceptively normal English gentleman as an archetype of Impressionist characterisation in *A Personal Remembrance* draws attention to this important shared theme of their fiction.[65]

Ford and Conrad were fascinated by Englishness in part because neither of them was fully naturalised to its norms and customs: they were resident aliens, keen ethnographers for whom English culture and society were at once intimately familiar and irreducibly strange. Ford described his own paradoxical position as an ethnographer of his own nation in his most frankly ethnographic book, *The Spirit of the People* (1907):

> He should be attached by very strong ties to the race of which he writes, or he will write without sympathy. He should, if possible, be attached to as many other races as may be by ties equally strong, or he will, lacking comprehension of other national manifestations, be unable to draw impartial comparisons.[66]

The Impressionist ethnographer must imagine his way into his object of study while preserving a sense of foreignness. In *Return to Yesterday* (1931), Ford recalls how H.G. Wells described the cluster of foreign writers living near Romney Marsh in south Kent as 'a ring of foreign conspirators plotting against British letters'.[67] This is an image worthy of Ford himself, who drew liberally on fictional tropes in his memoirs of literary life – not least *A Personal Remembrance*, which humorously presents Ford and Conrad's literary escapades as if they were episodes from an adventure novel. The writers Wells had in mind, in addition to Conrad, were the Americans Stephen Crane, W.H. Hudson and Henry James, an 'alien settlement' ringed in by the Englishmen Alfred Austin, Rudyard Kipling and Wells himself. It is often noted that modernism in England was not particularly English: the core of the Vorticist group, for example – England's first continental-style avant-

---

[64] Ford, 'Joseph Conrad', 78.
[65] On this major theme in Ford's fiction, see Chapter 13 in this volume; also Denis Brown and Jenny Plastow (eds), *Ford Madox Ford and Englishness*, International Ford Madox Ford Studies 5 (Amsterdam: Rodopi, 2006).
[66] Ford Madox Ford, *The Spirit of the People: An Analysis of the English Mind* (London: Alston Rivers, 1907), p. 5.
[67] Ford, *Return to Yesterday*, p. 21.

garde movement – was the Canadian-born painter and writer Wyndham Lewis, the French sculptor Henri Gaudier-Brzeska and the American poet Ezra Pound. Michael North has suggested that consciousness of racial and cultural difference were essential conditions for the linguistic experimentation that characterised literary modernism: 'writers who tamper with the English language are, ipso facto, racial aliens', disturbing the naturalness of national tongues and revealing their contingency.[68] North's argument suggests one way of seeing Ford and Conrad's friendship as a seminal chapter in the cultural history of modernism, bracketed by the milestones of Conrad's *Heart of Darkness* (serialised in 1899) and Ford's editorship of the *English Review* (1908–10). Ford does not insert himself into Wells's image of a subversive cell, but if he had featured in this picture his place would surely not have been among the outer shell of Englishmen, but rather in the nucleus with Conrad, two racial aliens, intent on bringing about a modernist revolution in England and in English.

---

[68] Michael North, *The Dialect of Modernism: Race, Language, and Twentieth-Century Literature* (Oxford: Oxford University Press, 1994), p. 27.

Chapter 3

Towards *The Good Soldier*: Ford's Edwardian Fiction

Rob Hawkes

On 22 January 1901, Queen Victoria died and was succeeded to the throne by her son, King Edward VII. Edward reigned until his death on 6 May 1910, and just as we know Victoria's time on the throne as the Victorian age, so we know Edward's as the Edwardian period. However, when we use a label such as this to describe a historical era we usually mean more than just the passage of time between two dates. In other words, when we describe an event or an artefact as 'Victorian' we do not just mean that it dates from the period between 1837 and 1901. Instead we allow the label to conjure up a whole host of characteristics including, perhaps, a particularly strict sense of morality, an excessive sexual prudishness, an ambitious and tirelessly confident approach to industry and empire-building, relatively austere fashions and, of course, a particular kind of literature. When we speak of Victorian fiction, we mean the novels of Dickens, Thackeray, Trollope, Gaskell, and George Eliot – in short, the major exponents of classic realism.[1] Furthermore, we often hear modernist writers such as James Joyce and Virginia Woolf charged with having overturned 'Victorian conventions' such as the linear plots, omniscient narration and detailed descriptions of characters and settings favoured by nineteenth-century novelists. We need to be cautious here since, in many ways, the outline I have just given is no more than a crude stereotype. Nevertheless, it is important to recognise the immediacy with which, for most of us, the term 'Victorian' evokes just this set of characteristics.

In this chapter we will examine a selection of Ford's Edwardian novels and, in doing so, we will ask: what, if anything, does 'Edwardian fiction' mean? While, as I have suggested, most of us are fairly clear about what we mean by 'Victorian', we are much less certain about the label 'Edwardian', and the fact that we do not even have a crude stereotype to fall back on provides an excellent indication of this. We will also sample the range of genres with which Ford experimented during the Edwardian years – from historical novels such as *The Fifth Queen* trilogy (1906–08) and the time-travel fantasy *Ladies Whose Bright Eyes* (1911) to novels of contemporary society such as *A Call* (1910) and *Mr. Fleight* (1913) –

---

[1]   For further discussion of realism, see Peter Brooks, *Realist Vision* (New Haven: Yale University Press, 2005); Pam Morris, *Realism* (London: Routledge, 2003); and Dennis Walder (ed.), *The Realist Novel* (London: Routledge, 1995).

and identify some of the characteristics that this diverse selection of books share. We will compare Ford to two of the best-known writers of the day, Arnold Bennett and H.G. Wells, and finally, as my title suggests, we will look at how Ford's Edwardian fiction shows him working 'towards' his modernist masterpiece, *The Good Soldier* (1915).

A Note on 'Edwardian'

By the time *The Good Soldier* appeared in 1915, Ford had already published more than forty books, eighteen of which were novels. Of these, only *The Shifting of the Fire* (1892) appeared before Edward VII became king and so, in one sense at least, almost all of Ford's fiction before *The Good Soldier* was Edwardian. Nevertheless, as I have already suggested, 'Edwardian' needs to mean more than just 'written between 1901 and 1910' to function as a useful category for our discussion. Samuel Hynes, whose work helped to establish Edwardian writing as category worthy of critical attention, observed in 1972 that:

> *Edwardian* scarcely exists as a literary term. [...] This may be because the Edwardian period was too short to attract scholarly specialists [...]. Or it may be that Victorian and Modern can be made to spread out, and cover the intervening years so completely that no transitional term seems necessary. [...] Yet the time between the turn of the century and the First World War does seem to have the qualities that make a literary period [...].[2]

Hynes's remarks are useful to us for several reasons. First, he focuses on Edwardian as a *literary* term (rather than as a strictly historical one). He also introduces the idea that 'Edwardian' may be seen as a *transitional* term, between 'Victorian' and 'Modern'. Trying to fix a definitive set of dates to a literary period is never straightforward, and our attempts to do so are often somewhat arbitrary. As Seamus O'Malley points out in the following chapter, a common set of dates for the age of modernism is 1900–1939, yet 1910–1945 and 1890–1925 are cited with equal frequency. Virginia Woolf famously claimed that: 'in or about December, 1910, human character changed',[3] suggesting that a decisive moment in the onset of the modernist era did indeed coincide with the end of Edward's time on the throne. From this perspective the Edwardian years were little more than an extension of the Victorian period. From another point of view, however, the age of modernism was already underway by 1890 just as, indeed, many of the social and cultural

    [2]   Samuel Hynes, 'Introduction: A Note on "Edwardian"', *Edwardian Occasions: Essays on English Writing in the Early Twentieth Century* (London: Routledge and Kegan Paul, 1972), p. 1.
    [3]   Virginia Woolf, 'Mr. Bennett and Mrs. Brown', *Collected Essays*, 4 vols (London: Hogarth Press, 1966–67), II, p. 320. If you are using *Selected Essays*, ed. David Bradshaw (Oxford: Oxford University Press, 2008), see the essay titled 'Character in Fiction' and p. xxvi for details of the essay's evolution.

conditions associated with the Victorian era were already on the wane. Either way, these views present the modernist age as following hard on the heels of the Victorian literary period without, as Hynes puts it, the need for a transitional term.

Since the publication of Hynes's *Edwardian Occasions* in 1972, critics have increasingly recognised the usefulness, if not the need for just such a literary term.[4] Like Hynes, these critics tend to position Edwardian writing *between* two cultural shifts: one signalling the end of the Victorian era at the close of the nineteenth century, and another signalling the beginning of the age of modernism in the early twentieth century. As Carola M. Kaplan and Anne B. Simpson point out: 'The year 1895, the time of the Wilde scandal, called into question prevailing norms of sexual behaviour and focused public attention on the definition of selfhood'.[5] John Batchelor also cites the Wilde trial as a turning point, suggesting that 'the Wilde *debâcle* and the first issue of *Blast* could be taken as the parameters' of the Edwardian literary period.[6] For the purposes of this discussion, then, we will accept the view that the Edwardian literary period began in the late nineteenth century, somewhere between 1895 and the death of Queen Victoria, but could not survive the twin onslaughts in 1914 of the outbreak of the First World War and the wave of new literary and artistic movements that Wyndham Lewis's radical modernist magazine *Blast* reflected and helped to foster.[7] Since we have already accepted that the boundaries between these periods are blurred, however, we have the advantage of some flexibility. We are not saying that there was no modernist fiction until after 1914: Joyce had written *Dubliners* (1914)[8] and Joseph Conrad produced his best and most challenging novels – *Nostromo* (1904) and *The Secret Agent* (1907) among them – during the Edwardian years. Nevertheless, positioning Edwardian fiction *between* Victorian and modernist fiction (both historically and aesthetically) allows us to see Edwardian as a literary category in its own right whilst recognising its connections and affinities with both neighbouring terms.

Mr Bennett and Mrs Brown

In 1924, Woolf's essay 'Mr. Bennett and Mrs. Brown' appeared. Along with the earlier 'Modern Fiction' (1919), this essay is now a standard entry in anthologies

---

[4]   See, for example, John Batchelor, *The Edwardian Novelists* (London: Duckworth, 1982); Jefferson Hunter, *Edwardian Fiction* (Cambridge, MA: Harvard University Press, 1982); and Carola M. Kaplan and Anne B. Simpson (eds), *Seeing Double: Revisioning Edwardian and Modernist Literature* (New York: St Martin's Press, 1996).

[5]   Kaplan and Simpson, Introduction, *Seeing Double*, p. xvii.

[6]   Batchelor, *The Edwardian Novelists*, p. 2.

[7]   For more on Ford and modernist magazines, see Chapter 7 of this volume and Jason Harding (ed.), *Ford Madox Ford, Modernist Magazines and Editing*, International Ford Madox Ford Studies 9 (Amsterdam: Rodopi, 2010).

[8]   Several of the stories that comprise *Dubliners* first appeared in *Irish Homestead* in 1904 and the manuscript for the full collection was completed in 1905.

of modernist writings, of twentieth-century literary criticism, and on the theory of the novel.[9] Both essays are also notable for the attacks Woolf makes on a trio of Edwardian writers: Arnold Bennett, John Galsworthy and H.G. Wells. In 'Modern Fiction', Woolf labels these writers 'materialists' and dismisses them as disappointing 'because they are concerned not with the spirit but with the body'.[10] Against the 'materialists' Woolf sets the 'moderns', singling out James Joyce as the prime example. Joyce, by contrast, 'is spiritual; he is concerned at all costs to reveal the flickerings of that innermost flame which flashes its messages through the brain'.[11] In 'Mr. Bennett and Mrs. Brown', Woolf continues her attack, focusing this time, as her title suggests, on Bennett. Criticising him, once again, for his interest in external appearances rather than in the inner lives of his characters, Woolf invents the fictional Mrs Brown – whom she places in a railway carriage travelling from Richmond to Waterloo – and imagines how Bennett would go about writing a novel about her. He would, according to Woolf, 'observe every detail with immense care':

> He would notice the advertisements; the pictures of Swanage and Portsmouth; the way in which the cushion bulged between the buttons; how Mrs. Brown wore a brooch which had cost three-and-ten at Whitworth's bazaar; and had mended both gloves – indeed the thumb of the left-hand glove had been replaced.[12]

Woolf's description of what Bennett 'would' do performs the criticism she wants to make of his writing: it focuses meticulously and painstakingly on increasingly minute, mundane and seemingly trivial details. In the end, Woolf complains that: 'With all his powers of observation, which are marvellous [...] Mr. Bennett has never once looked at Mrs. Brown in her corner', and she makes clear that not looking at Mrs. Brown also means avoiding looking at 'life' and 'human nature'.[13] As a result, as Woolf puts it in 'Modern Fiction', 'Life escapes'.[14] To those of us who first encounter the literature of the early twentieth century with modernism as the framing context (as I certainly did), this is familiar ground. Modernist writers, so the standard explanation goes, were interested in the mind rather than the body and so developed new methods – such as the stream-of-consciousness technique – for representing the psychological experiences of their characters. Their novels became more and more fragmented and obscure as they rejected chronological

---

9   See, for example, Vassiliki Kolocotroni, Jane Goldman and Olga Taxidoux (eds), *Modernism: An Anthology of Sources and Documents* (Edinburgh: Edinburgh University Press, 1998); Lawrence Rainey (ed.), *Modernism: An Anthology* (Oxford: Blackwell, 2005); Suman Gupta and David Johnson (eds), *A Twentieth-Century Literature Reader: Texts and Debates* (Abingdon: Routledge, 2005); and Michael J. Hoffman and Patrick D. Murphy (eds), *Essentials of the Theory of Fiction* (Durham: Duke University Press, 1996).

10   Virginia Woolf, 'Modern Fiction', *Collected Essays*, II, p. 104.

11   Woolf, 'Modern Fiction', p. 107.

12   Woolf, 'Mr. Bennett and Mrs. Brown', p. 328.

13   Woolf, 'Mr. Bennett and Mrs. Brown', p. 330.

14   Woolf, 'Modern Fiction', p. 105.

sequence in favour of new and freer approaches that more closely resembled the life of the mind. Woolf's attack on Bennett, Wells and Galsworthy helped to cement the view that Edwardian fiction was the polar opposite of this kind of modernist fiction: staid, outmoded and obsessed with physical details, skilfully observed, yes, but no longer fit for the task of representing life in the modern age. Because of the ubiquity of Woolf's remarks in discussions of modernist fiction, it is very difficult to avoid viewing Edwardian writing in the terms imposed on it by her attack. Our task, however, if we are to take a fresh look at Ford's Edwardian fiction, is to do just that.[15]

Edwardian and Modern?

Is Edwardian fiction really the polar opposite of modernist fiction? Is it not possible to be both Edwardian and modern? Of course, much depends on what we mean by the term 'modern'. It would require more space than we have here to do this matter justice, but broadly speaking 'modern' is best thought of as the opposite of 'traditional'.[16] Modernity, therefore, refers to a social order based on constant change and renewal rather than on traditions which remain fixed and unchanging. As Jesse Matz notes: 'The novel has always been modern – always concerned mainly with contemporary life, and, as the name suggests, always after the new thing. But some time around 1900 [...], to be modern meant something more, because suddenly modernity meant everything.'[17] For the early twentieth-century novelist, however, there was more than one way to respond to this newly all-encompassing sense of modernity. In terms of the basic distinction we often make when discussing literature between *content* and *form*, one way of being modern is to examine, worry over and seek to represent the experience of modern life at the level of *content* (that is, in terms of what happens in the novel, who it happens to, and how). Another is to reflect the newness of modern life at the level of *form* by seeking out new techniques, new styles, and new ways of constructing novels. The second of these options, of course, was the one favoured by modernists such as Joyce and Woolf. In keeping with our view of its position *between* Victorian and modernist, Edwardian fiction is best understood as resolutely modern at the

---

[15]   For more on Woolf vs. Bennett, see Rob Hawkes, *Ford Madox Ford and the Misfit Moderns: Edwardian Fiction and the First World War* (Basingstoke: Palgrave Macmillan, 2012), pp. 24–9.

[16]   For further discussion of the term 'modern' and the relationship between modernism and modernity, see Randall Stevenson, *Modernist Fiction*, revised edition (Hemel Hempstead: Prentice Hall, 1998); and Peter Childs, *Modernism* (London: Routledge, 2000). For more in-depth studies of the idea of modernity, see Marshall Berman, *All That is Solid Melts Into Air: The Experience of Modernity* (London: Verso, 2010); and Anthony Giddens, *The Consequences of Modernity* (Cambridge: Polity Press, 1990).

[17]   Jesse Matz, *The Modern Novel: A Short Introduction* (Oxford: Blackwell, 2004), p. 1.

level of content, whilst remaining relatively traditional in terms of style, structure and technique.

Phones, Trains and Automobiles

Ford's Edwardian novels are full of examples of the profound, rapid and bewildering changes that were sweeping through British society at the turn of the twentieth century. At the forefront of these changes were new technologies. In *A Call*, *Mr. Fleight* and *Ladies Whose Bright Eyes*, telephones, trains and motor cars play key roles in the narratives, more often than not threatening the protagonists in significant ways. The plot of *A Call* turns on a telephone call by which the recently married Dudley Leicester is discovered, late at night, in the house of an old flame. The telephone's ability to intrude into the seemingly private space of Etta Stackpole's hallway destroys Leicester's peace of mind and eventually leads to his complete mental breakdown. The historical fantasy *Ladies Whose Bright Eyes* has Mr Sorrell, a twentieth-century publisher, transported back to the fourteenth century where he must learn how to live without the trappings of modern life. The incident that flings him back in time is a railway crash, caused by the excessive speed of the train he is travelling on. Finally, *Mr. Fleight*, a satire on social climbing in political and literary circles, begins with Mr Blood, a figure who represents an outmoded sense of tradition, standing at the window of his club and tracking the advance of modernity by 'counting the motors against the horse traffic'.[18] Later on in the story, Mr Fleight, a young millionaire and parliamentary candidate, gives a poor tobacco seller named Gilda Leroy and her mother a lift home in his car:

> The town glided by them, the vibrating hands of the silver clock jumped to five, to ten; the country outside them grew dark, they seemed to be going into a dusky cave lit up by the enormous headlights. The pale faces of men, looking round, shot by them [...]. The vibrating hands of the dial jumped to thirty and trembled towards forty.
> 'Oh, mother!' Gilda exclaimed, 'we're going at forty miles an hour [...].'
> (p. 144)

It may be difficult for us today to recapture the striking novelty of this first ride in an automobile (and the extreme speed represented by forty miles an hour), but the images of the car disappearing into a cave and the faces of onlookers shooting by, along with the vibrating and trembling hands of the speedometer, emphasise the eerie combination of the exhilarating and threatening aspects of the journey for Gilda and her mother. As the story develops, Fleight's act of kindness leads indirectly to him being attacked and badly beaten by a gang of youths and, much worse, to Gilda's suicide.

---

[18]   Ford Madox Ford, *Mr. Fleight* (London: Howard Latimer, 1913), p. 2. All further references are to this edition.

Ford is not alone among Edwardian novelists in charting the impact of new technologies on his protagonists. The narrator of H.G. Wells's *Tono-Bungay* (1909), George Ponderevo, is a part-time inventor of flying machines. One of his early experiments with flight ends in a crash landing which leaves him bleeding and incapacitated for several days. Later, he and his uncle are forced to flee from England in another of his inventions (due to the discovery of his uncle's financial wrongdoing). Having dozed off in his airship overnight, George wakes to discover that their engine has failed and that they risk being swept out to sea:

> Then, indeed, for a time I felt the grim thrill of life. I crawled forward to the cords of the release valves, made my uncle crawl forward too, and let out the gas until we were falling down through the air like a clumsy glider towards the vague greyness that was land. [...]
> I remember coming down at last with a curious indifference, and actually rousing myself to steer. But the actual coming to earth was exciting enough.[19]

As we see here, despite the danger of death, George experiences the landing with 'a curious indifference'. His language itself betrays the same blend of excitement and menace – as encapsulated by the phrase 'the grim thrill of life' – familiar to us from Mr Fleight's car journey. Motor cars and hot air balloons are also among the key signals of modernity's gathering pace in Arnold Bennett's *The Old Wives' Tale* (1908). The novel follows two sisters, Sophia and Constance Baines, from girlhood in the 1860s to their deaths during the Edwardian years. It also charts the changes that take place in their hometown of Bursley, one of the fictionalised 'Five Towns' (based on Stoke-on-Trent). When, towards the end of the novel, as cars first begin to appear in the town, we are told of the sisters' 'natural prejudice against anything so new as a motor-car'.[20] This aversion is overcome, however, as Sophia eventually travels to Manchester by car to see her estranged husband. The journey back to Bursley is, once again, both tantalising and ominous: it is made 'under the spell of the changing beauty of nocturnal landscapes', and yet the narrator informs us that: 'under the melancholy arch of evening, the sadness of the earth seemed to possess Sophia anew' (pp. 580–81). By the end of the journey we learn that: 'Sophia was not asleep, but she was apparently not conscious' (p. 581), and soon afterwards she dies. Like Gilda Leroy in Ford's *Mr. Fleight*, Sophia is not, literally speaking, killed by an automobile, but there is a symbolic link between their deaths, their car journeys, and the broader sense of bewildering, exhilarating and yet profoundly unsettling societal change that these new technologies represent.

---

[19]   H.G. Wells, *Tono-Bungay* (London: Penguin, 2005), pp. 355–6. All further references are to this edition.

[20]   Arnold Bennett, *The Old Wives' Tale* (London: Penguin, 2007), p. 567. All further references are to this edition.

'All human relationships have shifted'

Of course, new technologies embody just one of the many rapidly changing aspects of early twentieth-century life with which the protagonists of Edwardian novels must grapple. Indeed, one of the reasons that new modes of transport and methods of communication play such disconcerting roles in the texts under discussion is that they very often amplify the instability of social relationships that were already precariously poised on the edge of irrevocable change. For example, the telephone call in *A Call* threatens to reveal the instabilities born of hidden passions and repressed desires in the network of relationships between Dudley Leicester, his new wife Pauline, Robert Grimshaw and Katya Lascarides. In *Mr. Fleight*, the speed with which Fleight's car travels reflects the speed with which the class barriers between himself and Gilda Leroy appear to have dissolved, giving her the false impression that he wishes to marry her. As noted earlier, Kaplan and Simpson suggest that the Wilde scandal ushered in the Edwardian era since it 'called into question prevailing norms of sexual behaviour',[21] and, of course, Woolf famously observed that: 'All human relationships have shifted – those between masters and servants, husbands and wives, parents and children' in 'Mr. Bennett and Mrs. Brown'.[22]

Edwardian fiction is replete with examples of social barriers and frameworks in a state of flux – such as class boundaries and gender roles – structures that just a generation or so earlier would have seemed fixed and immutable. *A Call* features the 'new woman' figure Katya Lascarides who is, as Max Saunders has pointed out, 'one of the first psychotherapist-characters in English fiction'.[23] What's more, as a formidable, independent, professional and above all unmarried woman, she poses a considerable threat to Robert Grimshaw's paternalistic desire to observe, control and manipulate those around him. Katya's most profound challenge to prevailing social norms is to refuse to marry but to insist that Grimshaw must allow her to live with and 'play the part of wife to him'.[24] A sense of the precariousness of the institution of marriage also comes into Wells's *Tono-Bungay* when George talks openly of his 'queer, unwise love relationship' with his wife and his 'bungle of a marriage':

> I'm enormously impressed by the ignorant, unguided way in which we two entangled ourselves with each other. It seems to me the queerest thing in all this network of misunderstandings and misstatements and faulty and ramshackle conventions which makes up our social order as the individual meets it, that we

[21] Kaplan and Simpson, Introduction, *Seeing Double*, p. xvii.

[22] Woolf, 'Mr. Bennett and Mrs. Brown', p. 321.

[23] Max Saunders, *Ford Madox Ford: A Dual Life*, 2 vols (Oxford: Oxford University Press, 1996), I, p. 301.

[24] Ford Madox Ford, *A Call: The Tale of Two Passions* (Manchester: Carcanet Press, 1984), p. 63. For more on gender in *A Call*, see Chapter 12 in this volume.

should have come together so accidentally and so blindly. Because we were no
more than samples of the common fate. (p. 163)

George's description of marriage as part of the 'network of [...] faulty and
ramshackle conventions which makes up our social order' is particularly important
because it suggests, first, that the failure of his marriage was not just a personal
failure but part of a wider pattern. Secondly, it suggests that this issue of how
the young 'pair off' is only one among many patterns of behaviour which have
begun to seem misguided and on the point of disintegration. Later, when George
comes to consider the reasons for an extramarital affair, he admits quite frankly
that: 'I was a young and fairly vigorous man; all my appetite for love had been
roused and whetted and none of it had been satisfied by my love affair and my
marriage' (p. 188). While marriages in Victorian novels are certainly not always
happy, and married characters do not always remain faithful, there is little sense
that the institution of marriage itself might be an empty and outmoded convention.
These tendencies – to criticise social conventions, to speak openly about sexual
desire, and to represent the ways in which social relationships were shifting – are
among the most striking ways in which Edwardian fiction exhibits its modernity.

Tradition versus Modernity

As well as focusing on the consequences of social and technological change,
Edwardian novels very often thematise the conflict between tradition and
modernity itself. The Baines family in *The Old Wives' Tale* stand, in many ways,
for tradition and stoical resistance in the face of change and in *Tono-Bungay*
tradition is embodied in Bladesover, the country mansion in which George grows
up. The novel charts the gradual destruction of all that Bladesover represents as
the modern age of advertising and commercialism takes over. Of course, the battle
between tradition and modernity is not a uniquely Edwardian preoccupation;
numerous Victorian novels present a similar set of conflicting values. However,
in Anthony Trollope's *Barchester Towers* (1857), for example, the representatives
of modernity – Mr Slope and Mrs Proudie – are made to appear both sinister
and ridiculous, and tradition is able to reassert itself unequivocally by the end of
the novel. In the Edwardian novel there are no such reassuring conclusions. The
Tudor trilogy *The Fifth Queen* (1906), *Privy Seal* (1907) and *The Fifth Queen
Crowned* (1908), with which Ford achieved his first major success as a novelist,
is no exception. The series is set in the court of Henry VIII and tells the story of
how Katharine Howard arrives at court, catches the eye of the King, becomes his
fifth queen, and is eventually accused of adultery and executed. As A.S. Byatt
notes in her introduction to *The Fifth Queen*, it is too simple to read the trilogy
as a straightforward allegory of Edwardian England.[25] Nevertheless, the world

---

[25] See A.S. Byatt, Introduction, in Ford Madox Ford, *The Fifth Queen* (London:
Penguin, 1999), p. vii. All further references are to this edition.

depicted in the trilogy is also one reeling from a profound sense of change. At the beginning, Henry has split from Rome, turning his back on the traditions of Catholicism, and is about to ally himself with German Lutherans by marrying Anne of Cleves. Thomas Cromwell, the King's most intimate adviser, represents a modern outlook based on political expediency, Machiavellian scheming and the 'New Learning', while Katharine remains committed to the traditions of the Catholic Church. As she tells Cromwell the first time they meet: 'I am for the Old Faith in the Old Way' (p. 54). Although the King turns against Cromwell at the end of the second novel in the series, *Privy Seal*, the forces of modernity win out in the end and, as the trilogy closes, Katharine dies along with any hope of a return to the 'Old Faith'. Time and again, Edwardian novels stage the conflict between tradition and modernity, and when they do so they invariably present the processes of modernisation as inexorable and the overturning of all traditions as inevitable. As Marshall Berman puts it in his seminal work on 'the experience of modernity': 'To be modern is to be part of a universe in which, as Marx said, "all that is solid melts into air"'.[26]

As I suggested earlier, despite being preoccupied with the conditions of modernity at the level of content, most Edwardian novels remain bound by the formal and stylistic conventions of the nineteenth-century novel. Of the texts discussed in this chapter, all but Wells's *Tono-Bungay* employs a third-person narrator. All contain stories with a beginning, a middle and an end (unlike modernist novels such as *Mrs Dalloway* and *Ulysses* which do not have a 'plot' in the traditional sense). Furthermore, Ford's Edwardian fiction often confirms rather than challenges Woolf's caricature of the obsessively detailed describer. Here, for example, is an early description of Katharine Howard from *The Fifth Queen*:

> She uncovered her face and sat looking at the ground. Her furs were all grey, she had had none new for four years, and they were tight to her young body that had grown into them. The roses embroidered on her glove had come unstitched, and, against the steely grey of the river, her face in its whiteness had the tint of mother of pearl and an expression of engrossed and grievous absence. (p. 50)

Just as Woolf imagines Bennett noticing Mrs Brown's brooch and mended gloves, Ford's narrator describes the tightness of Katherine's gown and the unstitched embroidery on her glove, details which indicate her relative poverty compared to the richness of the Tudor court. The observation that her face has a 'tint of mother of pearl' is not made from the perspective of anyone within the narrative itself, but from the detached, authoritative position of the omniscient narrator. Nevertheless, despite being relatively traditional in approach when compared to the experimental works that came later, Edwardian novels frequently show signs of the formal innovations and structural instabilities that modernist writers exploited to the full. The best way to bring these formal and structural signs of modernity

---

[26]   Berman, *All That is Solid Melts Into Air*, p. 15.

(if not modernism) in Ford's Edwardian novels into focus is to examine how they show Ford working towards *The Good Soldier*.

Towards *The Good Soldier*

Ford's own writing teaches us to be suspicious of straightforward linear narratives, of 'corrected chronicles' with all the inconsistencies and rough edges smoothed over.[27] We need, therefore, to be wary of overly simplistic, developmental readings of Ford's works in which all his novels before 1915 merely prefigure *The Good Soldier*. Nevertheless, as Ford himself said: 'I had never really tried to put into any novel of mine *all* that I knew about writing' before *The Good Soldier*.[28] These remarks would appear to endorse the view that all his previous novels had merely been dress rehearsals for the masterpiece he began writing on his fortieth birthday. On the other hand, many of Ford's Edwardian novels are so unlike *The Good Soldier* that we do them a considerable disservice if we read them simply for signs of what was to come rather than encountering them on their own terms. In the limited space remaining in this chapter we will look at some of the points of connection between the novels we have been discussing and Ford's modernist masterpiece, whilst avoiding reducing Ford's Edwardian fiction to a series of 'trial runs' for *The Good Soldier*.[29]

One of the ways in which *The Good Soldier* demonstrates its formal inventiveness most clearly is in its extensive use of the device Ford described as the 'time-shift'. This often involves sudden jumps from one point in narrative time to another without any explanation that might help to prepare the reader (for a flashback, for example) or apparent logic. The result is a reading experience that can be bewildering, but which also matches the confusion and disorientation of the novel's narrator, John Dowell. However, Ford employs this device throughout his Edwardian fiction. For example, *A Call* uses a time-shift to conceal the identity of the caller who discovers Dudley Leicester in Etta Stackpole's hallway until the penultimate chapter of the novel. If the passage revealing the caller's identity were to appear in its proper place in the chronology of the story, the novel would be robbed of its central enigma. In *Mr. Fleight*, the first we hear of Fleight's assault and the ride in the motor car that leads up to it is in Part II, Chapter 2, which begins: 'Mr. Fleight, with two enormous black eyes and three of his front teeth knocked

---

[27] See Ford Madox Ford, 'On Impressionism', *Critical Writings of Ford Madox Ford*, ed. Frank MacShane (Lincoln: University of Nebraska Press, 1964), pp. 33–55.

[28] Ford Madox Ford, 'Dedicatory Letter to Stella Ford', *The Good Soldier*, second edition, ed. Martin Stannard (New York: Norton, 2012), p. 3. All further references are to this edition.

[29] Vincent J. Cheng describes *A Call* as a 'trial run' for *The Good Soldier*: 'English Behaviour and Repression: *A Call: The Tale of Two Passions*', in Robert Hampson and Tony Davenport (eds), *Ford Madox Ford: A Reappraisal*, International Ford Madox Ford Studies 1 (Amsterdam: Rodopi, 2002), p. 105.

out, was in the backyard of Mrs Leroy's house' (p. 142). It is not until further down the page that we are situated in time with the phrase: 'That was on the Tuesday afternoon', and then taken back to the previous evening in order to fill in the gap in narrative time. In both of these examples the time-shift is used primarily as a story-telling device, allowing the omniscient narrator to withhold information in order to build intrigue or heighten narrative tension. In *The Good Soldier*, by contrast, the constant time-shifts are manifestations of the narrator's bewildered inability to control and to grasp the significance of the details of his narrative. Nevertheless, Ford's Edwardian time-shifts can still surprise and disorientate the reader and, although not used to the same extent as in Ford's later works, they still represent a rejection of the linear chronologies favoured by the Victorians.

At times, however, Ford goes even further. In the historical fantasy *Ladies Whose Bright Eyes*, with the transportation of Mr Sorrell back into the fourteenth century, Ford makes the time-shift into a central aspect of the story. At the end of the novel, as Sorrell begins to come back to the present, he has a curious vision of the fourteenth and twentieth centuries superimposed one on top of the other:

> Above his head were little fleecy clouds superimposed on a translucent and shining blue . . . . It became suddenly as if he saw them through an iridescent film of glass . . . . Tears in blue eyes that looked down on him! What did you know about that? . . . The Chronicles of Froissart? Of Shropshire? Of Wiltshire? A coif, white across the forehead? Nurse Dionissia, you read too much. A blond, broad face . . . . A little worn . . . . Bending over him against the sky . . . . No, against a shining ceiling . . . . 'We'll get him back.'[30]

This passage is a quite marvellous rendering of the confusion brought about by Sorrell's time-shift. From this point onwards the reader gradually realises that what is being described is Sorrell waking up in a hospital bed. At this stage, however, Sorrell is looking up at the 'fleecy clouds' in the fourteenth-century sky while simultaneously seeing the blue eyes of 'Nurse Dionissia' and the shining hospital ceiling. One way of interpreting this scene is to read Sorrell's time-travel experience as a coma-induced dream, and to conclude that he has really been in the hospital all along. However, the novel refuses to close down the possibility that Sorrell has genuinely travelled in time. For Robert Hampson, this makes the text 'a fiction of unresolved contradictions' and of 'modernist open-endedness'.[31]

Although this last example does not involve a time-shift as such (in that it does not involve a sudden jump in the chronology of the story), it does exemplify the way

---

    30   Ford Madox Ford, *Ladies Whose Bright Eyes* (Manchester: Carcanet Press, 1988), p. 259.
    31   Robert Hampson, 'Travellers, Dreamers and Visitors: Ford and Fantasy', in *Ford Madox Ford: A Reappraisal*, p. 51. For further discussion of Ford's manipulation of time in *Ladies Whose Bright Eyes* and *The Fifth Queen*, see Rob Hawkes, 'Visuality vs. Temporality: Plotting and Depiction in *The Fifth Queen* and *Ladies Whose Bright Eyes*', in Laura Colombino (ed.), *Ford Madox Ford and Visual Culture*, International Ford Madox Ford Studies 8 (Amsterdam: Rodopi, 2009), pp. 97–108.

that the time-shift works to bring about a disorientating sense of *not knowing* where one is in time. This brings me to the final aspect of Ford's Edwardian fiction that I wish to highlight, which is the widespread condition of not knowing. As readers of *The Good Soldier* will recall, the phrase 'I don't know' is Dowell's mantra. For example, the first chapter of the novel ends with Dowell asking whether a 'proper man' is 'a raging stallion forever neighing after his neighbour's womankind':

> I don't know. And there is nothing to guide us. And if everything is so nebulous about a matter so elementary as the morals of sex, what is there to guide us in the more subtle morality of all other personal contacts, associations, and activities? Or are we meant to act on impulse alone? It is all a darkness. (p. 15)

It is interesting to note the echoes here of George Ponderevo's description of the 'network of misunderstandings and misstatements and faulty and ramshackle conventions which makes up our social order' in *Tono-Bungay*. Like George, Dowell laments the fact that social conventions no longer provide an explanatory framework for sexual behaviour. In *The Good Soldier*, the condition of radical uncertainly is all-encompassing and it transcends the boundary between form and content: since Dowell is unsure of many of the details of his story, and his narrative method is erratic and fragmentary, uncertainty is part of the novel's structure as well as being its subject matter. Once again, this kind of uncertainty is to be found throughout Ford's Edwardian novels. When, mid-way through *Mr. Fleight*, Mrs Leroy asks Fleight what his intentions are (meaning his intentions towards Gilda), he misinterprets the question and replies: 'it really has become extremely difficult for me to decide what my intentions are, or whether it's even possible to have any intentions at all' (p. 167). Ann Barr Snitow describes this as the intervention of 'the voice of John Dowell in *The Good Soldier*, the voice of the modern man adrift'.[32] In its final scene, *Mr. Fleight* returns to the gentlemen's club where it began, with Mr Blood at the window 'counting the motors against the horse traffic' (p. 2). Just as he did in the opening scene, Fleight remarks that Blood's tally 'doesn't prove anything', prompting the following response from the minor character Cluny Macpherson:

> 'Proof!' he exclaimed; 'what sort of word is that to use in the twentieth century? Aren't we all just friendly agnostics? [...] There's not a single thing that we can know. We haven't any one of us got any religion; and science, that everybody used to be so frightened of, has given up the attempt to prove anything.' (p. 304)

The sense that 'there's not a single thing that we can know', and that this, furthermore, is a specifically modern phenomenon, is one that runs throughout Ford's Edwardian fiction. Indeed, despite the diverse range of genres, from historical fantasy to contemporary satire, and despite the wide variations in

---

[32] Ann Barr Snitow, *Ford Madox Ford and the Voice of Uncertainty* (Baton Rouge: Louisiana State University Press, 1984), p. 156.

tone, style, subject and quality, the novels Ford wrote between 1901–14 are both Edwardian and resolutely modern. All display a clear set of affinities with the novels of other Edwardians such as Bennett and Wells, whilst also demonstrating that, throughout the Edwardian years, Ford was working towards the modernism of *The Good Soldier*.[33]

---

[33] For more on Ford's Edwardian writing, see Laura Colombino and Max Saunders (eds), *The Edwardian Ford Madox Ford*, International Ford Madox Ford Studies 12 (Amsterdam: Rodopi, 2013).

Chapter 4
Ford and Modernism

Seamus O'Malley

Ford Madox Ford's writing career (1891–1939) is about equal to what most critics would say was the modernist period (a common one is 1900–1939).[1] Like modernism at large, his body of work responded to the emergence of psychoanalysis, the height and decline of the British Empire, the First World War and the rise of Fascism. Ford was also central to many of the modernist movements in London and Paris. As founder of the *English Review* (1909), he established a forum for emerging writers such as D.H. Lawrence, Wyndham Lewis and Ezra Pound. In 1924 he launched the short-lived *transatlantic review*, which again provided a meeting place for new talent: James Joyce, Gertrude Stein, Ernest Hemingway, William Carlos Williams and e.e. cummings were all included in Ford's Paris-based periodical.[2] He was also central to the informal networks of influence that were so crucial to modernism's growth. As friend of and collaborator with Joseph Conrad, Ford knew intimately, and was involved in various ways with, the texts that we now recognise as founding works in English modernism such as *Nostromo* (1904) and *The Secret Agent* (1907).[3] Ford's connections with Ezra Pound, one of modernism's most energetic champions and organisers, helped to shape the exciting world of modernist poetry in the decade of the war, to which Ford was both a contributor and advisor. And Ford's time in Paris in the twenties, recounted in his memoir *It Was the Nightingale* (1933), finds him immersed in the literary life of the 'capital' of cultural modernism.

This chapter will grapple with modernism as a set of aesthetic practices and techniques, and hopefully this will be useful not just in coming to a basic appreciation of Ford's unique version of modernism, but also to understand what modernism was all about. If we look at modernism as a set of practices, we notice several salient features that occur in most works of modernist art: non-linearity; fragmentation; a focus on subjectivity; unreliable sources of narration; and a sense of self-awareness. This chapter will explore how Ford experimented with

---

[1]   For further discussion of modernism, see Tim Armstrong, *Modernism: A Cultural History* (Cambridge, MA: Polity, 2005); Ann Ardis, *Modernism and Cultural Conflict, 1880–1922* (Cambridge: Cambridge University Press, 2008); and Peter Nicholls, *Modernisms: A Literary Guide* (Berkeley: University of California Press, 1995).

[2]   See Jason Harding (ed.), *Ford Madox Ford, Modernist Magazines and Editing*, International Ford Madox Ford Studies 9 (Amsterdam: Rodopi, 2010).

[3]   On Ford's work with and for Conrad, see Chapter 2 in this volume.

these techniques, mainly in his novels *The Good Soldier* (1915), *Parade's End* (1924–28) and *No Enemy* (1929).

Non-Linearity

Some of the stories we hear and tell are linear. In a linear narrative, events proceed in a chronological format. But just as often, we hear or tell stories that are non-linear, in which the events are out of order. If we say 'I went to the store because I had run out of milk', we put the going to the store before the running out of milk, even though we ran out of milk before we went to the store. While it is just as easy to arrange the events chronologically, telling the story non-linearly allows the teller to give priority to the trip, relegating the running-out of milk to a motivating backdrop.

Different literary eras and techniques tend to gravitate towards either way of telling a story. The epics of antiquity, for example, often started *in medias res* (in the middle of things), relating the backstory later on in the narrative. Nineteenth-century realism, on the other hand, perfected the linear narrative: classics such Jane Austen's *Pride and Prejudice* (1813), Charlotte Brontë's *Jane Eyre* (1847) and Charles Dickens's *Great Expectations* (1861) proceed, for the most part, from A to Z.

Many moderns desired to get beyond the linear techniques of the Victorians. Virginia Woolf's *Mrs Dalloway* (1924) employs periodic flashbacks to the characters' pasts. The first chapter of William Faulkner's *The Sound and the Fury* (1929) takes place over multiple generations simultaneously, in a style so baffling that the author toyed with the idea of using different coloured ink to indicate different time periods. And Joyce's *Finnegans Wake* (1939) is so temporally circular that the last sentence of the novel continues in the first sentence, so the entire work can be read in a never-ending loop.

But the first major experiment in the non-linear novel was Ford's *The Good Soldier*. First-time readers of this work would not necessarily know that they are dealing with a non-linear text until some way into it, but there are some hints early on that we are dealing with a tricky text. In describing their lives together as a group of four friends, our narrator John Dowell states:

> Upon my word, yes, our intimacy was like a minuet, simply because on every possible occasion and in every possible circumstance we knew where to go, where to sit, which table we unanimously should choose; and we could rise and go, all four together, without a signal from any one of us, always to the music of the Kur orchestra, always in the temperate sunshine, or if it rained, in discreet shelters.[4]

---

[4]   Ford Madox Ford, *The Good Soldier*, second edition, ed. Martin Stannard (New York: Norton, 2012), p. 11. All further references are to this edition.

The impression Dowell gives is of two couples very close, displaying bonds of affection and friendship. However, the next paragraph begins: 'No, by God it is false! It wasn't a minuet that we stepped; it was a prison – a prison full of screaming hysterics, tied down so that they might not outsound the rolling of our carriage wheels as we went along the shaded avenues of the Taunus Wald' (p. 12). Lunatics in an asylum are a far cry from the genteel, structured dance of the minuet. What Dowell has done is to tell us what he thought of the past, but then re-tell it, with drastic changes.[5]

The entire novel proceeds in this fashion, giving us an account of a past event, but then coming back to it later to revise it, adding details, cancelling some out. The result is an unstable text that refuses to proceed in a straightforward manner, but is constantly tugged into the past and then dragged back to the present. Dowell is quite aware of his methods, at one point pausing to reflect on his own storytelling:

> I have, I am aware, told this story in a very rambling way so that it may be difficult for anyone to find their path through what may be a sort of maze. I cannot help it. [...] And, when one discusses an affair – a long, sad affair – one goes back, one goes forward. One remembers points that one has forgotten and one explains them all the more minutely since one recognizes that one has forgotten to mention them in their proper places and that one may have given, by omitting them, a false impression. I console myself with thinking that this is a real story and that, after all, real stories are probably told best in the way a person telling a story would tell them. They will then seem most real. (pp. 124–5)

Here we see one reason for Dowell's non-linearity: to tell the story in a linear fashion would be a kind of falsehood, since Dowell did not know everything that was going on for the past ten years of his life. He did not know of his wife's infidelities, nor that her and Edward's heart conditions were faked. Thus the non-linearity of the novel is more 'real' than a 'realist' method might allow.[6] At one point he imagines what his story would be like if he told it chronologically:

> I wish I could put it down in diary form. Thus: On the 1st of September they returned from Nauheim. Leonora at once took to her bed. By the 1st of October they were all going to meets together. Nancy had already observed very fully that Edward was strange in his manner. About the 6th of that month Edward

---

[5]   For more on the revisionary nature of the novel, see Seamus O'Malley, *Making History New: Modernism and Historical Narrative* (New York: Oxford University Press, 2014), pp. 84–8.

[6]   This is the central premise of Theodor W. Adorno's essay 'The Position of the Narrator in the Contemporary Novel': '*If the novel wants to remain true to its realistic heritage and tell how things really are, it must abandon a realism that only aids the façade in its work of camouflage by reproducing it*' (author's italics): *Notes to Literature*, 2 vols, ed. Rolf Tiedeman, trans. Shierry Weber Nicholson (New York: Columbia University Press, 1991), I, p. 32.

> gave the horse to young Selmes, and Nancy had cause to believe that her aunt
> did not love her uncle. (p. 148)

This chronological ordering makes much less sense than the non-linear method that Dowell (and Ford) has adopted. As readers struggle through the time-shifts in *The Good Soldier*, then, they must always take into account the reason for the jumps: Ford has not simply taken a normal story and hacked it to bits, but rather crafted a narrative where Dowell's own discoveries and limitations play an important role in how the story gets transmitted.

When Ford turned to write a novel based partly on his own experience of war, *Parade's End*, he again decided to employ a non-linear format, although the overall plot of *Parade's End* proceeds more chronologically than *The Good Soldier* ever does. The four novels that comprise the tetralogy take place in historical order: *Some Do Not . . .* (1912–17); *No More Parades* (1916–17); *A Man Could Stand Up –* (1918); and *Last Post* (the post-war years). However, Ford's narrative style within each volume mixes up past and present in a manner that is often confounding, especially since, unlike *The Good Soldier*, *Parade's End* is narrated in the third person, although in a style narratologists refer to as 'free indirect discourse'. Free indirect discourse is when the third-person narration absorbs or assumes the thoughts of the characters it is describing. Gustave Flaubert is often recognised as the chief innovator of this style, incorporating his protagonist's thoughts into the third-person narration of *Madame Bovary* (1856). Many moderns extended his experiments, most notably Joyce in *A Portrait of the Artist as a Young Man* (1914) and Woolf in *Mrs Dalloway*. Ford, a lifelong devotee of Flaubert, employs free indirect discourse for much of *Parade's End*. For example, in a scene where Christopher Tietjens and Valentine Wannop are riding through the mists, the narration begins in third person but subtly registers what Tietjens is thinking:

> Actually, this mist was not silver, or was, perhaps, no longer silver: if you looked
> at it with the eye of the artist . . . With the exact eye! It was smirched with bars
> of purple; of red; of orange: delicate reflections: dark blue shadows from the
> upper sky where it formed drifts like snow. . . . The exact eye: exact observation:
> it was a man's work. The only work for a man. Why then, were artists soft:
> effeminate: not men at all: whilst the army officer, who had the inexact mind of
> the schoolteacher, was a manly man? Quite a manly man: until he became an
> old woman![7]

The passage never uses first-person markers like 'I' or 'me', and yet it is clear that it represents Tietjens's mind at work. It is Tietjens, not the narrator, who believes that artists are 'soft', but because of Ford's employment of free indirect discourse, Tietjens's thoughts inform how the narrative gets told.

---

[7]   Ford Madox Ford, *Some Do Not . . .*, ed. Max Saunders (Manchester: Carcanet Press, 2010), p. 159. All further references are to this edition.

This method accounts for how Ford mixes up time in *Parade's End*. A representative scene is from *Some Do Not . . .* when Tietjens and his brother Mark are meeting at the war office. They begin to have a conversation, and Tietjens insists that he is not having an affair with Valentine. Mark suddenly realises that his source for gossip, his roommate Ruggles, had been lying: "'Then Ruggles must be a liar." This neither distressed nor astonished him. For twenty years he and Ruggles had shared a floor of a large and rather gloomy building in Mayfair' (p. 250). Then follows several pages of narration of the past, centring around Mark's shared flat. Eventually we return to the present, and then Valentine arrives to try to say goodbye to Tietjens before he returns to the Front. But first she talks to Mark, who mentions that she used to be a servant, and the next paragraph begins: 'That had been the great shock, the turning-point, of Valentine Wannop's life. Her last year before that had been of great tranquility, tinged, of course, with melancholy because she loved Christopher Tietjens' (p. 279). Again, several pages of past events are recounted, this time through Valentine's memories. We then return to the present of the narrative, but it suddenly jumps forward to Tietjens' parting – we never 'see' the present tense of their goodbyes – and the skipped time, now the past, is conveyed to the reader as a remembrance.[8] Their last night together before he returns to the front is depicted as having happened in the past instead of narrated as if it is happening in the present or immediate past. Just as in *The Good Soldier*, memory informs narrative form.

Ford's other wartime novel, *No Enemy* (written in draft form in 1921 but finished in 1929), is the most non-linear of the three works we will consider. It depicts a poet named Gringoire, clearly modelled on Ford, humbly farming and writing after his wartime service. His words are given to us by the 'Compiler', a critic who has come to stay at Gringoire's cottage to interview him. As in *The Good Soldier*, we have at least two intertwined narratives, moving at different speeds: first there is Gringoire's war experiences, told non-linearly as fragments of his memory occur to him; and then there is the linear story of the Compiler's efforts to record Gringoire's personal history.[9] This history does not proceed in the order of time, but rather in the order of remembrance and importance. With these three novels, Ford was pioneering a method whereby a writer could choose other methods of ordering events beyond the mere temporal.

---

[8]   For more on time-shifts in *Parade's End*, see Anthony Fowles, *Ford Madox Ford: The Principal Fiction* (London: Greenwich Exchange, 2002), pp. 73–5.

[9]   See Paul Skinner, 'The Painful Processes of Reconstruction: History in *No Enemy* and *Last Post*', in Joseph Wiesenfarth (ed.), *History and Representation in Ford Madox Ford's Writings*, International Ford Madox Ford Studies 3 (Amsterdam: Rodopi, 2004), pp. 65–76; and Jonathan Boulter, '"After ... Armageddon": Trauma and History in Ford Madox Ford's *No Enemy*', in *History and Representation in Ford Madox Ford's Writings*, pp. 77–90.

Fragmentation

Any non-linear storyline is to a certain extent a fragmented narrative, as events do not proceed with temporal coherency and cohesion. But other aspects of art or literature can also be fragmented, not just time. Recall a Cubist painting by Picasso or the poetry of T.S. Eliot: fragmentation is at the heart of the modern.

Parade's End is a very fragmented text, but, interestingly, it does not begin as such. Note the famous opening of the first volume:

> The two young men – they were of the English public official class – sat in the perfectly appointed railway carriage. The leather straps to the windows were of virgin newness; the mirrors beneath the new luggage racks immaculate as if they had reflected very little; the bulging upholstery in its luxuriant, regulated curves was scarlet and yellow in an intricate, minute dragon pattern, the design of a geometrician in Cologne. The compartment smelt faintly, hygienically of admirable varnish; the train ran as smoothly – Tietjens remembered thinking – as British gilt-edged securities. It travelled fast; yet had it swayed or jolted over the rail joints, except at the curve before Tonbridge or over the points at Ashford where these eccentricities are expected and allowed for, Macmaster, Tietjens felt certain, would have written to the company. Perhaps he would even have written to the *Times*. (pp. 3–4)

This passage could easily fit into some of the classic realist texts of the Victorian age, as it gives us a seemingly fixed and stable picture of the world in which Tietjens lives. The two characters, despite travelling at high and dangerous speed, feel comfortable and contented, and the narrative reflects this with its firmness and coherence, its fixed point of view, its stable narrative style.

As the story proceeds, however, things start to fall apart, both in terms of Tietjens's life and the narrative that describes it. Tietjens finds out that his wife, Sylvia, has been unfaithful to him, and that his son may not be biologically his. He then goes to the front lines in France, suffers shell shock, and loses a large portion of his memory. Slowly, the steady realism that opened the novel disintegrates, fragmenting into the disjointed free indirect discourse that reminds some readers of Joyce's *Ulysses* (which was published two years before the first volume of *Parade's End*). Observe how the second novel, *No More Parades*, differs in its opening from the first:

> When you came in the space was desultory, rectangular, warm after the drip of the winter night, and transfused with a brown-orange dust that was light. It was shaped like the house a child draws. Three groups of brown limbs spotted with brass took dim high-lights from shafts that came from a bucket pierced with holes, filled with incandescent coke and covered in with a sheet of iron in the shape of a tunnel. Two men, as if hierarchically smaller, crouched on the floor beside the brazier; four, two at each end of the hut, drooped over tables in attitudes of extreme indifference. From the eaves above the parallelogram

of black that was the doorway fell intermittent drippings of collected moisture, persistent, with glass-like intervals of musical sound.[10]

This paragraph is as attuned to images and visuals as the previous, but note how the images it presents are mere fragments: we do not see men, but 'three groups of brown limbs'; the doorway is only a 'parallelogram of black'; somehow 'brown-orange dust that was light'; and the whole ensemble looks not like a realist portrait but a child's drawing. Sound, too, is fragmented, as the dialogue is 'hardly audible' and comes to us only as 'animal grunts', while the moisture produces 'glass-like intervals of musical sound'. The sounds and images seem like shattered shards that do not add up to a coherent whole.[11] From the first to second volume, we are witness to a mini-history of the transition from Victorian realism to twentieth-century modernism.[12]

One of the main challenges in reading *Parade's End* is grappling with this fragmented narrative. Walter Benjamin asks in 'The Storyteller' (1936): 'Was it not noticeable at the end of the war that men returned from the battlefield grown silent – not richer, but poorer in communicable experience?'[13] *Parade's End* reflects this societal difficulty, as modern war resists representation. However, Ford's oblique style is simultaneously one of the most rewarding things about the novel, and in fact Benjamin lauds the ability of modern writers 'to see a new beauty in what is vanishing'.[14] Note how, in the passage above, the soldiers' lives are so efficiently described by Ford: although we know nothing, plot-wise, about them at this point, we already understand the gloom and squalor in which they work. It is not important which battle they have fought in or what their individual names are. Instead, we get a sense of a world coming to pieces. The changes wrought by the war, both individual and social, are registered in the fractured narrative, and by comparing this to the stable opening of *Some Do Not . . .* we see just how much of their lives has been altered.

Sometimes Ford employs fragmentation to suggest the way the mind works. Note how Tietjens responds to sunrise at the Front:

---

[10]   Ford Madox Ford, *No More Parades*, ed. Joseph Wiesenfarth (Manchester: Carcanet Press, 2011), p. 9.

[11]   For more on visuals in *Parade's End*, see Alexandra Becquet, 'Modernity, Shock and Cinema: The Visual Aesthetics of Ford Madox Ford's *Parade's End*', in Laura Colombino (ed.), *Ford Madox Ford and Visual Culture*, International Ford Madox Ford Studies 8 (Amsterdam: Rodopi, 2009), pp. 191–204. On sound, see Tom Vandevelde, '"Are You Going to Mind the Noise?": Mapping the Soundscape of *Parade's End*', in Ashley Chantler and Rob Hawkes (eds), *Ford Madox Ford's Parade's End: The First World War, Culture, and Modernity*, International Ford Madox Ford Studies 13 (Amsterdam: Rodopi, 2014), pp. 53–66.

[12]   For more on this passage, see Adam Piette, 'War and Division in *Parade's End*', in *Ford Madox Ford's Parade's End*, pp. 141–52.

[13]   Walter Benjamin, 'The Storyteller', *Illuminations*, ed. Hannah Arendt, trans. Harry Zohn (New York: Harcourt, Brace and World, 1968), p. 84.

[14]   Benjamin, *Illuminations*, p. 87.

No doubt when the appalled soul left the weary body, the panting lungs. . . . Well, you can't go on with a sentence like that. . . . But you collapsed inwards. Like the dying pig they sold on trays in the street. Painter fellows doing battlefields never got that *intimate* effect. Intimate to them there. Unknown to the corridors in Whitehall. . . . Probably because they – the painters – drew from living models or had ideas as to the human form. . . . But these were not limbs, muscles, torsi. . . . Collections of tubular shapes in field-grey or mud-colour they were. Chucked about by Almighty God! As if He dropped them from on high to make them flatten into the earth. . . . Good gravel soil, that slope and relatively dry. No dew to speak of. The night had been covered. . . .[15]

Ford uses ellipses throughout his works, possibly suggesting the fragmented nature of thought, and these gaps and jumps render human consciousness with as much precision as the opening pages rendered a train car. Reading passages such as this, we should focus on how Tietjens's thinking operates, to see his train of thought even if it does not appear logical: thoughts of dying make him think of paintings of battle; then he thinks of how the painters would have worked; this makes him think of what he has seen, the dead bodies in the dirt; but this makes him think of soil, and how there was no dew this morning. Instead of the logical progression of realism, we have here the associative, fragmented juxtapositions of modernist narrative, one that prioritises the impressions of reality over reality itself.

To return to *The Good Soldier*: it too is a fragmented novel in terms of its chronology, but its fragmentation is also related to how the novel handles perspective. Dowell is giving us his own, but in order to attempt a complete story (whether or not he succeeds is open to debate) he must include the perspectives of the other characters. This involves interviews, eavesdropping and guesswork, but the other characters are just as dependent on the faulty processes of memory as Dowell himself, and thus the reader must be equally suspicious of the perspectives of Edward or Florence. Any picture that emerges from the novel will be an unstable and fragmented one.[16]

Subjectivity and Unreliability

John Dowell is trapped inside his own consciousness: for years he was ignorant about what was going on around him, and, as he states in the first paragraph, he 'had never sounded the depths of an English heart. I had known the shallows' (p. 9). This is an early indication that the novel we are reading will be concerned with

---

[15]   Ford Madox Ford, *A Man Could Stand Up –*, ed. Sara Haslam (Manchester: Carcanet Press, 2011), pp. 67–8.

[16]   See especially Sara Haslam, *Fragmenting Modernism: Ford Madox Ford, the Novel, and the Great War* (Manchester: Manchester University Press, 2002): '[Ford] is saying that memory fragments and tears apart the notion of a solid existence; it refracts, not reflects, light in many opposing directions. The more memory one possesses, then, or the more keenly one seeks for it, the more fragmented one becomes' (p. 210).

with accuracy and verisimilitude, modernism focuses instead on subjective impressions. All of these methods call attention to the fact that the narratives we read are not stories out there in the world, but words on a page.

No Enemy is Ford's most self-conscious text, full of footnotes, bracketed asides and even an appendix. Cornelia Cook notes that the novel 'calls attention to its own textuality at every opportunity and also alludes widely to other constructions: not only those of memory, but also of "history", myth, propaganda, architecture, cartography, poetry, fiction, political rhetoric and trench engineering'.[24] It seems appropriate that a novel about the difficulties of remembering and recounting should highlight its own struggles in storytelling. And, ultimately, one of the central subjects of Ford's entire *oeuvre* is storytelling itself: *The Good Soldier* is as much about how we tell stories as it is about a love quartet at a German spa. Dowell states:

> You may well ask why I write. And yet my reasons are quite many. For it is not unusual in human beings who have witnessed the sack of a city or the falling to pieces of a people to desire to set down what they have witnessed for the benefit of unknown heirs or of generations infinitely remote; or, if you please, just to get the sight out of their heads. (p. 11)

We might say that Ford pioneers a therapeutic model of fiction, as Dowell's reasons for writing are very similar to the reasons Vienna's middle-class families flocked to the new methods of Dr Sigmund Freud. Just as Freud was establishing the practices of twentieth-century psychoanalysis, Ford was establishing some of the aesthetic possibilities of the modern novel.

Other Modernisms

There are other common practices of literary modernism, however, in which Ford takes no part. Many moderns turned to myth, either for consolation for the lack of clear meaning in the modern world, or for a means of ordering the chaos of modern existence. Eliot's *The Waste Land* (1922) looks to myths across multiple cultures and times, dropping in fragments from the Bible, the *Bhagavad-Gita*, Greek narratives and medieval fertility rites. Joyce uses Homer's *The Odyssey* as his organising scheme for *Ulysses*, where every event in modern Dublin has a Homeric parallel. The poems of Ezra Pound, especially his epic poem *The Cantos*, include a dizzying array of references to obscure historical personages. Ford resists these mythic turns: despite his critiques of modern society, and his sometimes-nostalgia for a pre-modern way of life, he never shares in the modern embrace of the mythical.[25]

---

[24]   Cornelia Cook, 'Constructions and Reconstructions: *No Enemy*', in *Ford Madox Ford's Modernity*, p. 191.

[25]   The one exception is his novel *Mr. Apollo* (1908), which imagines the Greek god visiting modern-day London. But the plot is mostly for comic effect and light social critique, not a genuine investment in mythical structures or tropes.

Readers encountering the works of Eliot and Joyce are often put off by the amount of canonical reading they need to have accomplished to catch even a fraction of the allusions to myth, literature and history. (Those writers also included languages other than English in their texts.) Ford cannot be categorised in this way: despite the enormous demand he places on his readers, it is never directed to sources outside of the text we hold in our hands. The keys to unlocking *The Good Soldier*, *Parade's End* and *No Enemy* are found in the novels themselves, not in a historical allusion or encyclopaedic reference. As Paul Skinner has recently written: 'while Ford was excited and intrigued by what was being written in those years, some of it was incompatible with his own post-war vision of the world and the novel's place in it, a vision that never excluded or undervalued some interaction with his readers'.[26] Ford wanted what we now call modernism to be challenging and innovative, but he did not insist that only an elect few could enjoy these experiments in form and storytelling, and in fact wanted the new art of the early twentieth century to be accompanied by a spirit of openness and broad appeal.

---

[26]   Paul Skinner, 'Tietjens Walking, Ford Talking', in *Ford Madox Ford's Parade's End*, p. 134.

Chapter 5
Ford's Literary Impressionism

Laura Colombino

Literary Impressionism developed at the turn of the twentieth century, particularly in France and England, and derived its label from the one applied to French painters such as Claude Monet. Just like their counterparts in painting, Impressionist writers believed that (visual) experience is unstable and fragmented. Therefore, they concentrated on the casual and ever-changing aspects of experience, on highly subjective impressions (and memories) as they impinge on the mind in an indistinct flow. Sensations were to be rendered as truthfully as possible through a combination of a few carefully selected details. This explains why the Impressionists rejected both Emile Zola's sociological approach and the plotted and moralistic Victorian novel. Reading Ford's fiction, for example, you will realise that he dispenses with the cumbersome paraphernalia of realistic analysis (the accurate reproduction of facts) and avoids intruding into the story with his own voice to judge or comment on the characters. Through the use of intensely suggestive words, he wants impressions to speak for themselves and carry autonomous meanings. It is no accident that we often refer to the Impressionist subject as fundamentally passive and receptive. In the search for a spontaneous, unmediated presentation of experience, the protagonists of Ford's novels – like Dowell in *The Good Soldier* (1915) or Henry in *The Rash Act* (1933) and *Henry for Hugh* (1934) – and the author himself in works of autobiographical reminiscences[1] seem to dwindle to unobtrusive presences: Ford's typical narrating voice could be described, borrowing the words of his contemporary Arthur Symons, as a sort of 'disembodied voice, and yet the voice of a human soul'.[2]

Besides Ford, a considerable number of other writers are usually discussed in terms of literary Impressionism: Stephen Crane, Joseph Conrad, Katherine Mansfield, D.H. Lawrence, Marcel Proust, Dorothy Richardson and Virginia Woolf. But Ford is the major critical exponent of the 'movement', as shown by the bulk of his discussions of its meanings and aims throughout his career. Indeed, he was the first one who gave wide currency to the concept. So, you may wonder, why did it come to be so fundamental to *him* in particular? And what authors and movements smoothed the way for his aesthetic choices? Certainly, a major influence was Henry James, the 'master', whom Ford regarded as: 'the greatest of

---

[1] On Ford's reminiscences, see Chapter 1 in this volume.

[2] Arthur Symons, 'The Decadent Movement in Literature', *Harper's New Monthly Magazine*, 87 (1893), p. 867.

living writers and, in consequence, for me, the greatest of men'.[3] But how do the two authors differ on central issues such as the relationship between the author and his art work, or the author and his reader? And what are the specificities of Ford's techniques? These and other questions will be addressed in this chapter to tease out the fascinating mechanisms of Ford's writing as he himself describes them in his critical texts.

Ford dignifies writing by talking about it as an art requiring conscious craftsmanship. For him, technique has a 'freeing power', in that: 'It enable[s] those writers possessed of personality to discover the unique forms by which that personality, in its interaction with life, could most fully be expressed'.[4] Indeed, it is no accident that his views and practices have been and still are influential on writers: his critical texts seem like imaginative lessons on creative writing.[5]

Genealogy and Contexts

Compared to French discussions of fiction, in the 1870s British criticism was provincial – moralistic, theme-ridden, anti-formalist. Public outrage greeted the advent of such scandalous foreign writers as Zola, Gustave Flaubert and Henrik Ibsen: their books were stigmatised because they emphasised pluralism and complication, and did not manipulate their plots so that goodness and virtue would always triumph in the end. By the 1880s, however, things were starting to change in England. Particularly significant in this cultural turn was an essay which may already be familiar to you: James's 'The Art of Fiction' (1884). Here James objected to propriety of subject and tone and to a conscious moral purpose as preconditions for novel writing; rather, he claimed, formal exactitude in conveying the artist's experience of life should be privileged. He had formed this conviction during Flaubert's Sundays in Paris in 1875–76, when the craft of novel writing was discussed, writes Ford, by 'the Goncourts, Turgenev, Gautier, Maupassant and, in a lesser degree, Zola and the young James – the last as disciple of the gentle Russian genius'.[6] Dismissing social, moral or political aims, this literary coterie placed a new emphasis on conscious artistry: 'They discussed the *minutiae* of words and their economical employment; *charpente*, the architecture, of the novel; the handling of dialogue; the renderings of impressions; the impersonality

---

[3]   Ford Madox Ford, *Henry James: A Critical Study* (London: Martin Secker, 1913), p. 7.

[4]   John A. Meixner, *Ford Madox Ford's Novels: A Critical Study* (Minneapolis: University of Minnesota Press, 1962), p. 17.

[5]   On writers who have been admiring readers and eloquent critics of Ford, see Paul Skinner (ed.), *Ford Madox Ford's Literary Contacts*, International Ford Madox Ford Studies 6 (Amsterdam: Rodopi, 2006).

[6]   Ford Madox Ford, 'Techniques' (1935), *Critical Writings of Ford Madox Ford*, ed. Frank MacShane (Lincoln: University of Nebraska Press, 1964), p. 60.

of the author'.[7] In 1876, James would move to England, spreading the seeds of the French novel in the country of Victorian moralism.

The poet and critic Symons was a no less significant ambassador of literary innovations. He charted the latest artistic developments in Europe, with a special emphasis on France and England, in a seminal and useful article entitled 'The Decadent Movement in Literature' (1893). Here, he discussed and showed the importance of bringing into relation (in what we would define today as a comparative approach) the French Symbolists Paul Verlaine, Stéphane Mallarmé, Joris Karl Huysmans and the Impressionists Goncourts; the American painter James Abbott McNeill Whistler; and the English Walter Pater and W.E. Henley. Ford, too, was extremely sensible to the international quality of contemporary literary phenomena and this has always been recognised as one of his major virtues. In the following passage, he describes the cultural turn of the 1890s that occurred in the English capital and was brought about by a wide range of foreign influences:

> It was the London of the *Yellow Book*, of R.L. Stevenson, that sedulous ape, of W.E. Henley, that harsh-mouthed but very beneficent spreader of French influences.
>
> It was a city of infinite curiosity as to the new literary methods and of infinite readiness to assimilate new ideas, whether they came from Paris by way of Ernest Dowson, from Poland by way of Conrad, or from New York or New England by way of Henry James, Stephen Crane, Harold Frederick, or Whistler, Abbey, Sargent, George Boughton.[8]

But now I would like to draw your attention to what I feel is a major omission in Ford's reconstructions of the international genealogy of Impressionism: the influence of English Aestheticism. This exclusion is surprising, given that Pater's definition of the subject's solipsist experience of fleeting sensations is invariably referred to by critics as the closest antecedent to Ford's Impressionism. In the famous 'Conclusion' to *The Renaissance* (1868–73), Pater speaks of 'the narrow chamber of the individual mind' where 'impressions, unstable, flickering, inconsistent' appear 'in perpetual flight', in that they 'burn and are extinguished with our consciousness of them'.[9] If Ford never avows this legacy, it is because his concept of Impressionism was remote from the delights of the artificial nurtured by Aestheticism. In any case, as Ian Watt reminds us, the term Impressionism was rarely used to refer to epistemological solipsism; rather, its main usage, in England and France, 'was in reference to the French school of painters, and to their English counterparts who came to the fore with the foundation of the New

---

[7] Ford, 'Techniques', p. 60.

[8] Ford, 'Techniques', p. 62.

[9] Walter Pater, *The Renaissance: Studies in Art and Poetry* (Oxford: Oxford University Press 1998), p. 151.

English Art Club in 1886'.[10] When applied to writing, the term indicated works which appeared as fresh, spontaneous and rapid executions. Symptomatically, Symons himself prefers the more general definition of Decadent when he refers to Pater's over-elaborate style whereas he insists on the 'purely impressionistic' quality of Henley's poetry: his *London Voluntaries*, says Symons, 'flash upon us certain aspects of the poetry of London as only Whistler had ever done, and in another art'.[11] Ford's *The Soul of London* (1905) is part of the same tradition of urban Impressionist aesthetics and was written when Monet was in the capital to paint his series of London pictures (1902–04).

Also, James and Conrad are regarded as responsive to the concerns of this tradition. In the preface to *The Nigger of the 'Narcissus'* (1897), Conrad's only statement on his approach to writing, he emphasises that art must 'make its appeal through the senses': 'My task which I am trying to achieve is, by the power of the written word, to make you hear, to make you feel – it is, before all, to make you *see!*'[12] Equally well known is James's metaphor of the house of fiction in his preface to the New York Edition (1908) of *Portrait of a Lady* (1881), where he theorises that reality can be seen and known only through subjective, partial points of view: 'The house of fiction has in short not one window, but a million [...] every one of which has been pierced, or is still pierceable, in its vast front'.[13]

Pictorial Influences and Literary Techniques

To understand why Impressionism – with its emphasis on visual appearances and its relationship with painting – was so central to Ford's concerns, you just need to look at his biography and cultural background.[14] He grew up in a Pre-Raphaelite milieu and, later in life, was the partner of two painters, Stella Bowen and Janice Biala. His knowledge of painting is testified by his early art monographs on his grandfather Ford Madox Brown, Dante Gabriel Rossetti and the Pre-Raphaelites as well as Hans Holbein. In later writings and until his death, Ford wrote repeatedly on Futurism, Vorticism, Cubism and Paul Cézanne. Doubtless, his sensitivity to visual impressions and his concern for style and technique in literature were nourished by this direct and constant experience of painterly craft. Art movements helped him redefine his concept of the literary and shaped his writings to a large extent. In the crucial years between the famous exhibition in London, 'Manet

---

[10] Ian Watt, *Conrad in the Nineteenth Century* (Berkeley: University of California Press, 1979), p. 172.

[11] Symons, 'The Decadent Movement in Literature', p. 867.

[12] Joseph Conrad, Preface, *The Nigger of the 'Narcissus'*, ed. Robert Kimbrough (New York: Norton, 1979), p. 147.

[13] Henry James, 'Preface to *Portrait of a Lady*', *The Art of Criticism: Henry James on the Theory and Practice of Fiction*, ed. William Veeder and Susan M. Griffin (Chicago: University of Chicago Press, 1986), p. 290.

[14] For details of Ford's life, see Chapter 1 in this volume.

and the Post-Impressionists' (November 1910–January 1911) – the time when, according to Virginia Woolf, 'human character changed'[15] – and the First World War, the avant-gardes had a powerful impact on English literature. This influence is particularly evident in Ford, not only in the refined techniques he uses to render the visual but also in the spatial metaphors he deploys to visualise his novels as if they were art objects: 'What we need, what we should strive to produce', he writes shortly before the publication of *The Good Soldier*, 'is a novel uniform in key, in tone, in progression, as hard in texture as a mosaic, as flawless in surface as a polished steel helmet of the fifteenth century'.[16]

Further pictorial influences can be inferred from the analysis of his main narrative techniques, to which we are now moving. Their examination will be conducted mainly with the help of some key Fordian texts through which you may gain a fairly complete view of his main ideas and narrative devices: the essay 'On Impressionism' (which appeared in *Poetry and Drama* in June and December 1914); *Joseph Conrad: A Personal Remembrance* (1924); and 'Techniques' (*Southern Review*, 1935).

(1) Effects of Vibration and the Time-Shift

> Indeed, I suppose that Impressionism exists to render those queer effects of real life that are like so many views seen through bright glass – through glass so bright that whilst you perceive through it a landscape or a backyard, you are aware that, on its surface, it reflects a face of a person behind you. For the whole of life is really like that; we are almost always in one place with our minds somewhere quite other.[17]

This extract from 'On Impressionism' is one of the numerous enticing visual metaphors you may find in Ford and it depicts the experience of being lured into a space of displacements. The reflecting surface of the glass allows the overlap of the landscape outside and the 'person behind' who would remain invisible otherwise. The image is reminiscent of a Cubist collage where fragments taken from different points of view are boldly juxtaposed. But does the passage also

---

[15] Virginia Woolf, 'Mr. Bennett and Mrs. Brown', *Collected Essays*, 4 vols (London: Hogarth Press, 1966–67), II, p. 320. If you are using *Selected Essays*, ed. David Bradshaw (Oxford: Oxford University Press, 2008), see the essay titled 'Character in Fiction' and p. xxvi for details of the essay's evolution. For an assessment of the way Ford engages with painting, see Laura Colombino (ed.), *Ford Madox Ford and Visual Culture*, International Ford Madox Ford Studies 8 (Amsterdam: Rodopi, 2009).

[16] Ford Madox Ford, 'Literary Portraits – XX: Mr. Gilbert Cannan and "Old Mole"', *Outlook*, 33 (24 Jan. 1914), 110. For an investigation of the relationship in Ford's main novels between his literary techniques and painting, music, sculpture, visual technologies and forms of popular entertainment, see Laura Colombino, *Ford Madox Ford: Vision, Visuality and Writing* (Oxford: Peter Lang, 2008).

[17] Ford Madox Ford, 'On Impressionism' (1914), *Critical Writings of Ford Madox Ford*, p. 41.

suggest the superimposition of physical space and mental space? Or perhaps the instability of our consciousness moving between alertness and distraction? Or could that 'somewhere quite other' refer to our selves in the past and, therefore, bring the dimension of time into the picture? These interpretations are all possible and equally correct: indeed, if this passage is a successful example of Ford's 'vibration' of 'superimposed emotions',[18] it is precisely because so many displacements are encapsulated in a simple but carefully devised image (see below for the discussion of the principle of selection). Similar fractured visions were practised by avant-garde movements. Futurist paintings, for example, tell stories by juxtaposing sensations and memories, presenting, as Ford says, 'fragments of impressions gathered during a period of time, during a period of emotion, or during a period of travel'.[19] This movement backwards and forwards is the time-shift, a basic device of Ford's storytelling, which disrupts the chronological sequence of events of Victorian fiction, as you may find in novels by Charles Dickens or Thomas Hardy.[20] John A. Meixner notices that, in Ford, its 'use varied considerably from novel to novel. In *The Good Soldier*, it shifted from the focus of a disturbed and disordered narrator; in *Some Do Not*, from the point of view of the author'.[21]

(2) Surprise

Ford believed that literature should be 'exceptional, vivid, or startling' and, through its disruption of conventions, produce a fresh and gripping look upon reality. 'A picture should come out of its frame and seize the spectator'.[22] Wrestling attention and arousing interest from the weary and distracted modern reader is imperative; and in this sense, a connection can be established with Walter Benjamin's seminal 1936 essay 'The Work of Art in the Age of Technological Reproduction' which famously discusses reception in distraction as a fundamental phenomenon of the new mass culture. Ford's diagnosis is that this distraction is an effect of the baffling dispersal of knowledge in a society which is getting more and more complex and specialised: 'We know so much, we know so many little things that we are beginning to realise how much there is in the world to know, and how little of all there is, is the much that we know'.[23] As T.S. Eliot's writes: 'Our civilization comprehends great complexity, and this variety and complexity, playing upon a refined sensibility, must produce various and complex results'.[24] The awareness that

---

[18] Ford, 'On Impressionism', pp. 42, 41.

[19] Ford Madox Ford, 'Les Jeunes and *Des Imagistes* (Second Notice)' (1914), *Critical Essays*, ed. Max Saunders and Richard Stang (Manchester: Carcanet Press, 2002), p. 155.

[20] For more on Ford's use of time-shift, see Chapter 4 in this volume.

[21] Meixner, *Ford Madox Ford's Novels*, p. 11.

[22] Ford, 'On Impressionism', pp. 51, 48.

[23] Ford Madox Ford, *The Critical Attitude* (London: Duckworth, 1911), p. 178.

[24] T.S. Eliot, 'The Metaphysical Poets' (1921), *Selected Prose of T.S. Eliot*, ed. Frank Kermode (New York: Harvest, 1975), p. 65.

reality is illimitable and its general meaning ungraspable makes it impossible for the individual to achieve a coherent vision and produces a profound epistemological crisis. Nowadays, 'any connected thought is almost an impossibility', suggests Ford, there is a 'disease of thoughtlessness'.[25] This explains both his abandonment of an encompassing point of view (fragmentation) and his need to take the reader by surprise. Finally, you should consider that Ford and his contemporaries were aware of their changing reading public in a society increasingly standardised and democratic. In this context, Ford feels that artists should address themselves not to 'intellectuals', 'persons of very conventional mind' who are not ready to accept and be struck by fresh and original impressions, but 'to the cabmen round the corner' whose minds are untrammelled by cultural dogmas.[26]

(3) Selection

Ford's narration is so fluid and natural that it may deceive you into thinking that there is nothing studied about it. And yet, if you engage in a close reading of his prose, you will realise how sophisticated his style is and wonder at the burden that the attainment of this naturalness must have laid on his power of expression. Writing is a titanic effort for him, which should be pushed to one's limits in search for the exactitude of expression. For the rendition of a scene, for example, he relies on the accurate selection of few details whose evocative power, though, will be so strong as to allow our mind's eye to complete the picture. Ford provides a potent example of this technique in 'On Impressionism', where he underscores the evocative power of carefully selected words:

> In that way you would attain to the sort of odd vibration that scenes in real life really have; you would give your reader the impression that he was witnessing something real, that he was passing through an experience. . . . You will observe also that you will have produced something that is very like a Futurist picture – not a Cubist picture, but one of those canvases that show you in one corner a pair of stays, in another a bit of the foyer of a music hall, in another a fragment of early morning landscape, and in the middle a pair of eyes, the whole bearing the title of 'A Night Out'.[27]

This aspect of Ford's craftsmanship is a lesson learnt mainly from French poetry, from Verlaine's, Mallarmé's and Arthur Rimbaud's exactly chiselled and yet intensely suggestive words capable of expanding imagination. A fine example of Ford's ability to conjure up complex images through economical precision is this sketchy portrait of Leonora in *The Good Soldier*: 'She was the great Mrs. Ashburnham of Branshaw and she lay all day upon her bed in her marvellous, light airy bedroom with the chintzes and the Chippendale and the portraits of deceased

---

25   Ford Madox Ford, *The Critical Attitude*, p. 123.
26   Ford, 'On Impressionism', pp. 50, 49.
27   Ford, 'On Impressionism', p. 42.

Ashburnhams by Zoffany and Zucchero'.[28] In this description the atmosphere is recreated through scanty objects but the highly evocative words and the multiple, suggestive rhythms generated by the repetition of consonant and vowel sounds (alliterations, assonances and consonances) convey the lyricism and richness of the room. This passage also allows us to appreciate that beside the selection (a tenet which features prominently also in James) of the *mots justes* (exact words), Ford is also interested in their skilful arrangement, whereby they might acquire rhythmic strength just as primary colours do when they are boldly juxtaposed – you may remember, in this connection, Dowell's vision of the world in *The Good Soldier* as 'spots of colour in an immense canvas' (p. 17). As Ezra Pound and the Imagists also knew well, it is through the friction, the electricity produced by an artful selection and combination that words come alive.

(4) Progression d'Effet and Cadence

The 'sense of inevitability' of the story (which Ford also refers to as its 'justification') is mainly conveyed through the technique of the *progression d'effet*, that is the steady rise to climax: through 'every word set on paper', he writes, 'the story must be carried forward faster and faster and with more and more intensity'.[29] An illuminating example is this extract from the final pages of *The Good Soldier*, which shows that the initial incommunicability but quiet and well-mannered relationship between the protagonists has developed into a frantic and almost deranged sort of communication: what 'had happened was just Hell. Leonora had spoken to Nancy; Nancy had spoken to Edward; Edward had spoken to Leonora – and they had talked and talked. And talked' (p. 135). Tellingly, a similar effect of increasing intensity can be found in the very final pages of *A Man Could Stand Up* –, when Valentine and Tietjens meet. Their stories and points of view – which so far have been kept separate in this novel and treated in Part I and Part II respectively – are rapidly juxtaposed in a sort of short circuit. This effect combines with the roar of euphoric crowds celebrating the end of the war on the streets, to produce a sense of electricity.[30]

Ford believes that style should reflect the writer's personal rhythms: 'everyone has a natural cadence of his own from which in the end he cannot escape'.[31] It is no accident that his writings display intense aural effects and in this Ford is influenced by his profound knowledge and appreciation of music.[32] His ambition

---

[28]   Ford, *The Good Soldier*, second edition, ed. Martin Stannard (New York: Norton, 2012), p. 137. All further references are to this edition.

[29]   Ford Madox Ford, *Joseph Conrad: A Personal Remembrance* (London: Duckworth, 1924), p. 210.

[30]   Ford Madox Ford, *A Man Could Stand Up* –, ed. Sara Haslam (Manchester: Carcanet Press, 2011), pp. 217–18.

[31]   Ford, *Joseph Conrad*, p. 200.

[32]   See Sondra J. Stang and Carl Smith, '"Music for a While": Ford's Compositions for Voice and Piano', *Contemporary Literature*, 30.2 (1989), 183–223.

is to achieve a style authentically his own: so simple and naturally cadenced that it will pass unnoticed. These features, he feels, will make the author's presence unobtrusive (attaining the Flaubertian aim of impersonality) while at the same time they will vouchsafe that the work be the genuine expression of his/her personality (for a discussion of the author's subjectivity, see below). This intensely rhythmical quality is particularly pleasant as you will find out if you try and read Ford's prose out loud. This quality is particularly true of his late works, such as *Provence* (1935) or *Great Trade Route* (1937), and, undoubtedly, of *The Good Soldier*, where Dowell, the narrating voice, suggests to the reader-listener what kind of aural atmosphere Ford has imagined for the novel:

> I shall just imagine myself for a fortnight or so at one side of the fireplace of a country cottage, with a sympathetic soul opposite me. And I shall go on talking, in a low voice while the sea sounds in the distance and overhead the great black flood of wind polishes the bright stars. (p. 15)

Ford's most subtle way of arousing our interest is by turning reading into a 'seductive occupation'[33] where the very substance of writing (its sounds, rhythms and formal arrangements) becomes a physical, sensuous reality capable of creating intense enjoyment. He expresses this concept in the following passage, which sounds like a striking anticipation of the theories formulated by Roland Barthes in *The Pleasure of the Text* (1973):

> You will do this by methods of surprise, of fatigue, by passages of sweetness in your language, by passages suggesting the sudden and brutal shock of suicide. You will give him passages of dulness, so that your bright effects may seem more bright; you will alternate, you will dwell for a long time upon an intimate point; you will seek to exasperate so that you may the better enchant. You will, in short, employ all the devices of the prostitute.[34]

Subjectivity and Objectivity: A Comparison with James

A major epistemological dilemma for both James and Ford is the problematic oscillation in their theoretical texts between two competing concepts of novel writing, which sometimes is described as a process of projection of the author's personality and at other times as a process of recording of outer reality. According to Dorothy J. Hale:

> In the Prefaces, it seems, James outlines two competing ideals of novelistic authorship: on the one hand the successful novelist is one who most transparently expresses his unique 'impression' of life; on the other hand, the successful

---

[33] Ford, 'On Impressionism', p. 39.
[34] Ford, 'On Impressionism', p. 54.

novelist is the one who does not allow his own views to prevent life from making its 'impression' on him.[35]

Similarly, Ford holds in tension the need for writers to efface themselves and their need to interest the reader by impressing themselves upon him/her. In Ford's words: 'the Impressionist author is sedulous to avoid letting his personality appear in the course of his book. On the other hand, his whole book, his whole poem is merely an expression of his personality'.[36]

In James, this productive tension tends to be resolved in favour of self-expression: he believes in the artist's superior subjectivity and that 'the greater' his 'capacity for appreciation, the more capable he is of representation'.[37] In turn, the qualities of his art work will provide a clear enough indication of his subjectivity. Writing becomes for him a mirror where 'The desire to grasp the "secret" of what interests him' allows 'James to plumb the "deeps" of his "personal" premises', so that, guided by the contents and treatment of his subject matter, he may be led 'to an objective assessment of the material within him'.[38] In a similar vein, Ford conceives writing as a form of 'egotism': 'I do not see how Impressionism can be anything else. [...] It recognises, frankly, that all art must be the expression of an ego'.[39] Compared to James, though, he places a far stronger emphasis on the artist as a *receptive* personality. Even his styling himself as an Impressionist, in the 1914 essay, is presented in less self-assertive terms than you might expect from what is to all intents and purposes a literary manifesto: 'one person and another in the last ten years has called me an Impressionist with such persistence that I have given up resistance'.[40] He claims to have adopted the label just because it has been repeatedly attached to his writing; to have accepted it because it responds to a widely shared impression of his style. If this was the actual reason it is very hard to tell: Ford's programmatic disregard for facts (but faithfulness to impressions) is well known.[41] In any case, you should be aware that this humble attitude is a skilful rhetorical move: it allows Ford to posit the artist's identity within his Impressionist poetic frame, that is, to conceive him or her as reflected in and constructed out of other people's impressions. So if, for James, 'the artist discovers himself in the process of representation',[42] for Ford he discovers himself in the process of being represented.

---

35 Dorothy J. Hale, 'Henry James and the Invention of Novel Theory', in Jonathan Freedman (ed.), *The Cambridge Companion to Henry James* (Cambridge: Cambridge University Press, 1998), pp. 84–5.

36 Ford, 'On Impressionism', p. 43.

37 Hale, 'Henry James and the Invention of Novel Theory', p. 86.

38 Hale, 'Henry James and the Invention of Novel Theory', p. 87.

39 Ford, 'On Impressionism', p. 34.

40 Ford, 'On Impressionism', p. 34.

41 See Chapter 1 in this volume.

42 Hale, 'Henry James and the Invention of Novel Theory', p. 87.

But this is not Ford's only or major mirroring strategy. Far more consequential, for example, is the one which vouchsafes, in the frame of egotistical impressions to which consciousness is confined, that the writer's or the narrator's experience may be nonetheless communicated to the reader; that it will not live and fade away within the individual mind. The fact is that Ford's is no longer Pater's solipsism but an egotism shared with a 'sympathetic soul' (*The Good Soldier*, p. 15): its preconditions are that the writer's personality be close enough to the experience and emotions of a standard individual, the '*homme moyen sensuel*',[43] to establish a contact with him or her.

Ford thinks that reality and characters are no longer stable identities: there is no answer to what the truth of other people's desires, concerns and motivations may be or what objective truth might be attained through a painstaking reconstruction of facts. This accounts for his belief that what writing should be about is the rendering of impressions as they impinge on the consciousness; so if, in James's view, for the great artist 'to know the "thing" is irresistibly to reproduce it',[44] for Ford *not* to know the thing is irresistibly *to let it reproduce itself*. Introducing 'On Impressionism', Frank MacShane states that: 'the Impressionist could not tell the reader what was going on, either internally or externally. Instead he had to show the reader these things'.[45] Outer reality and the inner self are equally elusive for Ford and cause a bewilderment, which is epitomised by the sentence Dowell pronounces repeatedly as if it were a musical refrain: 'I don't know'. All the writer can offer is the *manner* in which these elusive contents are perceived by a central consciousness. It follows that the *way* in which the experience of these bewildering substances of consciousness is conveyed, the faithfulness and effectiveness of rendition become paramount. Hence Ford's insistence on technique and his describing himself as a perfectly conscious writer.

Part of the ungraspable quality of reality is its illimitability (an issue which, you will remember, came to the fore with the epistemological crisis). In the preface to the New York Edition (1907) of *Roderick Hudson* (1876), James suggests: 'Really, universally, relations stop nowhere, and the exquisite problem of the artist is eternally but to draw, by a geometry of his own, the circle within which they shall happily *appear* to do so' by virtue of the work's self-contained architectural structure.[46] And here a major difference between James and Ford should be noticed. For James, art 'enacts the formal illusion of life's limitability' so that 'well-made works of art redeem "life" by giving it meaning'.[47] Ford's challenge, however, is to defy life's illimitability, by turning his protagonist's consciousness into a device where the manifold impressions of reality, his or her own as well as those of other characters, seem to refract endlessly. But life's illimitability is rendered

---

43 Ford, 'On Impressionism', p. 49.
44 Hale, 'Henry James and the Invention of Novel Theory', pp. 86–7.
45 Frank McShane, Introduction, Ford, 'On Impressionism', p. 33.
46 Henry James, 'Preface to *Roderick Hudson*', *The Art of Criticism*, pp. 260–61.
47 Hale, 'Henry James and the Invention of Novel Theory', p. 80.

also through a writing which Ford aspires to make itself virtually illimitable: prose should be made 'interesting at the third and fourth reading', contrived to generate each time new facets and meanings.[48] This gradual enrichment produces in the reader's memory the progressive overlaying of present and past impressions of the story; an effect which recalls the technique of the time-shift. The difference is that this time the superimposition occurs not so much in the text as in our own mind. In this way, Ford transforms reading into an intense act of reflection, involving us in the process of interpretation of the text and production of its meanings. It is mainly Ford's reliance on our intermittent attention that allows him to produce such effects. Let me provide an example drawn from my own experience. When I first read *The Good Soldier*, my attention was immediately gripped by the profound sadness that Ford conveys in the stunning opening sentence: 'This is the saddest story I have ever heard' (p. 9). I took the alternating tragedy and quietness of it to be the main emotional notes of the book, or in musical terms Ford would certainly subscribe to – being also a musicologist and composer – as the key of the tonic and the key of the dominant in a sonata (a musical genre he loved to equate with the novel). Predictably, my alertness to these features meant that the comic effects of the story mainly escaped my notice. Of these I became fully conscious only at a second and third reading, which, therefore, enriched and partly revised my initial impressions. This awareness made me feel that the unsettling vibrations of Dowell's consciousness had combined with those of my own in a sort of fascinating kaleidoscope.

How to 'Establish Your Own Critical Attitude': The Legacy of Ford's Criticism

Critics have often underscored the dual qualities of Ford's writing.[49] His Impressionism has been shown as vacillating between opposite terms: present perceptions and past memories; subjective expression and objective rendition; the impermanence of ever-changing sensations and the arresting quality of first impressions. This 'vibration', as Ford often refers to it, is meant to present life as the shimmering affair it actually is and to reproduce the bewilderment we feel when passing through an experience whose meaning we cannot fully grasp. Such oscillations, found throughout his work, are responsible for the most widely varying interpretations critics have given of his *oeuvre*, most notably of *The Good Soldier*.[50]

But these conceptual instabilities might appear no longer as an enticing interpretative challenge when found in critical and theoretical writings that

---

[48]   Ford Madox Ford, Preface, in Guy de Maupassant, *Stories from De Maupassant*, trans. E[lsie] M[artindale] (London: Duckworth, 1903), p. xii.

[49]   See, for example, Max Saunders, *Ford Madox Ford: A Dual Life*, 2 vols (Oxford: Oxford University Press, 1996).

[50]   See Chapter 6 in this volume.

we normally expect to be notable for their clear-cut definitions and consistent statements. Therefore, we may find Ford's vacillations particularly difficult to account for when appearing in his expositions of Impressionist techniques. Here, his antipathetic statements seem to frustrate our attempt to arrange his observations into a coherent theoretical frame. Yet this insecurity we feel is not a symptom of inaccuracy but an objective deliberately pursued by Ford and is in tune with his aesthetic beliefs. Indeed, it is precisely by recognising that his texts on the theory and practice of literature are themselves forms of Impressionist writing that we can make sense of their apparent contradictions. Far from betraying a lack of rigour or stylistic recklessness, these texts are sophisticated applications of his methods meant to convey Impressionist tenets in an Impressionist way. In other words, they are forms of meta-Impressionism.

Ford's theoretical and critical discussions of the art of the novel are grounded in relativism and suspicious of stable, unswerving assertions as to the truth to be achieved through the writing of fiction. Frank MacShane is correct that: 'Ford was not, of course, a critic like John Ransom or Dr. Leavis: as an enthusiastic pioneer, he was incapable of the balanced and scholarly assessment that characterises their criticism. [...] As a critic, Ford was too much the experimental writer to dogmatize'.[51] Ford's constant experimentation – meant to alter and extend the possibilities of Impressionist aesthetics to which he was faithful to the end – is part and parcel of his fundamental insight that experience is unstable and reality subject to the richness of interpretations elaborated by different individuals or by the same individual through time. For this reason: 'In his preface to *The English Novel*, he warned students of literature not to accept his judgements as incontestably true. Instead, he hoped that his statements would so excite the reader that he would himself start to think seriously about them and thus establish his own critical attitude'.[52] We may conclude that the controlled instability of his critical texts is a further profession of his aesthetic beliefs (a form of meta-Impressionism) and also an instrument to engender new ideas.

Finally, it should be noted that, as a literary historian and critic, Ford was most influential especially in the United States where *The English Novel* (1929) proved his most successful assessment of literature. MacShane suggests that Ford's 'pioneering efforts as a critic [...] helped plant the seeds for the New Criticism',[53] a school of criticism that would no longer focus on the *meaning* of literary texts but provide *interpretations*, paying particular attention to the formal aspects of literature whilst ignoring the author's life. For the New Critics, 'literature offers the most profound insights into human nature and the human condition that are available to us'; thanks to its insightfulness and authenticity, literature 'offers us a vantage point from which to criticize the superficial,

---

[51] Frank MacShane, Introduction, *Critical Writings of Ford Madox Ford*, pp. xii, xiv.
[52] MacShane, Introduction, pp. xiii-xiv.
[53] MacShane, Introduction, p. iii.

rationalized, and commercialized world we live in'.[54] Ford is similarly critical of the mechanisation of contemporary society – as he shows in late works such as *Provence: From Minstrels to the Machine* and *Great Trade Route* – as well as sceptical of comprehensive, organicist philosophies of reality. In a new epistemic context characterised by complexity and uncertainty, Ford feels he should posit 'the novel' as 'absolutely the only vehicle for the thought of our day. With the novel you can do anything: you can inquire into every department of life, you can explore every department of the world of thought'.[55]

---

[54]   Hans Bertens, *Literary Theory: The Basics* (London: Routledge, 2010), p. 22.

[55]   Ford, *Joseph Conrad*, p. 208.

Chapter 6

The Good Soldier

Martin Stannard

Graham Greene thought *The Good Soldier* 'one of the finest novels of our century'.[1] On its publication in March 1915, however, critical opinion was divided. Rebecca West praised its 'extreme beauty and wisdom',[2] the *New York Times* described it as 'a novel which extorts admiration',[3] and the *Observer* found it 'absorbing'.[4] Others had objections, some of which those now reading *The Good Soldier* for the first time might share: that it can seem 'terribly long-winded and prosy',[5] with the 'semblance of a plot carelessly flung together'.[6] Indeed, when one asks such apparently simple questions as 'What is the plot?' and 'What is it about?', they are surprisingly difficult to answer. Everything, as Julian Barnes suggests, shifts beneath our feet as we read.[7]

The Good Soldier looks like a realist first-person narrative. Indeed, Greene re-read it and *Great Expectations* (1861) before embarking on *The End of the Affair* (1953), to accustom himself to the limitations of first-person perspective, only to find that he needed other points of view to complicate Bendrix's interpretation of the facts. But the supposed 'facts' of any novel are, of course, merely inventions. In realist fiction we are asked to suspend disbelief and to accept the data *as though* they were facts. Jane Austen, Charles Dickens and George Eliot do not invite us to question the honesty, intelligence or sensitivity of their narrators who, we assume, are attempting to tell the truth. We have to trust them. In *The Good Soldier*, however, we (might) have something quite different. Critics often see John Dowell as unreliable. What his story is 'about', then, depends on *how* the story is told, and

---

[1] Graham Greene, Introduction, in Ford Madox Ford, *The Bodley Head Ford Madox Ford*, 5 vols (London: Bodley Head, 1962–71), I, p. 7.

[2] Rebecca West, 'Mr. Hueffer's New Novel', *Daily News and Leader*, 2 Apr. 1915, 6, in Ford Madox Ford, *The Good Soldier*, second edition, ed. Martin Stannard (New York: Norton, 2012), p. 237. All further references are to this edition.

[3] Anon, [Untitled], *New York Times Book Review* (7 Mar. 1915), 86, in *The Good Soldier*, p. 234.

[4] Anon, [Untitled], *Observer*, 28 Mar. 1915, 5, in *The Good Soldier*, p. 236

[5] Anon, [Untitled], *Times Literary Supplement* (25 Mar. 1915), 103, in *The Good Soldier*, p. 235.

[6] Anon, [Untitled], *Independent* (US), 22 Mar. 1915, 432, in *The Good Soldier*, p. 235.

[7] Julian Barnes, '[On Lostness]', in *The Good Soldier*, p. 420.

the supposed 'facts' of the novel are not facts at all but part of a fiction that he is constructing in a form of autobiography.

Dowell is attempting to 'figure out' (p. 53), as he puts it (he is an American), how it was that for nine years his wife, Florence, and his best friend, Edward Ashburnham, managed to conduct a heated affair without his (Dowell's) noticing anything. He is reflecting on the happiest years of his life but, in the narrative present, these have become for him years during which he was continuously betrayed by those he loved best. And of these two people, he had loved Ashburnham the most because he made him feel 'comfortable' (p. 69). Now he (Dowell) feels radically uncomfortable, destabilised. He has one set of memories of contentment which he must re-read in the light of a new set relating to knowledge only recently acquired. As a result, one of the things that the novel might be 'about' is how Dowell *now* feels about Florence and Ashburnham. One might expect him to hate them. In fact, he struggles not to. Put another way, if he does admit resentment to himself, he doesn't (often) to us and then frequently changes his mind; or, although he might not admit it to himself or to us, we might detect it as a suppressed emotion, which to acknowledge would drive him mad. He is governed by what might be described as an almost paranoid terror of hatred, or something which might equally be defined as a near-beatific (or anaemic?) Christian forgiveness.

A great deal depends, then, on what we make of Dowell himself. If he is unreliable, is he also weak and self-deceiving? Is he trying to tell the truth or to avoid telling the truth? Since 1915, literary criticism on *The Good Soldier* has tended to divide between those who believe the former and those who believe the latter. Even more confusing is the idea that both camps can be right. Two essays by American scholars, Mark Schorer (1948) and Samuel Hynes (1961), set the tone of this debate. Schorer finds Dowell inert, passionless and devoid of a sense of humour. As a result, Dowell is seen to tell a po-faced story about his own cuckoldry that is amusing at his own expense to those of us reading between the lines. His narration might thus be interpreted as unconsciously ironical, like Pooter's in *Diary of a Nobody* (1892). For Schorer, this anti-hero exhibits 'the madness of moral inertia'.[8] He suffers from a kind of mental paralysis and reveals himself as a dullard without realising it. This reading detects the story of a fool trying to be reflective. He is, therefore, Schorer argues, an unreliable narrator. He has to be. How else might one explain the opacity of Dowell's reactions *at the time* and his failure to react passionately when the truth is revealed?

Hynes's essay agues directly against this. 'What', he asks, 'are we to make of the novel's narrator? Or, to put it more formally, what authority should we allow to the version of events which he narrates?' 'In a novel which postulates such severe limits to human knowledge – a novel of doubt, that is, in which the narrator's fallibility *is* the norm – the problem of authority cannot be settled directly, because the question which authority answers: "How can we know what is true?" is itself

---

[8]   Mark Schorer, '[*The Good Soldier* as Comedy]', in *The Good Soldier*, p. 325.

what the novel is about'.[9] Hynes therefore thinks Schorer's interpretation to be misguided: first because Dowell's failings are shared by all the characters, and second because he displays a self-lacerating honesty and an admirable capacity for love which endears him to us. He is thus not an idiot whom we despise but a fellow human being whose failings everyone shares.

Other chapters in this volume deal with Ford as an Impressionist and a modernist: his use of point of view, disrupted chronology, fractured dialogue, free indirect discourse, the collapse of stable 'characters', and so on. Ford himself wrote extensively on the limitations of literary realism, and at the back of the Norton edition there is a section on what he termed 'Literary Impressionism' (pp. 251–315). I want rather to concentrate here on the Russian Formalist distinction between 'story' and 'plot'. This describes 'story' as the temporal/causal sequence of events (the chronological order of events relating cause to effect) and 'plot' as the defamiliarising, the making strange, of that sequence through the transformations of art: a particularly useful distinction when discussing *The Good Soldier*.[10] If we attempt a resumé of the 'story', the temporal/causal sequence of events in the 'right' chronological order, we discover a gap between what the narrator tells us and what we may, or may not, believe. There is even a sense in which Dowell himself does not know what 'happened'. The plot, the *telling* of the narrative, defamiliarises the story in such radical fashion as to render the original events chimeric, and as to the meaning of those events, there are as many versions as there are readers.

The essays at the back of the Norton edition thus present a wide range of interpretations. The novel is seen as a comedy, a tragedy, a comi-tragedy and, as Eugene Goodheart suggests, it might even offer a pre-vision of the philosophical and linguistic questions raised by structuralist and post-structuralist thought.[11] Is it, therefore, postmodern rather than modernist? Frank Kermode and Carol Jacobs regard its central concern as the arbitrary nature of the word, of written or spoken signification.[12] Does Dowell learn anything from his experience? Perhaps a more complicated question is: if he does, does he only learn things in the process of writing them down or dictating them or, to stay with the device of the novel, imagining himself speaking them to a 'sympathetic soul' (p. 15) on the other side of the fireplace? Or is he, as he maintains, as bemused at the end of his tale as he was at the beginning? Is it possible for the reader to learn anything from his

[9]   Samuel Hynes, '[The Epistemology of *The Good Soldier*]', in *The Good Soldier*, pp. 327, 329.

[10]   For further discussion of the story/plot distinction (using the French terms '*histoire*' and '*récit*') in relation to *The Good Soldier*'s narrative structure, see Rob Hawkes, *Ford Madox Ford and the Misfit Moderns: Edwardian Fiction and the First World War* (Basingstoke: Palgrave Macmillan, 2012), pp. 93–7.

[11]   Eugene Goodheart, 'What Dowell Knew: A Reading of *The Good Soldier*', in *The Good Soldier*, pp. 382–91.

[12]   Frank Kermode, '[Recognition and Deception]' and 'Carol Jacobs, '[The Passion for Talk]', in *The Good Soldier*, pp. 347–54 and 354–61, respectively.

experience, whether or not he can quantify it, in the way in which we might expect to learn from the experience of the central figure of a realist *Bildungsroman*? A recurrent phrase runs throughout: 'I don't know'. It is the polar opposite of the omniscient, omnipresent, omnipotent presence of the realist narrator, and gains much of its effect from defamiliarising that convention.

The Good Soldier, then, is a fascinating text to examine when discussing the form of the modern novel because it can shift between classifications: realist; Impressionist; modernist; postmodern. It displays many of the formal features of modernism yet it is much more immediately accessible than, say, James Joyce's *Ulysses* (1922) or Virginia Woolf's *The Waves* (1931). Goodheart's analysis states that:

> *The Good Soldier* remains one of the most puzzling works of modern fiction, because it has none of the anchoring affirmations or negations that control the works of the classic modernists [...]. If the classic modernists had a vision of the abyss, they also knew the compensations of aesthetic consciousness or moral commitment or spiritual transcendence. A moral fecklessness provides *The Good Soldier* with a paradoxical energy that makes the novel seem well in advance of its time: postmodern rather than modern. The fecklessness determines the character of the narration.[13]

It is worth pausing over Goodhart's use of that word 'fecklessness'. Its dictionary definition is: 'ineffectiveness', 'futility', 'weakness or impotence'. And if fecklessness determines 'the character of the narration' i.e. how Dowell tells his story, it also determines the character, such as it is, of the narrator. In Russian Formalist terms, we might say that the story, the temporal/causal sequence of events, is lost to us for ever. We cannot reconstruct it from the impressions Dowell renders. And if we try (it's a favourite party game of Ford scholars) to replace the narrative units in chronological order, as does Vincent J. Cheng,[14] we find that the chronology does not add up. We have, then, not only a narrative in which Dowell's 'plot' defamiliarises the 'story' by recounting it in 'unordered pictures',[15] but also one in which our possible mistrust of the narrative stance defamiliarises the story he *thinks* he is telling, or is, consciously or unconsciously, fabricating to protect himself from damnation as a complete idiot or failure, someone who is 'less than a man' (p. 85). Even if he is telling the truth as he has heard it, he has often only *heard* it, not witnessed it for himself, from a variety of prejudiced witnesses such as Leonora, Ashburnham's wife. Kermode has famously remarked that *The Good Soldier* defies '*the single right reading*'.[16] The reader must complete it, fill the

---

13   Goodheart, 'What Dowell Knew', p. 382.

14   Vincent J. Cheng, 'A Chronology of *The Good Soldier*', in *The Good Soldier*, pp. 391–5.

15   Ford Madox Ford, '[Developing the Theory of Impressionism with Conrad]', in *The Good Soldier*, p. 290.

16   Kermode, '[Recognition and Deception]', p. 353.

ideological gaps and even the gaps in what can be known of material detail. It is an open, 'writerly' text, to use Roland Barthes's term, that resists reduction.[17] There is no escape from this.

What 'happens' here, as it does in other modernist narratives, is that the link between the original event and its narration becomes increasingly frail. First-person narrative in the hands of a realist novelist carries an air of greater authenticity than does third-person narration because it appears to be coming to us more directly. It is a kind of fake autobiography or confession. Impressionist and modernist first-person narratives such as Henry James's *The Turn of the Screw* (1898), Joseph Conrad's *Heart of Darkness* (1899; 1902) and *The Good Soldier* subvert these assumptions of authenticity and authority. The narrator is no longer a wiser personality standing outside the recorded events and putting them into moral order; he or she is deeply implicated in a narrative present in which there is no moral order and authority itself is an illusion. It was precisely the absence of moral order that enraged some of *The Good Soldier*'s contemporary critics who saw the book as being distorted by a 'sex-morbid atmosphere'[18] and the work of 'an unpleasant imagination'.[19] All the links we have come to expect from realist practice are broken: between intention and action; between cause and effect; between guilt and punishment. The black-and-white world, like the black-and-white cow Dowell sees out of the train window, is upended.

Everything, then, hinges upon how we interpret this controlling voice that is constantly running out of control, and it is on this 'speaking' voice as a register of the narrator's cultural consciousness that this chapter will concentrate. Why is it that so few critics have discussed Dowell *as an American*? One reason might be that they find him an unconvincing or, at best, token American. Grover Smith notes Dowell's misuse of the term 'Pennsylvania Dutch' (p. 37) but only to decide that this must be a deliberate mistake on Ford's part, thus condemning his hero as 'ignorant and pretentious'.[20] Karen Hoffmann examines Dowell's American credentials in an interesting reading of 'the novel's treatment of imperialism [and] its reflection upon the mutually re-enforcing relationship between imperialism and patriarchy'.[21] However, although she notes that 'Dowell is presented as a Jamesian American who looks to Europe and specifically England as the superior Old World – a world he wishes to be a part of',[22] this element of his psychological conflict is not developed. The essay is rather, and quite legitimately, focussed on Ashburnham as a representative of British imperial masculinity who effeminises Dowell.

---

[17]   See Roland Barthes, *S/Z: An Essay*, trans. Richard Miller (New York: Hill and Wang, 1974), p. 4.

[18]   Anon, [Untitled], *Boston Transcript* (17 Mar. 1915), 24, in *The Good Soldier*, p. 235.

[19]   Anon, [Untitled], *Independent* (US), 432, in *The Good Soldier*, p. 235.

[20]   Grover Smith, '[Dowell as Untrustworthy Narrator]', in *The Good Soldier*, pp. 343–4.

[21]   Karen A. Hoffmann, '[Masculinity and Empire in *The Good Soldier*]', in *The Good Soldier*, p. 404.

[22]   Hoffmann, '[Masculinity and Empire in *The Good Soldier*]', p. 405.

Hoffmann discusses Dowell's 'sense of inferiority [about] being an American':

> By creating an American narrator who aspires to be British, Ford can examine
> Dowell's anxieties in relation to specific intersections of nationality, class, and
> gender. Defining himself and Florence as 'leisured Americans, which is as much
> as to say that we were un-American' [p. 9], Dowell finds his own conception
> of his class [and gender] identity to be out of place in America. [His choices to
> move to Europe and] define himself as closely as possible in terms of the nicer
> English [allow him to] salvage his masculinity yet [maintain his self-definition
> as leisured; after all, in the United States where middle- and upper-class
> masculinity is defined in terms of 'wrestling with men of business',] Florence's
> aunts [simply see Dowell as] 'the laziest man in Philadelphia' [pp. 9, 87, 17].[23]

In other words, to all intents and purposes, he is *not* American. He is a faked-up
Briton trying hopelessly to imitate Ashburnham, an effete Anglophile, and we end
with an intriguing reading not dissimilar to Schorer's but this time updated in the
context of postcolonial and gender theory. He is a man typical of his generation:
frightened by the new power of women and by the old power of colonial men.
Even so, that phrase 'un-American' carries ironical resonance (particularly after
Senator McCarthy's House Committee on Un-American Activities, 1938–44). For
it is not that Dowell is effectively not an American, but that he is a cultured East-
Coast American out of kilter with what he takes to be the brasher commercialism
that now supports his country's elite. Henry James and T.S. Eliot felt much the
same as they gravitated towards Britain as a cultural refuge.

Ford, in fact, went to great lengths to establish Dowell's (and Florence's)
American context. The whole book is written in an American voice, not that of
Huckleberry Finn but that of James's cultivated protagonists. It is not hugely
different from an educated British voice – Florence, he tells us, 'wanted her husband
to have an English accent' (p. 60) – but it is quietly littered with Americanisms:
'sidewalk' (p. 22); 'two dollars fifty' (p. 28); 'the whole rest of the day' (p. 36);
'thank'ee-marms' (p. 40); 'figure out' (p. 53); 'lay awake nights' (p. 101); 'on the
hop' (p. 115); 'twenty thousand a year English' (p. 134), and so on. They render
the tone noticeably more colloquial and intimate than James's: more 'American'.
The question is whether this easiness, this telling the story 'in a very rambling
way' (p. 124), signals mental laxity or even stupidity.

Dowell is, of course, well aware that 'casual Yankees' (p. 43) like him and
Florence might often appear vulgarly 'bright' (p. 28) in conversation with stylish
Europeans, invasive and over-intimate on slight acquaintance. He knows that the
British landed gentry can be snobs, and that Leonora might regard Americans as
little more than 'a carpet beneath her feet'. 'You may well ask what she had to
be proud of. Well', he remarks, 'she was a Powys married to an Ashburnham. I
suppose that gave her the right to despise casual Americans as long as she did it
unostentatiously' (p. 43). Is this the voice of a weak man trying to buy into the

---

[23]   Hoffmann, '[Masculinity and Empire in *The Good Soldier*]', pp. 409–10.

social exclusiveness of the 'nicer English' (p. 9)? If so, how do we explain the sentence that immediately follows: 'I don't know what anyone has to be proud of'? The book is in part a study of pride from an American perspective, by a man whose pride has been wrecked; a study of the tension between the performative, dignified public behaviour of the characters, English and American alike, and the silent tensions that are tearing them all apart on the rack of monogamy and good form. Ford once noted that his novel was a 'serious [...] analysis of the polygamous desires that underlie all men'.[24] 'I suppose that I should really like to be a polygamist', Dowell admits somewhat unconvincingly, 'with Nancy, and with Leonora and with Maisie Maidan and possibly even with Florence. I am no doubt like every other man; only, probably because of my American origin I am fainter. [...] I have only followed, faintly, and in my unconscious desires – Edward Ashburnham' (p. 157).

We shall return to Dowell's relations to the other protagonists but first let us take a step back to establish the American context of his remarks. What does it mean to say that, as a man of 'American origin', he is 'fainter'? The first point is that there might well be a level of irony, often mordantly humorous, in everything he says (or leaves unsaid) which derives from a cultivated intelligence. Although he plays down his intellectual accomplishments, he has a good knowledge of literature, the Bible and theology; there are shades of Dante in his allusions to the various dark woods; he quotes Latin, speaks fluent German and obviously knows French. He is well-read in fiction, serious and light, cites the Troubadours, Herrick and Swinburne, and he has a good knowledge of European painting. In fact, the whole book is painterly, presented as a sequence of Impressionist canvases. Take, for instance, the famous black-and-white cow scene. Dowell is on a train with his wife and the Ashburnhams, looking out of the window:

> The sun shines, the earth is blood red and purple and red and green and red. And the oxen in the ploughlands are bright varnished brown and black and blackish purple; and the peasants are dressed in the black and white of magpies; and there are great flocks of magpies too. Or the peasants' dresses in another field where there are little mounds of hay that will be grey-green on the sunny side and purple in the shadows – the peasants' dresses are vermillion with emerald green ribbons and purple skirts and white shirts and black velvet stomachers. Still, the impression is that you are drawn through brilliant green meadows that run away on each side to the dark purple fir-woods; the basalt pinnacles; the immense forests. And there is meadow-sweet at the edge of the streams and cattle. (p. 36)

Is this the voice of an anaemic or 'fainter' and passionless observer? True, it is a rare expression of delight but all the other 'pictures' that structure the narrative display equal sensitivity. As he says early on: 'That will give you the measure of how much I was in the landscape' (p. 22). And he is: acutely describing the

---

[24]   Ford to John Lane (28 Mar. 1915), *The Ford Madox Ford Reader*, ed. Sondra J. Stang (Manchester: Carcanet Press, 1986), p. 477.

inflections of colour above as a reflection of the vivacious interconnectness of the peasants and their land but, more importantly, he is embedded in the cultural landscape leading up to the outbreak of the First World War, a landscape in which all Edwardian certainty about gendered and national identity, all feudal and gentlemanly interconnectedness, is collapsing.

As an 'innocent' American, Dowell regards the performance of the Europeans and of his corrupt American wife with distant bemusement, as though watching a dance, 'a minuet de la cour' (p. 11), a slow, stately court dance in pairs, the steps of which he has not been taught. It is the light, refracting their strangeness, that catches his attention. 'Over her throat', we hear of Nancy, 'there played the reflection from a little pool of water, left by a thunderstorm of the night before, and all the rest of her features were in the diffused and luminous shade of her white parasol' (p. 91). In the photograph of Leonora with her six Irish sisters a 'black shadow from one of the branches of the apple-tree cuts right across her face which is all but invisible' (p. 97). Mrs Basil meets Ashburnham 'in the Burmese garden, under the pale sky, with sheafs of severed vegetation, misty and odorous in the night around their feet' (p. 117). 'You have to imagine horrible pictures of gloom and half light', he warns, invoking Nancy's rising up by Ashburnham's bed, 'her long hair falling, like a split cone of shadow, in the glimmer of a night-light that burned beside him' (p. 135). Dowell can't have *known* the emotional intensity of any of this from first-hand experience. No one, least of all the largely silent Ashburnham, has provided him with these interpretations. Dowell is imagining it. He is, in short, an artist, unconsciously so but an artist nevertheless. This might leave us with the old interpretative problem. Do we trust his painterly constructions? But whatever we decide, it seems difficult to avoid sympathy for the mind that created them, and its bemusement does not easily equate with dullardry.

Dowell, then, seems far from the kind of *nouveau-riche* American described by Hoffmann as appropriating the *chic* of old-money British estates. Acquiring Bramshaw Manor is almost an afterthought, seems manifestly absurd to Dowell himself, and brings him nothing but misery. The 'old-fashionedness in [his] phraseology' (p. 91) is that of a New Englander of Republican stock who can trace his ancestry back to William Penn, owns whole blocks of property in Philadelphia and, although he makes nothing of it, must be extremely wealthy. He feels as divorced from the getting-and-spending economic energy of modern commercial America as he does from its thrusting masculinity. As a Quaker he is tormented by his Protestant conscience and its stringent demands of Christian forgiveness and charity. Yet, although he struggles to forgive Florence (the only central figure not to be granted one of those 'pictures' suggesting secret distress), ultimately he is unable to because she has betrayed their shared American ideology. For Dowell, this is rooted in 'the liberty of a free American citizen' to think what he pleases (p. 54) about anything. 'You cannot [...] have acted as nurse to a person for twelve years without wishing to go on nursing them', he explains, battling against negativity, 'even though you hate them with the hatred of the adder':

But, in the nights, with that vision of Judgement before me, I know that I hold myself back. For I hate Florence. I hate Florence with such a hatred that I would not spare her an eternity of loneliness. She need not have done what she did. She was an American, a New Englander. She had not the hot passions of these Europeans. (p. 55)

To him, she now appears to have been merely 'a common flirt' (p. 125), a 'whore' (p. 56), an 'unstoppable talker' (p. 126), presenting her 'bright, American point of view' (p. 56) full of flapdoodle uplift about leaving the world a better place for her presence when really all she was trying to do was to raise herself socially and be free to seduce whomsoever she chose. *She* is the 'Anglo-maniac' (p. 31), not him. Leonora is right, he thinks, to despise her and, although he has a visceral distaste for the 'unscrupulous' (p. 49), 'shifty' (p. 164) 'Continental papists' (p. 49) that is bred in the bone of his Quakerism, he prefers, sometimes even loves, Leonora and her (albeit misguided) attempts to do her duty. After her revelations at Bramshaw, although he cannot *like* her (p. 167), she remains an object of his respect.

Dowell's wild protestations about Catholics are precisely the sort of statements that can make him seem unreliable. Does he not protest too much, a stuffed-shirt conservative riddled with archaic prejudice running under the flag of American liberty, equality and fraternity while abusing his black servant and sucking up to Ashburnham? Does he not lack any attractive *virility*? What woman married to such a man would *not* want to find a lover? Does he not almost *deserve* to be deceived? In this light, Florence might be construed as a New Woman to Dowell's Old Man locked in the lumber room of nineteenth-century masculinity: out of date, out of touch, untouchable to the point of being physically repulsive. In detaching himself from Florence's gaudy Protestantism in the Schloss scene, and in his sheer myopia in not being able to *see* what is going on when Florence places her finger on Ashburnham's wrist, he might seem to be unbearably stupid. The text is certainly open to such a reading (see Schorer). But what if (this novel is full of 'What ifs'), what if Dowell's vision of Florence is as near to the truth as we can get? What if she is, beneath that attractive exterior, a brash, manipulative sex-maniac, not only exploitative but also sadistic, relishing the embarrassment she causes to Leonora in the Schloss, taking positive pleasure in playing Dowell for a fool in public? There is plenty of evidence for this, too, and the American context of the novel gives it some force.

The central punning metaphor is the question of 'having a heart'. 'Have a heart' is a colloquialism for 'Be sympathetic'. In *The Good Soldier*, however, to 'have a heart' means to have a heart condition. That is what Florence is doing at these German spas: fabricating coronary disease in order to be with Ashburnham while simultaneously keeping her husband at a distance because she is supposedly too fragile to suffer his advances. So, paradoxically, she both has 'a heart' in that she is there for an affair of the heart, and she is heartless because she has no illness and treats Dowell despicably, rendering him a eunuch and an unconscious pander. What man (to echo the rhetoric of the anti-Dowell camp above) would not hate such a woman and find it difficult to forgive her? This issue, however, is both complicated and made more interesting as a moral problem by Dowell's struggle to forgive, which springs directly from his American Quakerism. For it is not only Florence who deceives him. Both Leonora and Ashburnham are complicit. Leonora knows exactly what is going on and, although she tries to tell Dowell after she storms out of the Schloss in a rage at Florence's behaviour (p. 39), she then bites her tongue until Florence and Ashburnham are dead. Ashburnham is also pretending to 'have a heart' and has presumably been behind those locked doors excluding Dowell in Bad Nauheim, preparing to undress his friend's wife. Yet Dowell forgives them. Why?

Leonora's is the easiest case to explain. She was, in Dowell's view, a tormented, betrayed wife who had come from the impoverished Irish gentry and found herself hitched to a serial philanderer and gambler, rich but unstable. She fears the total waste of their estate, needs to keep Ashburnham under financial control and does this with an allowance of money and by turning a blind eye (once she has burnt out her initial sense of betrayal) to his women. As a devout Irish Catholic, she sees adultery as a cardinal sin and marriage as indissoluble. She does not condone what her husband does but divorce is never an option for her. She wishes both to protect Dowell's innocence and her husband's (and her own) reputation. As a theological and social position, Dowell finds this understandable. She is cold and proud, sexually frozen (the putative cause of Ashburnham's waywardness) and, in her way, she is as cruel to Ashburnham as Florence is to Dowell. But she is trapped in one kind of gender performance: 'She saw life as a perpetual sex-battle between husbands who desire to be unfaithful to their wives, and wives who desire to recapture their husbands [...]. That was her sad and modest view of matrimony. Man, for her, was a sort of brute who must have his divagations, his moments of excess, his nights out, his, let us say, rutting seasons' (p. 126). This is not, however, the sort of man Dowell has been brought up to be in Philadelphia and not the sort of man he wants to be, except 'faintly'. Throughout he thus feels a lack, a sense of emasculation. After Leonora has revealed two hideous facts that had somehow escaped his attention – his wife's suicide and her adultery with his best friend – he heads for America apparently determined to remasculinise himself with some tough financial dealing (p. 87). But his heart is not in it. His heart is not in anything any more.

And when he regards Ashburnham, what does he see? The narrative expresses many hesitations over Ashburnham, points at which Dowell says that if he has given the impression of his friend as a heartless philanderer, that would be wrong (see, for example, p. 47). Despite Ashburnham's affair with Florence, despite the Kilsyte Case, Mrs Basil, Maisie Maidan, La Dolciquita, Nancy and, implicitly, numerous other casual seductions, Dowell, this quiet Philadelphia Quaker, refuses to cast the first stone or even, in Seamus Heaney's words, 'the stones of silence'.[25] Thus the novel is, perhaps, abstractly focussed on a central, unanswerable question: why is it that Dowell loves Ashburnham?

---

[25]   Seamus Heaney, 'Punishment', *North* (London: Faber and Faber, 1975), p. 35.

Here, we might return to the issue of irony in Dowell's narrative, for, in terms of what he tells us, there is nothing in Ashburnham for this cultivated American to love. The 'warm good-heartedness' of his eyes is immediately subverted by 'such a touch of stupidity' (p. 13). It is Ashburnham rather than Dowell who has no sense of irony or humour. Ashburnham reads sentimental romantic novels (p. 26), is happy to have the foolish Florence educate him (pp. 34–5), is usually bored, has a blankly expressionless face (p. 24), no conversation and is interested only in sport. When Leonora easily wrong-foots him with her teasing, he takes Dowell aside in the smoking room to ask quite seriously whether 'having too much in one's head would really interfere with one's quickness in polo. It struck him, he said, that brainy Johnnies generally were rather muffs when they got on to four legs' (p. 34). At face value, he is like a P.G. Wodehouse caricature. While Ashburnham knows everything about Chiffney bits and loose-boxes (pp. 24, 169), Western civilisation seems to have passed him by.

When Dowell thinks about Ashburnham, he thinks of him in images of absurdity. He stands by his array of designer luggage (an unwanted present from Leonora who was trying to promote an aura of manly control and style in her disgraced husband), opening and closing each case arbitrarily. He stares out over the hotel dining room with his vacuous sexual magnetism. He fiddles with a penknife just moments before he cuts his throat with it. Yet somehow Dowell detects nobility, and his 'picture' of Ashburnham tells its own intriguing story of the man's complexity:

> Edward was sunk in his chair; there were in the room two candles hidden by green glass shades. The green shades were reflected in the glasses of the bookcases that contained not books but guns with gleaming brown barrels and fishing rods in green baize over-covers. There was dimly to be seen, above a mantel-piece encumbered with spurs, hooves and bronze models of horses, a dark brown picture of a white horse. (p. 142)

Ashburnham here is in his den (hardly a study), 'sunk' (probably drunk) amid a philistine litter of masculinity, books displaced by sporting gear, and Leonora, for the first time in nine years, has entered this sanctuary to savage him for seducing Nancy's affections. It is the *coup de grace*, the final bust-up. Leaving him, Leonora goes to the girl's room to insist that she commit adultery to 'save' him. He is, Leonora says, 'dying for love of you' (p. 144), as Nancy and Leonora, and Dowell himself, are dying for love of him. Why? Why is it that Leonora, after telling him that 'This is the most atrocious thing you have done in your atrocious life' (p. 142), can say to Nancy: 'He's worth more than either of us' (p. 144) – and mean it? And why is it that Dowell, a man apparently so much cleverer, more accomplished and morally subtle, cannot conceal from himself that he loves the man 'because he was just myself' (p. 168)?

One reading of this might be ironical: that Dowell is being magnificently self-deceiving. Trying to appropriate Ashburnham's charm and recklessness but, really enervated, emasculated, by it, he appears as merely overshadowed and pathetically besotted by the aura of English upper-middle-class 'style'. In this reading, Dowell is a small man trying on a giant's clothes. Another take on it is that Dowell sees us all in Ashburnham. We would all do what he did if we had the nerve and were not 'normal, [...] virtuous, and [...] slightly-deceitful' members of society, those who 'flourish', rather than the 'passionate, the headstrong, and the too-truthful [who] are condemned to suicide and to madness' (p. 167–8). Dowell thinks that in his 'fainter way' he belongs to the latter category and that if he had 'had the courage and the virility and possibly also the physique of Edward Ashburnham I should, I fancy, have done much what he did. He seems to me like a large elder brother who took me out on several excursions and did many dashing things while I just watched him robbing the orchards, from a distance' (p. 168). But what, exactly, was it that Ashburnham 'did'?

Dowell is quite clear that he is not talking about 'free love' (p. 167). It is not the man's sexual adventures that he envies. Is it his courage to break the silence that enshrouds all the characters of this tale, to *talk*, to reach out for 'tenderness' (p. 56)? Is it his Christ-like endurance and simplicity under the lash of so many detractors? Is it his virility, his sheer attractiveness to women where, throughout, Dowell tends to be ignored? We shall never know because Dowell himself doesn't know. That rider – 'I fancy' – suggests the essence of the problem. If Dowell fancies that he belongs to the headstrong who are exterminated by the supposedly virtuous, how is it that he doesn't kill himself (it is a book strewn with suicides) and instead remains:

> that absurd figure, an American millionaire, who has bought one of the ancient haunts of English peace. I sit here, in Edward's gun-room, all day and all day in a house that is absolutely quiet. No one visits me, for I visit no one. No one is interested in me, for I have no interests. (p. 168)

Opposite him at dinner, the mad Nancy, a woman he cannot marry because she is too crazy to understand the Anglican ceremony, stares into space only to shout 'Shuttlecocks' periodically and to declare her belief in an omnipotent God (p. 168). It is like a scene from Beckett. There is no peace in this ancient haunt, no love, only silence. Above all he feels his nakedness, his exposure. '[A]nd to think', he concludes, 'that it all means nothing – that it is a picture without a meaning. Yes, it is queer' (p. 168).

The American voice behind *The Good Soldier*, then, is both astutely observant and baffled, courageous yet fearful, talkative yet silent. There is, of course, no friendly presence across the fireside, and he is not in a country cottage. He can only imagine being in such a place. He is an isolated, ageing virgin. His first and last 'embrace of [...] warmth' came from Florence 'lying for some moments in [his] arms' (p. 63) during the farcical elopement scene. He cannot but be aware that 'lying' here has a terrible double meaning. He touches no one and no one touches him. His narrative is painfully strung, as it were, between two cultures like the speaker of T.S. Eliot's 'The Love Song of J. Alfred Prufrock' (1917).

Indeed, it offers us the first quintessentially modernist voice, two years before Eliot presented us with Prufrock's tragedy of indecision.

Prufrock's invitation – 'Let us go then, you and I'[26] – is also Dowell's, beckoning us towards the befogged and shattered unreal city of the modern mind tempted by both the devalued ideology of high culture and the more tangible vulgarities of the streets, unable to affiliate with either. Prufrock's is a neurotic, rather priggish American consciousness, anxious about women, about wasting his life on trivia, about his unheroic status. 'No! I am not Prince Hamlet', he remarks, 'nor was meant to be'. He is, rather, an 'attendant lord',[27] just as Dowell is 'the attendant, not the husband' (p. 157), the nurse, the poodle, the ignored, the unheard. And yet we listen to both because they are telling us something important. Dowell paradoxically describes Leonora regarding him, rather than Florence, 'as if I were an invalid' (p. 29) and that final word becomes another acid pun as it wobbles in grammatical status between noun and adjective. Like Prufrock, Dowell feels somehow 'invalid', worthless, inauthentic. Theirs are not heroic tales with happy endings. They are narratives about the absurdity of such a construction of human behaviour, the 'realist', uplifting construction that assumes there to be intrinsic meaning or moral equity in life. 'I am not going to be so American', Dowell remarks, 'as to say that all true love demands some sacrifice. It doesn't' (p. 83). There can be 'true love' but rarely are both parties available simultaneously. Sacrifice won't salvage it. 'Why can't people have what they want? The things were all there to content everybody; yet everybody has the wrong thing' (p. 158).

At the heart of *The Good Soldier*, as at the centre of 'Prufrock', lies an incalculable isolation, alienation amid 'broken, tumultuous, agonised and unromantic lives, periods punctuated by screams, by imbecilities, by deaths, by agonies' (p. 158), which remain screened by the silences of polite discourse. Both are sardonic 'love stories', tales of passion by loveless men, but love stories nevertheless, celebrating the courageous and tragic search for identity through love, for connectedness, in time of total war. '[T]he real fierceness of desire', Dowell observes dispassionately,

> the real heat of a passion long continued and withering up the soul of a man is the craving for identity with the woman that he loves. He desires to see with the same eyes [...], to lose his identity, to be enveloped, to be supported. For, whatever may be said of the relation of the sexes, there is no man who loves a woman that does not desire to come to her for the renewal of his courage [...]. We are all so afraid, we are all so alone, we all so need from the outside the assurance of our own worthiness to exist. (pp. 82–3)

Is this weakness? Or self-lacerating honesty? The novel won't decide for us. But perhaps this rare expression of ardour helps to explain why Dowell loves

---

26   T.S. Eliot, 'The Love Song of J. Alfred Prufrock', *Collected Poems: 1909–1962* (London: Faber and Faber, 2002), p. 3.

27   Eliot, 'The Love Song of J. Alfred Prufrock', p. 7.

Ashburnham: because he is the one person in the novel who does not settle for alienation but seeks, like some crazed knight errant, absolute love, the only thing that might make life worth living, the only guarantee of identity.

At the end of a recent essay, I suggested that: 'oddly, [Dowell] writes a love story without realising it: not about Ashburnham's infatuations or Leonora's passion for the institution of marriage; not about Florence's possessive lust or Nancy's idealised hero-worship; but about the love of an American for Europe'.[28] The novel is, as it was in its creation (it was largely dictated), a 'spoken' text by someone trying to articulate the unspeakable, and it is, as it was not in its creation, spoken with American inflection, albeit in an English accent. Is it a closet homosexual text like Oscar Wilde's *The Picture of Dorian Gray* (1891)? Possibly. But that would surely be a restrictive '*single right reading*',[29] for it is, like 'Prufrock', also about masculinity and shyness, cultural confidence and hesitation. Both texts provide us with mock-heroic echoes of the supposedly grander loves of the classical and neo-classical tradition; both focus on men whose timidity is representative of a widespread Western sense of epistemological collapse.

Our responses to the problem that Goodheart investigates, then, 'What Dowell Knew', are likely to be various, but because the novel presents itself as an enigma, a puzzle, it continues to tease critics with the possibility of a 'key' to a single right reading. One of the more intriguing of these approaches was supplied by the late Roger Poole, a brilliant literary theorist from the University of Nottingham and a Ford fanatic. The novel's 'story', Poole argued, its temporal-causal sequence of events, was so ridiculously improbable that it plainly called into question Dowell's truthfulness. Poole thus regarded him not merely as an unreliable narrator, a moneyed dupe, but as a penniless adventurer who marries Florence believing that she will die from her supposed heart condition. When it is discovered at Uncle Hurlbird's death that he (Hurlbird) also did not 'have a heart', and that Florence has therefore been lying about this as an inherited condition, Dowell kills her by substituting her nitrate of amyl with prussic acid to make it appear that she has committed suicide. He has also killed Maisie Maidan. Leonora and he are co-conspirators. Jimmy does not exist. Nancy is either Ashburnham's daughter, or Dowell's. The story, in short, is a tale told by a murderer attempting to cover his tracks. It is a detective story with false clues, narrated not by an idiot but by someone who knows everything and is not telling us.

When Poole and I first discussed his theory, a fascinating correspondence ensued. He insisted that there was no evidence that Dowell had any money of his own before he met Florence. I replied saying that there is evidence: he has valuable properties in America. But, Poole protested, we only hear this from Dowell. True, I responded, but we only hear anything from Dowell. We can't thus

---

28   Martin Stannard, 'Cutting Remarks: What Went Missing From *The Good Soldier*', in Jason Harding (ed.), *Ford Madox Ford, Modernist Magazines and Editing*, International Ford Madox Ford Studies 9 (Amsterdam: Rodopi, 2010), p. 241.

29   Kermode, '[Recognition and Deception]', p. 353.

believe the sections of the narrative we choose to and ignore the rest. On this basis, we might just as well say that there is no evidence for Florence or her uncle having any money. And how does the supposed murder of Maisie Maidan relate to this motive of greed or revenge? I was quite happy with Poole's notion that Dowell might be saturated with inarticulate longings: homosexual ones for Ashburnham, heterosexual ones for Leonora, for Nancy, even for Maisie. Dowell admits that he wants Ashburnham's women, possibly even wants Ashburnham himself. As an American, it seems, he wants, indeed, to *be* Ashburnham: to have his European style and *sang-froid*, his sexual success. But to suggest that he says 'Now I can marry the girl' (p. 75) merely to throw the reader off the scent that Nancy is his daughter seemed to me to lose the complexity of the nightmare of repression inhabited by all the characters. If Dowell and Leonora were engaged in serial murder, is it not more credible that their loyalty to one another in felony (or their fear of one betraying the other's secrets) would have caused them to stick together, to get married as soon as decently possible and thus to seal up the mystery within the family? And why would Dowell tell this story at all? He is rich. He is installed in Ashburnham's house with Florence's money. He has got away with it. From whom is he trying to disguise the truth? No one is asking him anything. A man so cunning would surely realise that the very act of elaborating the details would lay him open both to suspicion and to making mistakes. He would simply remain silent unless the text we read is a form of disguised confession from a man tortured by conscience.

Is he, then, like the Ancient Mariner who must tell his tale as a form of expiation? I had no objection to this proposition: that what we hear is a form of purgation, that he must grasp the listener and force him to pay attention. But to do this and then to lie about everything would seem to defeat the object. To my mind, Poole's reading was reductive, limiting the text to a murder mystery, no matter how subtle. Bafflement, I argued, was surely the essential ingredient: the fact that Dowell does not understand the story he is telling until he tells it – and that, even then, it becomes more terrifyingly complicated than he dares contemplate, changing *as* he tells it.

It did no good. Poole remained adamant. He had a right reading to which he was wedded.[30] It is a useful example, however, of just how volatile this text is, how partisan readers can become, and how much our reading of it depends on what we believe to be the limits of Dowell's knowledge. Another interpretation might run as follows: to begin with, perhaps, Dowell thinks he knows, or could

---

[30] See Roger Poole, 'The Real Plot-Line of Ford Madox Ford's *The Good Soldier*: An Essay in Applied Deconstruction', *Textual Practice*, 4.3 (1990), 391–427; also 'The Unknown Ford Madox Ford', in Robert Hampson and Max Saunders (eds), *Ford Madox Ford's Modernity*, International Ford Madox Ford Studies 2 (Amsterdam: Rodopi, 2003), pp. 117–36. John Sutherland's 'Whose Daughter is Nancy?', in his *Can Jane Eyre Be Happy?* (Oxford: Oxford University Press, 1997), also picks up on the idea of Nancy's possibly dubious parentage, an idea first raised by Max Saunders in *Ford Madox Ford: A Dual Life*, 2 vols (Oxford: Oxford University Press, 1996), I, pp. 421–2.

know, everything, and thus provides detailed documentary evidence about dates and places. He is attempting to put what he now knows in order, to make a *lisible*, 'readerly' tale out of disordered pictures, to rescue the 'story' from the 'plot' Ashburnham, Leonora and Florence imposed on it. In the process of narration, however, this realist, empiricist version of the truth, and his sense of self, fail him. He has nothing to replace them. What he ultimately knows, then, is that he knows nothing and has no existence. Yet he knows that he knows nothing, which is something, and he has a form of existence in the narration he has created. So he is a 'fainter' (p. 157) figure than Ashburnham and, like Prufrock, is in limbo, suspended between integration and disintegration, a ghost or zombie haunting his old life. 'I was', as Dowell puts it, 'the walking dead' (p. 79).

Chapter 7

Ford Among the 'Movements, Magazines and Manifestos'

Stephen Rogers

London at least and possibly the world appeared to be passing under the dominion of writers newer and much more vivid. Those were the passionate days of the literary Cubists, Vorticists, Imagistes and the rest of the tapageur and riotous Jeunes of that young decade. [...] I prepared to stand aside in favour of our good friends – yours and mine – Ezra, Eliot, Wyndham Lewis, H.D., and the rest of the clamorous young writers who were then knocking at the door.

But greater clamours beset London and the world which till then had seemed to lie at the proud feet of those conquerors; Cubism, Vorticism, Imagism and the rest never had their fair chance amid the voices of the cannon [...].[1]

To the generation of writers emerging at the end of the nineteenth century it seemed that the tone of the Victorian age was complacent and conventional. The radical innovation in sensibility of the Romantics had been absorbed and diluted into the mainstream of Victorian culture, and was often seen to be associated with the sentimental and commercial aspects of a self-consciously respectable society. However, during the latter part of the nineteenth century, new movements and ideas developed among coteries of intellectuals and artists. The Pre-Raphaelites were perhaps the earliest to challenge accepted notions, and they attempted to express their vision through not just their paintings but also through literature. To do this they launched a magazine called *The Germ* in 1850, which would provide an opportunity for them to disseminate their ideas. Whilst this magazine was not especially successful at the time, lasting for just four issues, it was later seen to be a distinct prototype for what we may now term the modernist magazine. William Michael Rossetti, the brother of Dante Gabriel and Christina, was the editor and was responsible for producing a facsimile of the original magazine in 1901, when it became clear that its reputation was growing among the younger generation. By this time, other magazines such as *The Yellow Book* (1894–97) and *The Savoy* (1896) had appeared, making a stand for the exclusively aesthetic values of art in an age of increasing commercialisation. The Pre-Raphaelites were pioneers of this tendency and also felt that it was necessary to explain their aims and objectives,

---

[1] Ford Madox Ford, 'Dedicatory Letter to Stella Ford', *The Good Soldier*, second edition, ed. Martin Stannard (New York: Norton, 2012), p. 4.

and in this idea of outlining a programme and making a statement of beliefs they initiated the sort of manifesto that was to be repeated by future movements.

Meanwhile, Victorian novels had become, to use Henry James's phrase, 'large loose baggy monsters'.[2] In response to a perceived carelessness among writers, Ford promoted the idea of the 'critical attitude', which was an attempt to oppose 'sloppy' thinking about the writing of novels and poems, with a clear understanding of literary techniques – of how writers get their effects. By taking the example of Gustave Flaubert and Guy de Maupassant, he was at pains to demonstrate that the aspiring writer ought to consider their methods and take their art as seriously as a craftsman would; and this was an obsession that remained with him throughout his career.

Ford managed to express his sense of the dynamism of the times and the unsettling chaos in his poem 'To All the Dead' (1912): 'When my mind's all reeling with Modern Movements', he takes refuge in an elevated position above the turmoil below. As Ford makes clear in this poem, it is a time of speeding minutes, of 'Dead faiths, dead loves, lost friends' and 'pomps go down and queens go down'; and yet in this radically changing world 'I don't feel a spark of regret / not a spark'.[3] It was a period when the certainties of the past had been eroded, leaving in their place the hope for greater freedom. It was Ford's conviction that this opening world would make it possible for the artist to express his or her vision with exactitude and with the technical innovation necessary in order to render accurately the experience of modern life, which is 'so extraordinary, so hazy, so tenuous, with still such definite and concrete spots in it'.[4]

Making It New: *English Review* (1908–1910)

Ford's importance in the evolution of the modern literary 'revival' was initially established by his role as founder and editor of the *English Review*. At this time, Ford was living at 84 Holland Park Avenue, occupying three floors above a grocer's shop. This became his headquarters and where he held an open house, which was entered from round the corner in Portland Road. Joseph Conrad, Wyndham Lewis and Ezra Pound all visited Ford here. The *English Review* gave him a platform not only from which to publish new writers, but also to be active as an influential critic. It has perhaps been overlooked that Ford's criticisms anticipated the re-assessment of literature which is more often attributed to his younger contemporaries, especially Pound and T.S. Eliot. These criticisms, which began as a series of

---

[2]   Henry James, Preface, *The Tragic Muse* (Harmondsworth: Penguin, 1995), p. 4. The preface was first published in 1908, when the novel was re-published in the famous New York Edition of James's novels.

[3]   Ford Madox Ford, 'To All the Dead', *Selected Poems*, ed. Max Saunders (Manchester: Carcanet Press, 1997), pp. 75, 76.

[4]   Ford Madox Ford, 'Impressionism – Some Speculations', *Critical Writings of Ford Madox Ford*, ed. Frank MacShane (Lincoln: University of Nebraska Press, 1964), p. 142.

articles on what Ford termed 'the Critical Attitude' in the *English Review*, were later collected in book form in 1911. He was, after all, among the first critics to understand the significance of Thomas Hardy's poetry, stating that 'first Browning and then [...] Hardy, showed the way for the Imagiste group'.[5] Ford understood the crosscurrents that lay at the bottom of the urge to reform, and its origins in the minor poets of the Victorian age. He had a dislike for the great literary figures, instead preferring the poetry of Christina Rossetti because 'she held aloof from all the problems of her day'.[6] This comment indicates Ford's critique of the tendency of Victorian writers to vitiate their work by getting involved in the questions of the day (the result of nineteenth-century Positivism), which he regarded as detrimental to their work as creative artists concerned with presenting the truth as they saw it without intrusive comment. It was this objectivity that Ford found in the work of the French novelist Gustave Flaubert. However, such eminent Victorians as George Meredith, as poet, and Algernon Charles Swinburne could also receive sympathetic obituaries in the *English Review*.[7]

Ford's early journalism had been concerned with searching for signs that the life of the world of the early twentieth century finally made its way into the literature of the period. He stated, writing in the *Tribune* in January 1908:

> Will this year begin to show us English Literature registering and presenting in a great body, Modern Life? Will it begin to show us that Literature can still do for this Age what it has done for all that preceded it? Will it register and give to our time a form and an abiding shape and stamp? I wonder. We have, of course, the three or four writers. But are they enough to form an impulse, to found a school, to turn a tide? I wonder.[8]

It should be noted that Ford places his emphasis not on the one or two figures, but on a group of writers emerging together, strengthening each other's purpose, to establish a new canon. He had not at this point the confidence that such a group would appear, but was determined to analyse current conditions to see if such a group could emerge. By writing about the need for a new school of writers he hoped to attract new young writers who were working towards a similar conception and that they could be consolidated through their awareness that they were not in fact working in isolation but in interrelation with each other. In this sense they would serve not themselves but what Ford understood to be the only kingdom

---

[5]   Ford Madox Ford, *Thus to Revisit: Some Reminiscences* (London: Chapman and Hall, 1921), p. 153. Lionel Johnson's book-length study, *The Art of Thomas Hardy* (1894), was concerned with Hardy's fiction; and although the 1923 reprint included an essay on the poetry by J.E. Barton, it was not until later in the century that Hardy received serious critical attention for his poetry.

[6]   Ford Madox Ford, 'The Collected Poems of Christina Rossetti', *Critical Essays*, ed. Max Saunders and Richard Stang (Manchester: Carcanet Press, 2002), p. 26.

[7]   See Ford Madox Ford, 'Algernon Charles Swinburne' and 'George Meredith, OM', *Critical Essays*, pp. 71–3.

[8]   Ford Madox Ford, 'The Year 1908', *Critical Essays*, p. 52.

worth serving – the kingdom of the arts – and the everlasting Republic of Letters, an apparent attempt to subvert the imperial jingoism of the period. Quite clearly, Ford was of the opinion that new movements were necessary, that manifestos gave direction to groups, and saw the literary magazine as the platform on which the new writers of the future could introduce themselves to the wider world.

So Ford founded the *English Review* in December 1908, with the intention to establish a new school of writers. He claimed that the immediate reason for the magazine's foundation was that not one of the existing literary periodicals of the day would print a poem by Hardy.[9] Although Hardy had been a popular Victorian novelist, he had encountered controversy with his later novels, which seemed to challenge the accepted morality of the times. In particular, *Tess of the D'Urbervilles* (1891) and *Jude the Obscure* (1895) had been censured for their relatively frank depiction of sexual relationships.[10] Rebecca West linked this predicament to the reaction that had resulted from the trial of Oscar Wilde, stating that 'the revulsion against Wilde [...] spilled over', so that 'any writer who dealt with clashes between an individual and society or moral issues found a chill creeping over their careers'.[11] This state of affairs had led Hardy to abandon his career as a novelist and concentrate on what had always been his desire to write poetry. *Wessex Poems* had appeared in 1898: however, the poem that Hardy had now written, 'A Sunday Morning Tragedy', was about the birth of an illegitimate child and the tragic consequences of a mother's care for her daughter's reputation, which ironically commented on prevailing attitudes to sexual morality and the rigidity of traditional attitudes. It was this poem that Ford printed at the beginning of the first number of the *English Review* (December 1908). Characteristically, Ford recounted the episode in *Return to Yesterday* (1931), giving emphasis that it was Arthur Marwood's (the review's financial backer and the model for Christopher Tietjens) view that if Hardy's poem was not published in any of the monthly, weekly or daily papers, then he was 'of opinion that the rest of the world must guffaw if it heard'.[12] The point that Ford wanted to emphasise, here as elsewhere, was that in terms of literary matters, Britain was lagging behind other continental countries – particularly his beloved France. Ford felt that there was not a critical attitude.

It is often suggested that the *English Review* was amongst the foremost of modernist magazines – and Cyril Connolly, in an influential essay on 'Little Magazines', argued that it was indeed the first little magazine of the modern movement.[13] The authority for this comment was taken from Pound's observation

[9] See Max Saunders, *Ford Madox Ford: A Dual Life*, 2 vols (Oxford: Oxford University Press, 1996), I, p. 242.

[10] See Dale Kramer (ed.), *The Cambridge Companion to Thomas Hardy* (Cambridge: Cambridge University Press, 2003).

[11] Rebecca West, *1900* (London: Weidenfeld and Nicolson, 1982), p. 125.

[12] Ford Madox Ford, *Return to Yesterday* (Manchester: Carcanet Press, 1999), p. 288.

[13] Cyril Connolly, 'Little Magazines' (first published in *Art and Literature*, 1964), *The Evening Colonnade* (San Diego: Harcourt Jovanovich, 1975), p. 372.

that the key literary event of 1909–10 was Ford's periodical.[14] It holds this reputation because within its pages Ford introduced the work of Pound, D.H. Lawrence and Wyndham Lewis to the British public, rather than through any more advanced methods of shock such as was adopted by Lewis when he launched *Blast* (July 1914) with its striking typography and bright puce cover. Instead, Ford's editorial strategy was to introduce new work by the best young writers whilst also publishing work from the established names of the Edwardian literary scene: Arnold Bennett, Conrad, John Galsworthy, Hardy, Henry James and H.G. Wells.[15] This had the effect of consolidating the positions of new talent by placing it alongside the work of those who had already established a reputation in the public's consciousness. Such a juxtaposition meant that new writers appearing in the pages of the *English Review* were presented in such a way as to have the same status and therefore impact as those from a slightly older generation. It was because *les jeunes*, as Ford called them – Richard Aldington, H.D. (Hilda Doolittle), Norman Douglas, Eliot, F.S. Flint, Lawrence and Pound – were already knocking at the door that the periodical could offer a mouthpiece to an emerging generation (although some of this generation, as it turned out, would need to wait before their first works saw publication). Ford later wrote: 'Les Jeunes made a very pretty movement for themselves, only the war cut it short'.[16] In the pages of the magazine appeared a number of significant contributions, among them poems by Pound (including 'Sestina: Altaforte'), stories by Lewis ('The "Pole"', 'Some Innkeepers and Bestre' and 'Les Saltimbanques') and a poem and story by Lawrence ('A Still Afternoon' and 'Goose Fair').

The history of the *English Review* under Ford's editorship is discussed at length in *Ford Madox Ford, Modernist Magazines and Editing* (2010). Especially recommended are Nora Tomlinson's discussion about the economic difficulties of running such a review, Simon Grimble's essay on the perspectives that found voice in the *English Review*, and John Attridge's examination of the political writings that appeared in its pages. Other essays touch upon Ford's relations with James and Wells during his editorship.

---

[14] Ezra Pound, 'This Hulme Business', *Townsman*, 2.5 (Jan. 1939): quoted in Brita Lindberg-Seyersted (ed.), *Pound/Ford: The Story of a Literary Friendship: The Correspondence Between Ezra Pound and Ford Madox Ford and Their Writings About Each Other* (New York: New Directions, 1982), p. 164.

[15] Conrad's 'Some Reminiscences', which were dictated to Ford and later published as *A Personal Record* (1912), are Conrad's fullest autobiographical writing and a manifesto of his approach to the art of fiction. Wells's condition-of-England novel *Tono-Bungay* (1909) was serialised, as was Ford's own novel of contemporary life, *A Call* (1910). James had three stories published: 'The Velvet Glove', 'Mora Montravers' and 'The Jolly Corner'.

[16] Ford, *Thus to Revisit*, p. 59.

Literary Impressionism

So far we have looked at Ford's role among the movements of modernism, but we should also remember that Ford was not content just to let *les jeunes* have all the fun. Together with Conrad he evolved a method of narrative that he called Impressionism. Ford's Impressionism is sometimes a difficult concept because it is a theory that evades simplistic analysis. However, in the magazine *Poetry and Drama*, edited by Harold Monro, Ford did try to make his ideas clear, writing a two-part essay, 'On Impressionism', in 1914. This is really a manifesto espousing Ford's artistic credo. For a fuller discussion of Ford's Impressionism, you should turn to Chapter 5 in this volume. Here, it should be noted that Monro was a poet with a passionate and idealistic belief in poetry, and who was interested in the new approaches to the writing of poetry that were emerging in continental Europe, and had given space in *Poetry and Drama* to discussions about Marinetti and Futurist poetry, as well as chronicles by F.S. Flint of emerging tendencies in French poetry. In 1912, Monro had become the first editor of the Poetry Society's journal, the *Poetry Review*, and in the following winter had opened the Poetry Bookshop, in a rundown street off Theobalds Road, near the British Museum. The Museum was an important place in the development of modernism at this time. As well as housing extensive collections of art and artefacts, including objects associated with various ethnicities, it was the home of the famous circular reading room – once frequented by Karl Marx – and a place visited by nearly all the significant personalities of the times. By opening the Bookshop, Monro hoped to stimulate lively debate about poetry, by organising gatherings and poetry readings. Being placed close to the intellectual life surrounding the reading room at the Museum meant that the shop was able to attract all sorts of writers and artists. Ford was among those that came to the Bookshop to share his work.

Ford was, as we have already seen, concerned with recording the modern world, and was open to new influences and to exploring the new technologies emerging in the early twentieth century (for example, he constructs *A Call* around the use of the telephone as a means of communication). As a result, 'On Impressionism' was in part an attempt to write a manifesto outlining a method of composition that would allow the writer to convey the actuality of modern life as it was experienced by the individual.

The term 'Impressionism' had been carried into English literary discourse because it had been applied to the poems of Arthur Symons. Symons, a critic as well as poet, responsible for mediating between French movements and the London literary world, had been responsible for explaining Symbolism to British and American readers in *The Symbolist Movement in Literature* (1899). Symons's Impressionism was closely associated with his subject matter; as Donald Davie suggests, 'it seemed to have to do chiefly with sad prostitutes sheltering in London doorways from the London rain'. However, Davie also asks: 'was not the young Ford Madox Hueffer (Ford) an impressionist in a rather less restricted and more significant sense than Arthur Symons?'[17] Ford was far more able to develop a theory of writing than was Symons, who tended to import his literary theories from his experience gained during continental excursions. However, it should be noted that among Ford's earliest magazine publications was a poem, 'The Song of the Women: A Wealden Trio', published in the 1890s periodical *The Savoy* (1896), which was edited by Symons. This magazine is usually associated with the Decadent movement as manifested in England, and the magazine's art editor was Aubrey Beardsley, perhaps the most distinctive artistic figure to be noted among English artists linked with Decadence. Although Ford did not contribute to the *Yellow Book*, the most noted of the Aesthetic magazines, it is clear from his writings that the writers and artists that were to be found among its pages did provide Ford with some sort of conception of what a movement among English writers might look like. In *The English Novel* (1930), he notes that:

> The idea that writing was an art and as such had its dignity, that it had methods to be studied and was therefore such another acknowledged craft as shoe-making – such ideas acted for a time, in the days of the *Yellow Book*, like magic on a whole horde of English – and still more of American – writers.[18]

Ford's concern for craftsmanship seems, therefore, to have initiated interest that led him in the direction of what we may call Impressionism. It was in this context that Ford and Conrad developed their technique, rendering an affair through the capacity of making the reader see. Conrad famously wrote in his preface to *The Nigger of the 'Narcissus'* (1897): 'My task which I am trying to achieve is, by the power of the written word to make you hear, to make you feel – it is, before all, to make you *see*'.[19] Writing in *Thus to Revisit* (1921), Ford makes the comparison with a trickster who performs his task without drawing attention to himself or his methods, so that he can claim that the 'main canon of the doctrine of Impressionism had been this: The artist must aim at the absolute suppression of himself in his rendering of his Subject'.[20] It might also be claimed that the sophisticated methods of narration and perspective adopted by Ford and Conrad have something in common with Cubism, in that their concern was with rendering the affairs of mankind with objectivism.

However, Ford's own definition of this method, of adherence to the 'accuracies of my impressions',[21] is problematic in that it locates the 'truth' in that which cannot be objectified, as one person's 'impression' will differ from another's. In Fordian aesthetics it was the point of view that determined how an episode was

---

[17] Donald Davie, *Ezra Pound* (Chicago: University of Chicago Press, 1982), pp. 30–31.

[18] Ford Madox Ford, *The English Novel* (Manchester: Carcanet Press, 1997), p. 133.

[19] Joseph Conrad, Preface, *The Nigger of the 'Narcissus'*, ed. Robert Kimbrough (New York: Norton, 1979), p. 147.

[20] Ford, *Thus to Revisit*, p. 138.

[21] Ford, *Return to Yesterday*, p. 4.

understood. Rather than trusting to the omniscient narrator, as in much nineteenth-century realist fiction, Ford was concerned with rendering the way in which all phenomena is seen through a temperament.

'Those Were the Days': Imagism

We should not forget that Ford continued to write verse. Ford felt that much of the poetry of the late nineteenth and early twentieth century too easily adopted conventional commonplaces instead of finding subjects in contemporary life. In 1913, shortly before the publication of his first *Collected Poems* (1914),[22] Ford expressed his dissatisfaction with the general vogue for pastoral sentiment:

> the song of birds, moonlight – these the poet playing for safety and the critic trying to find something to praise, will deem the sure cards of the poetic pack. They seem the safe things to sentimentalise over and it is taken for granted that sentimentality is the business of poetry.[23]

In questioning these prevailing attitudes, Ford found himself aligned with an emerging group of poets who were forming themselves into a modern movement. Discussions between T.E. Hulme and F.S. Flint were leading in a direction similar to that adopted by Ford at this moment.[24] Ford later claimed that it was he who was responsible for instilling the notion into the minds of Hulme and Pound that 'poetic ideas are best expressed by the rendering of concrete objects'.[25]

Pound was at this point made the foreign representative of a new magazine simply called *Poetry*, founded in Chicago by Harriet Monroe. In this capacity he was on the lookout for good poetry. When he re-met H.D. (they had first met in the US when she had been a student at Bryn Mawr) together with Richard Aldington, he declared that the poetry that they showed him at their regular meetings in a tea-shop in Kensington in the spring of 1912 was the work of Imagistes.[26] This was the first use of the term, and was perhaps chosen to reflect the interest in the revolutionary movement of French Symbolists. It was a way of launching H.D. and Aldington when neither were finding any interest in their poetry, and were not being considered to be published by the conventional outlets of the day. Following the appearance of six poems in *Poetry* (three by H.D., three by Aldington), attention was directed at the fledgling movement. This was largely due to Pound's skill in promotion (and self-promotion). Any new artistic movement has to justify itself, and in the period before the First World War there were a number of coteries

---

[22]   See Chapter 8 in this volume.

[23]   Ford, 'Impressionism – Some Speculations', p. 143.

[24]   See Peter Jones, Introduction, *Imagist Poetry*, ed. Peter Jones (Harmondsworth: Penguin, 1972), pp. 14–18.

[25]   Ford Madox Ford, 'Those Were the Days', in *Imagist Anthology 1930* (London: Chatto and Windus, 1930), p. xiii.

[26]   Jones, Introduction, p. 17.

competing for attention: Imagism, Vorticism and Georgianism were to some extent illustrative of this social dynamic. Pound adopted an eccentric style of dress – Ford noted that he appeared in Holland Park Avenue wearing 'trousers made of green billiard cloth, a pink coat, a blue shirt, a tie hand-painted by a Japanese friend, an immense sombrero, a flaming beard cut to a point, and a single, large blue earring'.[27] Pound also promoted apparently eccentric ideas about poetry, as his 'explanations' about what Imagism was or was not must have appeared at the time. In March 1913, Flint published an article in *Poetry* that purported to be an attempt to find out, in response to public curiosity, what he could about Imagism and Imagistes. The article referred to Imagism as a 'movement' (in telling 'scare quotations') and also noted that the Imagists admitted to belonging to the era of the Post-Impressionists and the Futurists, whilst not having anything in common with those movements, and also having not published a manifesto. Instead, Flint offered a few remarks gleaned from having spoken to 'an *imagiste*'.[28] These statements were followed by some observations by Pound, given under the casual heading 'A Few Don'ts By An Imagiste', illustrating the method by which the poet could produce poetry that presented 'an intellectual and emotional complex in an instant of time'.[29] The attempt was, as Rebecca West boldly expressed it, to write a poetry that 'should be burned to the bone by austere fires and washed white with rains of affliction'.[30]

To launch the movement properly, Pound decided to bring out an anthology of poems by Imagists. Among those asked to contribute was Ford, then still known as Hueffer. Ford was included as one who was a sympathiser. Apart from Pound himself, who included those of his own poems that were closest to the principles of Imagism, the other sympathisers were: Skipwith Cannell, John Cournos, Flint, Joyce, Amy Lowell, Allen Upward and William Carlos Williams. The anthology was published in the American little magazine *The Glebe* in February 1914 (which was edited by Alfred Kreymborg, a poet active in New York's Greenwich Village, which had already established a reputation for being the centre of American bohemia), then independently by Monro's Poetry Bookshop in March, titled *Des Imagistes*. Retaining the French form for the title gave the volume the necessary appearance of Parisian chic.

Ford claimed in a review for *Outlook* that he did not know what Imagism was, although he was able to detect influences as diverse as what he characterised as being either Hellenic or Chinese. The reader of this article might have had cause to take issue with Ford's ability to be a guide in the new poetry. He acknowledged that Flint's poems were 'upon the whole most what I want, since

---

[27]   Ford, *Return to Yesterday*, p. 277.

[28]   F.S. Flint, 'Imagisme', in *Imagist Poetry*, pp. 129–30.

[29]   Ezra Pound, 'A Few Don'ts By An Imagiste', in *Imagist Poetry*, p. 130.

[30]   Rebecca West, 'Imagisme', *New Freewoman*, 1.5 (15 Aug. 1913), 86.

they are about the city'.[31] Thus far, so good, perhaps, because he here makes a stand for modern poetry being able to find subjects in the environment of the city, the cosmopolitan, dynamic, fast-paced location that most seemed to express the energies of the contemporary world. However, Ford is not really cut out to be dogmatic like Pound, and when he makes apparently dogmatic statements they are almost immediately undercut. So he refers in this article to Flint's 'The Swan' – a compacted version of an earlier poem called 'A Swan Song' – as being 'the truest piece of Imagisme, at any rate in this volume', and then proceeds to declare that Pound's 'Liu Ch'e' 'is more valuable as an example of what Imagisme really is'.[32] What interests Ford, apart from the beauty of individual poems, is that an attempt has been made to found a school of poetry along lines that he had desired to see. Not that he admits that his own work quite fits in with the poems of his younger contemporaries, on the contrary, he emphasises that he has tended to write long poems that have needed rhyme in order to speed them up. In contrast, the poems in *Des Imagistes* are usually short and written in *vers libre*. Ford finds that this 'allows a freer play for self-expression than even narrative prose; at the same time it calls for an even greater precision in that self-expression'.[33] As such, the Imagist poem is the intimate expression of the author's thought.

As has been frequently recorded, Pound quickly lost interest in his fledgling movement, and his place was effectively taken over by the American poet Amy Lowell. It was under her direction that the later anthologies were produced, appearing at yearly intervals like the popular Georgian anthologies. Ford's association with Imagism continued beyond the period of *Some Imagist Poets* (1915, 1916, 1917) when he was invited to write a piece ('Those Were the Days') by way of foreword for *Imagist Anthology 1930: New Poetry By the Imagists*, which included work by Aldington, Cournos, H.D., John Gould Fletcher, Flint, Ford, Lawrence and Williams. This provided something of a curious moment in literary history, with the anthology appearing just prior to the publication of the first academic study of Imagism, Glenn Hughes's *Imagism and the Imagists: A Study in Modern Poetry* (1931). Hughes was an academic at the University of Washington, who had forged contacts with Yeats and Eliot whilst on a Guggenheim Fellowship to Europe in 1928. He had produced a series of chapbooks and was fascinated by modern poetry – and was the force behind the 1930 anthology.

Into the Vortex

Pound, having ushered in a new poetry movement, promptly turned aside, as we have seen, and concentrated his energies in promoting a pan artistic movement that owed much to the example of Futurism, and which became known as

---

[31]   Ford Madox Ford, 'Les Jeunes and *Des Imagistes*', *Outlook*, 33 (May 1914), in *Critical Essays*, p. 151.

[32]   Ford, 'Les Jeunes and *Des Imagistes*', p. 151.

[33]   Ford, 'Les Jeunes and *Des Imagistes*', p. 153.

Vorticism. British Edwardian society had experienced a period of increased anxiety and nervousness, characterised by the clamour for equal voting rights for women, an arms race with Germany (particularly a struggle for naval superiority), an increased competition for imperial expansion in overseas possessions with rival powers, and the slipping of the prestige of being the dominant world power, with economic and manufacturing prowess increasingly felt to be threatened. These factors disrupted the social cohesion and in turn shifted attention towards an attempt to come to terms with the condition of modernity. The artist Charles Ginner, writing in the *New Age* in 1914, called for a 'Neo-Realism', declaring: 'Each age has its landscape, its atmosphere, its cities, its people'.[34] Ginner's manifesto was one that sought an art that would be part of the history of the epoch, even suspecting that the craze for Post-Impressionism and Cubism coming from France was a new academism in the making. In that year, 1914, the Vorticists emerged attempting a more radical assault on a culture that was already breaking apart. *BLAST* was the message that was proclaimed across the puce cover of their magazine. Magazines had been used as propaganda tools in this sort of way in continental Europe and were often the medium by which new groups of artists could disseminate their ideas. The Vorticists announced: 'Long live the great art vortex sprung up in the centre of this town!' Vorticism was therefore among the very few British art movements to respond to the European avant-garde, and its members have been described as being an exclusively English variety of Cubists and Futurists.[35] Among these Vorticists were three remarkable women whose work has only recently started to receive its due: Jessica Dismorr, Helen Saunders and Dorothy Shakespear. It is notable that *Blast* responded to the spirit of the times by supporting female suffrage – although with a tone that is patronising, suggesting that works of art should not be made targets for attack as had recently occurred when Velásquez's only known nude, the *Rokeby Venus* (c. 1647–51), had been slashed by a suffragette in the National Gallery.

The Vorticists, as has been noted, began as a British response to the impact of Post-Impressionism, Cubism and Futurism in the years immediately following the influential art critic Roger Fry's Post-Impressionist Exhibition in 1910. As an avant-garde art movement it was quickly overtaken by the events of the First World War. However, its origins go back to 1913, when the future Vorticists had been included in a exhibition held in Brighton by the Camden Town group. Wyndham Lewis, whose early stories Ford had published in the *English Review*, was the leading personality in the group and was responsible for editing *Blast*. Although Vorticism is most easily identified as being an art movement, it was also a label under which writers found a place from which to experiment and engage with the dynamics of the culture that

---

[34]   Charles Ginner, 'Neo-Realism', *New Age*, 14.9 (1 Jan. 1914), 272.
[35]   'Vorticism is a story of the acceptance and transformation of contemporary European art by young artists working in London': Philip Rylands, Introduction, in Mark Antliff and Vivien Greene (eds), *The Vorticists: Manifesto for a Modern World* (London: Tate, 2010), p. 15.

they found themselves amidst. Ford contributed the opening of *The Good Soldier* (1915), under the working title 'The Saddest Story', to *Blast* no. 1 (1914), which also included a suffragist story by West, 'Indissoluble Matrimony'; and Eliot was represented by poetry in *Blast* no. 2 (1915). Ford was to write of the period that:

> It was like an opening world. . . . For, if you have worried your poor dear brain for at least a quarter of a century over the hopelessness of finding, in Anglo-Saxondom, any traces of the operation of conscious art – it was amazing to find these young creatures not only evolving theories of writing and the plastic arts, but receiving in addition an immense amount of what is called 'public support'.[36]

Blast no. 1 contained, in addition to the fiction and poetry, a collection of statements of attitude, which were aimed to shock the polite culture of the day. These were arranged as a series of blasts and blesses, with the principle target of the blasts being the years of Queen Victoria's reign, 1837–1901. The magazine therefore was a medium by which publicity could be courted and also a platform for the dissemination of manifestos. Copies were left provocatively in restaurants and on trains, and this strategy was successful in creating a sensation that in turn led to numerous newspaper and magazine articles which sought to react to the apparent challenge manifested by its sudden appearance.

Making It New (Again): *transatlantic review* (1924)

Ford found that the promise of the pre-war period was revived when he left England and settled in Paris in the 1920s, just as a young generation of expatriate Americans also arrived, and helped to establish a transatlantic avant-garde. The disillusion of the war years had given rise to new developments in the European avant-garde, and the result was that Paris was alive with the spirit of bohemian experimentation and anarchism – both in art and life. Many people who wanted to find new ways of living were attracted by the spirit of the times as it existed among those who found their way to the bars and restaurants located on the Left Bank. Leading figures of the pre-war avant-garde such as Picasso were already firmly established, and they were soon joined by the Surrealists and Dadaists. Ford's friend Pound moved to Paris in 1920, having decided that the prevailing mood in London was likely to be harmful to the experimental forms of art and movements that had briefly flourished there in the years before the war. Gertrude Stein was already present, and Joyce had arrived in 1920 from Trieste, where he had moved from Zurich, the city where he had lived from 1915 to 1919, whilst he continued working on *Ulysses* (1922). Others associated with international modernism – Constantin Brancusi, Jean Cocteau and Francis Picabia – were also drawn to the French capital.

---

[36] Ford, *Thus to Revisit*, pp. 136–7.

Apart from Pound, the most important figure Ford published in his new literary periodical, the *transatlantic review*, was Joyce. There is a famous photo of Ford, Joyce, Pound and the American lawyer and patron John Quinn, taken in Paris in 1923, which has contributed to the association of Ford with the most advanced movements flourishing at that time.[37] Ford appears as something of an elderly Edwardian gentleman, posing alongside two of the most controversial writers of the period. However, this photo demonstrates Ford's close interest in what we now know as high modernism. The magazine's very title, *transatlantic review*, of course suggests the kind of cosmopolitan outlook that is one of the characteristics of modernism; and more than that, the decision taken to use lower-case letters can be seen as an attempt to demonstrate the magazine's credentials as an egalitarian avant-garde periodical breaking the rules of grammar. The American poet e.e. cummings, a contributor to the *transatlantic review*, was known for the radical use of lower-case letters in his poems, which appeared at the time to have modernist chic. Anthony Burgess, in his novel *Earthly Powers* (1980), made reference to this aspect of the magazine's design: 'Ford Madox Ford was starting a new magazine called *transatlantic review* (the lower case initial letters were modish, the Charvet cravat of modernism)'.[38]

In fact the magazine was probably not as revolutionary as it may have appeared – and was probably less significant than magazines such as *Broom*, *This Quarter* and *transition*, which shared a similar background, though it did allow Ernest Hemingway and a few other American expatriates a platform to announce themselves to the literary world. Andrew Thacker has drawn attention to the fact that the *transatlantic review* by its very title attempted to defy specific geographical affiliations and instead made its appeal in terms of 'an imagined community of international modernism'.[39] In this respect it was a place for the best writing of the contemporary moment to find an outlet. However, in Ford's view this meant work that was not necessarily avant-garde – he insisted on maintaining links between the literary tradition of the past and the future (best seen in the series of articles he wrote for the magazine under the pseudonym 'Daniel Chaucer', which attempted a 'Stocktaking' to see what still could be said to have survived the war as literature that retained its value to a generation who had their illusions shattered on the Western Front), although he did publish Jean Rhys for the first time in the magazine; whereas Hemingway, who was Ford's assistant, sought to offer an opportunity to those writers who had been rejected by the mainstream commercial magazines, such as Elsa von Freytag-Loringhoven. These tensions did not prevent the *transatlantic* from publishing, as Andrzej Gąsiorek has noted, 'such "advanced" English and American writers as

---

[37]   See Saunders, *Ford Madox Ford*, II, between pp. 290 and 291. For more on Ford's founding and editing of the *transatlantic review*, see Saunders, *Ford Madox Ford*, II, pp. 144–62.

[38]   Anthony Burgess, *Earthly Powers* (Harmondsworth: Penguin, 1997), p. 189.

[39]   Andrew Thacker, General Introduction, in Peter Brooker and Andrew Thacker (eds), *The Oxford Critical and Cultural History of Modernist Magazines: Volume II, North America 1894–1960* (Oxford: Oxford University Press, 2012), p. 4.

Djuna Barnes, Mary Butts, e.e. cummings, John Dos Passos, James Joyce, Robert McAlmon, Dorothy Richardson, Gertrude Stein, and William Carlos Williams'.[40] Indeed, the magazine published 'Work in Progress', extracts of what would become Joyce's final masterpiece: *Finnegans Wake* (1939).

Conclusion

What can we conclude regarding Ford's association with the movements, manifestoes and magazines of modernism? One thing that is immediately apparent is the extent to which he was directly involved with the most important movements of English language modernism. He was the editor of two of the most significant magazines of the modern movement, and as such was responsible for launching the literary careers of Ernest Hemingway, D.H. Lawrence, Wyndham Lewis and Jean Rhys. He was also responsible for supporting and promoting the work of James Joyce, Ezra Pound and William Carlos Williams, when they were still finding their way along the road to recognition. It was Ford's opinion that:

> A Movement in the Arts – *any* Movement – leavens a whole Nation with astonishing rapidity; its ideas pour through the daily, the weekly and the monthly press with the rapidity of water pouring through interstices, until at last they reach the Quarterlies and disturb even the Academicians asleep over their paper-baskets.[41]

So if movements can find a way into the general debate that is conducted in the periodical literature of the time, they can have an influence that goes beyond the journalistic necessity of the time into the more serious shaping of ideas. Ford's phrasing here, from *Thus to Revisit*, suggests something of T.S. Eliot's famous description, in the essay 'Tradition and the Individual Talent' (1919), of the emergence of a new work of art as being like a chemical that effects a change not just on the present moment but also causes a re-evaluation of what is already in existence. Ford's conception is expressed with far less caution, indeed it suggests that the effect of a movement's ideas can be such that the existing superstructure is eroded, forcing an awareness of the ideas upon those remotely complacent. Interestingly, both envision a sense of displacement, but it is Ford that understands this in relation to the social activity of journalism, whereas Eliot's view leads to the New Critical emphasis on the work of art seen in isolation. Ford's view is that cultural shifts are achieved not primarily through works of art on their own but in relation to the discussion that they are able to generate. It is worth noting that when Edward Thomas, in 1914, wrote to Walter de la Mare (both contributors to Ford's *English Review*) that he was doubtful if the 'Blast poets' had

---

40   Andrzej Gąsiorek, 'Exiles', in *The Oxford Critical and Cultural History of Modernist Magazines*, p. 700.

41   Ford, *Thus to Revisit*, pp. 63–4.

joined up, he was indirectly revealing how useful labels can be in locating groups within the complex dialogues of modernity:[42] the 'Blast poets' being primarily Pound, but perhaps meant here to include Ford and Rebecca West, and identified by association of course with Lewis's *Blast*. This form of labelling or notation therefore reveals the way in which the 'new' in art and literature could become located in the consciousness of the public through the associational influence of movements, magazines and manifestos. This could operate at the level of shock and the sensational, but the implications tended towards a re-evaluation of cultural norms and artistic practice. As Malcolm Bradbury has asserted: 'experimentalism [...] made its way by spectacle, establishing its practices and its norms, asserting its distinctive significance for the times'.[43] Ford played his part in this process; but it is equally significant to stress how he understood these dynamics, making the conscious effort to engineer a shift in perspective. This included an understanding that if art wants an audience then it needs to make a dramatic impact – and movements, magazines and manifestos were the means in the early twentieth century of achieving such an aim.

---

[42]   Thomas to Walter de la Mare (30 Aug. 1914), *Poet to Poet: Edward Thomas's Letters to Walter de la Mare*, ed. Judy Kendall (Bridgend: Seren, 2012), p. 188.

[43]   Malcolm Bradbury, 'Movements, Magazines and Manifestos', in Malcolm Bradbury and James McFarlane (eds), *Modernism: A Guide to European Literature 1890–1930* (Harmondsworth: Penguin, 1991), p. 204.

Chapter 8

In the 'Twentieth-Century Fashion':
Ford and Modern Poetry

Paul Skinner

When Ezra Pound published *Des Imagistes*, the first Imagist anthology, in 1914, it was mostly given over to work by Richard Aldington, H.D. (Hilda Doolittle), F.S. Flint and Pound himself; but he found room also for single poems by seven others, among them James Joyce, William Carlos Williams and Ford Madox Ford. Ford's contribution was 'In the Little Old Market-Place', which begins:

> It rains, it rains,
> From gutters and drains
> And gargoyles and gables:
> It drips from the tables
> That tell us the tolls upon grains,
> Oxen, asses, sheep, turkeys and fowls
> Set into the rain-soaked wall
> Of the old Town Hall.[1]

Forty words: thirty of them monosyllables, a drumming or pattering, like rain on a roof; no consistent pattern of syllables, nor of stresses beyond the first four lines; and, for all the relentless rhyming and chiming, the half-rhymes, sibilants and alliteration, the dominant impression is really one of relaxedness, enjoyment, even perhaps an unselfconsciousness about 'modernity'. Nobody could mistake it for anything other than a poem, yet there's no word here that wouldn't be used in conversation, nothing 'that you couldn't, in some circumstance, in the stress of some emotion, actually say', as Pound would write in a 1915 letter that consists very largely of assertions taken from Ford's writings and conversation.[2] The poem is also filled with concrete objects, with named *things*. The rendering of such ordinary material details and the language of everyday speech as the language of poetry: these are the issues of central importance to understanding both Ford's

---

[1] Ford Madox Ford, 'In the Little Old Market-Place', *Selected Poems*, ed. Max Saunders (Manchester: Carcanet Press, 1997), p. 68. Unless indicated otherwise, all poems by Ford quoted in this chapter are from *Selected Poems*.

[2] Pound to Harriet Monroe (Jan. 1915), *Selected Letters of Ezra Pound, 1907–1941*, ed. D.D. Paige (New Directions: New York, 1971), p. 49.

view of modern poetry's proper concerns and how far that view differed from those of his contemporaries.

When *Des Imagistes* appeared, Ford had not only published far more books than the other ten contributors (some of whom had yet to produce a volume at all), he had also published far more *poetry* than any of them: seven volumes, including a *Collected Poems* (1914).[3] Now, a hundred years on, despite the efforts of several eminent advocates, that poetry stubbornly remains little-known. And it's true that, when we confront it on the page it may seem, for the most part, far from revolutionary: the forms are largely conventional, the language generally unexceptional, the rhymes unfashionably frequent. So it may puzzle many twenty-first-century readers of Ford's 'On Heaven' to learn that Pound, arch-modernist, described it (also in 1914) as 'the best poem yet written in the "twentieth-century fashion"'.[4] In a 1917 review, T.S. Eliot would praise Ford's *Antwerp* (1915) as 'the only good poem I have met with on the subject of the war thus far',[5] while *A House* (1921) won the prize for best poem of the year, awarded by Harriet Monroe's influential magazine *Poetry* (Chicago).

We might note that both Pound's and Eliot's comments have their qualifiers, 'yet' and 'thus far', implying their authors' awareness that those judgements are provisional, each made at a specific juncture in what was recognisably, even then, a period of dramatic political, social and cultural change. Nevertheless, there is clearly an implication that Ford had achieved something significant and something new, not only in his 'first' art, that of the novel, but in his poetry too.

Victorian and Edwardian Ford

Ford's early poems have often been dismissed or ignored, probably because critics are looking primarily for evidence of the writer he had not yet become, the qualities and inclinations that would involve him with the major movements and figures of the modernist 'revolution'.[6] That early work is strongly marked by a sense of place: its context was overwhelmingly rural for a decade from the mid-1890s. Much of Ford's imagery is drawn from the country around Romney Marsh, showing a keen awareness of the weather, of the unremitting labours of agricultural

---

3   The volume's title page has '1914' but it seems to have been published in November 1913 and post-dated, a fairly common practice at that time.

4   Ezra Pound, 'The Prose Tradition in Verse', *Literary Essays of Ezra Pound*, ed. T.S. Eliot (London: Faber and Faber, 1960), p. 373.

5   T.S. Eliot, 'Reflections on Contemporary Poetry', *Egoist*, 4.10 (1917), 151.

6   A notable exception here is Ashley Chantler: see his 'Ford's Pre-War Poetry and the "Rotting City"', in Sara Haslam (ed.), *Ford Madox Ford and the City*, International Ford Madox Ford Studies 4 (Amsterdam: Rodopi, 2005), pp. 111–29; and '"In This Dead-Dawning Century": Ford Madox Ford's Edwardian Poetry', in Max Saunders and Laura Colombino (eds), *The Edwardian Ford Madox Ford*, International Ford Madox Ford Studies 12 (Amsterdam: Rodopi, 2013), pp. 91–103.

workers, of trees and clouds and hedges and birds. He ranges widely over poetic forms, using song, dialogue, ballad, pastiche and dramatic monologue. At first sight, these poems often appear very simple, perhaps unexciting, but many reward a careful reading. Some representative examples are 'From the Soil', 'The Great View' and 'Gray: For a Picture' (1900), in part an elegy for a ploughman, William Mead, good at his work, good too at teaching others but otherwise unremarkable – which is, of course, the point. The last two stanzas run:

> Thus when his work was done and done his days
> He left a school of workers – to this day
> We recognize their touch – and owe due praise
> For bread and thought to such as he and Gray.
>
> Who ploughed such furrows each in his own field,
> Who sowed such seed and gathered in such grain,
> That we still batten on their well-sown yield,
> And wonder who shall do the like again.[7]

The poem honours the unexceptional yet indispensable in both its subject and its method (ten monosyllables in each of the opening and closing lines of the first quoted stanza). There is that slight element of risk in the rhymewords falling so closely together on the ear – 'days' / 'day' – but separated just sufficiently by each word's exact matching with its partner ('praise' and 'Gray'); risk also in the repetition of 'done' which is offset by recognition of the line's effective economy. The phrase 'bread and thought' not only stresses the reliance of everyone, poets as well as labourers, sculptors as well as draymen, on the producers of food but it also emphasises the metaphorical closeness of the ploughman's work to the writer's which Ford has indicated: ploughing furrows in one's own field, sowing seed, tending and harvesting. Finally, the last line points us to an important contextual factor: that Ford had been born at the beginning of a period conventionally regarded as the Great Agricultural Depression (roughly, from the mid-1870s to the late 1890s); and that, when he wrote this poem, he was seeing all around him the continued depopulation of the countryside as young men in particular moved into the cities; and widespread poverty and desperation among those who remained. In 'Every Man: A Sequence' (1905), the first section is titled 'The Ploughman':

> I am the ruler of all Kings
> Who bear the State upon my back;
> All wealth comes from my furrowings;
> If I should stay my hand what lack
> What dearth and what despair, what death,
> Where now waves wheat, what bitter heath!

---

[7] Ford Madox Ford, 'Gray: For a Picture', *Collected Poems* (New York: Oxford University Press, 1936), p. 212.

> I plough green lands, by shaws all brown,
> Whilst knaves rise up and kings fall down. (p. 52)

The implied political point here was probably less important to Ford than the fact that he was writing of what he knew at first-hand, a countryside he had inhabited and familiarised himself with, an informed insider's view rather than that of weekender, the urban poet seeking material outside his or her normal run. The assertion that the producers of food (and of poetry) were the true ruling class of a country was one that recurred several times in his later work.[8] Ford would also have been aware of the long tradition of the ploughman as symbolic figure, from classical and Christian sources through to Shakespeare, Wordsworth and, of course, Thomas Gray.[9]

In addition to novelist, poet and critic, Ford was musician and composer,[10] and that interest strongly informs the first dozen or so years of his poetry, in its rhythms, its strong and often monosyllabic rhymewords, its frequent use of regular stanzaic forms – and its titles, both of individual poems and of volumes: *The Questions at the Well: With Sundry Other Verses for Notes of Music* (1893); *Poems for Pictures: And for Notes of Music* (1900); *The Face of the Night: A Second Series of Poems for Pictures* (1904); and *Songs from London* (1910).

That constant pairing of the poetry with another art, painting or music, while not an unusual feature of the *fin-de-siècle* period (such as Arthur Symons's 1892 *Silhouettes* and his 1905 *A Book of Twenty Songs*), may imply Ford's doubts about the ability of the poetry to stand entirely alone, less perhaps a matter of personal self-confidence than a questioning of the current health of poetry itself. In his 1909 essay 'Modern Poetry', later included in *The Critical Attitude* (1911), Ford confessed to liking, of Victorian poetry, 'really only a few poems of Browning's and a very considerable number of Christina Rossetti's'. He stressed the small scale of modern poetry, which he saw as 'a thing not very sturdy, but extraordinarily tenacious of life. We have not got any great poet, but we have an extraordinary amount of lyric ability'.[11] Algernon Charles Swinburne had died in April 1909, whereupon W.B. Yeats said to his sister Lily: 'And now I am King of the Cats.'[12] But the volumes that marked Yeats's own shift to a more modern idiom, *The Green Helmet* (1910) and (even more so) *Responsibilities* (1914) were yet to come. Ford's essay mentions Yeats (and Walter de la Mare) in passing but essentially looks forward: 'It does not much matter where the poet goes or what he

---

[8]   See Chantler, '"In This Dead-Dawning Century"', p. 94.

[9]   See Thomas Gray's 'Elegy Written in a Country Churchyard' (1751). The literary history of the ploughman is usefully summarised in Michael Ferber, *A Dictionary of Literary Symbols* (Cambridge: Cambridge University Press, 1999), pp. 157–9.

[10]   See Sondra J. Stang and Carl Smith, '"Music for a While": Ford's Compositions for Voice and Piano', *Contemporary Literature*, 30.2 (1989), 183–223.

[11]   Ford Madox Ford, *The Critical Attitude* (London: Duckworth, 1911), pp. 179, 182.

[12]   R.F. Foster, *W.B. Yeats: A Life, I: The Apprentice Mage: 1865–1914* (Oxford: Oxford University Press, 1997), p. 616, n. 69.

does, so long as he turns inquiring, sincere, and properly humble eyes upon the life that is around him. In that case poetry would come entirely into its own again.'[13]

Pound, Prose and the 'Documentary Tradition'

We can see now how ready Ford was to engage with the new writers of the pre-war period of Imagism and Vorticism. As editor of the *English Review*, he published several of them himself: Pound, D.H. Lawrence, Wyndham Lewis. Pound, whom he met early in 1909, valued Ford's criticism highly and reviewed his poetry: *High Germany*, in 1912, as well as his *Collected Poems*, in December 1913 and again in June 1914. The second of these, 'Mr. Hueffer and the Prose Tradition in Verse', reprinted as 'The Prose Tradition in Verse', is one of Pound's most significant essays. He singles out Ford's musical ability, the true lyric to be set to music; but, as his title indicates, is concerned to stress the value of prose training, the recognition of poetry 'as an art, not merely a vehicle for the propagation of doctrine', and his view of Ford as 'significant and revolutionary because of his insistence upon clarity and precision, upon the prose tradition', that is 'the importance of good writing as opposed to the opalescent word, the rhetorical tradition'.[14]

In a letter of early 1913, criticising a friend's work, Ford concluded:

> That is what is the matter with all the verse of to-day; it is too much practised in temples and too little in motorbuses – LITERARY! LITERARY! Now that is the last thing that verse should ever be, for the moment a medium becomes literary it is remote from the life of the people, it is dulled, languishing, moribund and at last dead.[15]

So a clearer picture emerges of the qualities and characteristics that Ford was seeking, both positively and negatively, in modern poetry. His childhood had been dominated by his Pre-Raphaelite family connections and the frequent presence, in conversation and in person, of many great Victorian figures, and Ford certainly reacted against that. He didn't want oratory or loud self-importance. He especially didn't want the moralising commentary that he associated with Ruskin's criticism of painting, with Pre-Raphaelite art and with many nineteenth-century writers. He was opposed to self-consciously 'poetic', artificial language and the conventional *subjects* of poetry. 'Love in country lanes, the song of birds, moonlight – these the poet, playing for safety, and the critic trying to find something safe to praise, will deem the sure cards of the poetic pack'. Ford wanted, rather, a poetry of – especially – modern urban life, able to confront and to render 'the portable zinc

---

[13] Ford, *The Critical Attitude*, p. 190.

[14] Pound, 'The Prose Tradition in Verse', pp. 373, 377, 371.

[15] Ford to Lucy Masterman (23 Jan. 1913), *Letters of Ford Madox Ford*, ed. Richard M. Ludwig (Princeton: Princeton University Press, 1965), p. 54.

dustbin left at dawn for the dustman to take'.[16] Or, as he put it elsewhere: 'I want the poetry of cafés, of automobiles, of kisses, and of absinthe.'[17]

The value of studying the best prose writers, he believed, was that they avoided the tangled and over-decorative styles he identified with authors such as Carlyle, which 'interfered with the precise articulation of thought and feeling and therefore with the advent of a modern literature'.[18] Ford claimed that, in England, 'we have a literary jargon in which we must write',[19] and that this threatened to rule out not only a great deal of the subject-matter offered by modern life but also much of the language that people habitually used to describe or assess that subject-matter, both to others and to themselves.

Though some distance remained for a while between Ford and Pound on just how colloquial the language of poetry should be, the essential principles were established. It should not be artificially 'literary', it should avoid abstractions, it should aim for a certain directness, it should reflect contemporary life. Ford would describe his contribution to the Imagist anthology as 'more conversational' than those by H.D. or William Carlos Williams or Pound himself;[20] and this remained a significant element in his discussions of the methods and motives involved in his writing, an attitude towards his assumed audience which he came to feel was not always shared by some of his fellow modernists.[21]

Ford's summed up his artistic credo thus: 'I may really say that, for a quarter of a century I have kept before me one unflinching aim – to register my own times in terms of my own time'.[22] That determination to render accurately the ordinary processes of life and their material details has prompted several critics to place him firmly in 'the documentary tradition', as against 'the aesthetic tradition': on the one hand, Hardy, Kipling, Browning, Wordsworth, going back to Crabbe, the Augustans and Ben Jonson; and on the other, Yeats, Swinburne, Tennyson, Coleridge, Keats.[23]

---

[16]   Ford Madox Ford, Preface, *Collected Poems* (London: Max Goschen, 1914), p. 16. The preface was reprinted as an appendix in the 1936 *Collected Poems*.

[17]   Ford Madox Ford, 'Literary Portraits – XXXIII. Mr. Sturge Moore and "The Sea is Kind"', *Outlook*, 33 (25 Apr. 1914), 560.

[18]   Joseph Wiesenfarth, 'The Ash-Bucket at Dawn: Ford's Art of Poetry', *Contemporary Literature*, 30.2 (1989), 241.

[19]   Ford, Preface, p. 16.

[20]   See Ford Madox Ford, *Thus to Revisit: Some Reminiscences* (London: Chapman and Hall, 1921), pp. 157–9.

[21]   See Paul Skinner, 'Poor Dan Robin: Ford Madox Ford's Poetry', in Robert Hampson and Tony Davenport (eds), *Ford Madox Ford: A Reappraisal*, International Ford Madox Ford Studies 1 (Amsterdam: Rodopi, 2002), pp. 88–9.

[22]   Ford Madox Ford, 'The Poet's Eye', *New Freewoman*, 1.6 (1 Sept. 1913), 108.

[23]   This draws closely on Hugh Kenner's 'The Poetics of Speech', in Richard A. Cassell (ed.), *Ford Madox Ford: Modern Judgements* (London: Macmillan, 1972), pp. 178–9. See also Colin Edwards, 'Dancing in the Mud: Bunting's Documentary Tradition and the

If Ford's poetic practice lagged behind his own critical statements for some years, it was in part because he found, at the outset, few usable English models. He did, though, have the advantage of a knowledge of other poetries, particularly German. 'Tandaradei', his version of Walther von der Vogelweide's 'Under der Linden', begins:

> Under the lindens on the heather,
> There was our double resting-place,
> Side by side and close together
> Garnered blossoms, crushed, and grass
> Nigh a shaw in such a vale,
> Tandaradei,
> Sweetly sang the nightingale. (p. 14)

This appeared in the 1900 volume *Poems for Pictures*. The fifth line may read a little 'poetically' to a modern reader and there is an inversion in the last line, though not one that grates on the ear; but, for the most part, the work of translation has simplified and naturalised the language, more than was the case with much of Ford's original poetry at that time, although the dialect poems and the dramatic monologues often obscure the fact. A similar case occurs in Pound's translations of Heinrich Heine ('O what comfort is it for me / To find him such, when the days bring / No comfort, at my time of life when / All good things go vanishing'),[24] which were included in his *Canzoni* (1911). This was the book which prompted Ford, when Pound showed it to him in Germany, to roll '(physically, and if you look at it as mere superficial snob, ridiculously) on the floor of his temporary quarters'. Pound added: 'And that roll saved me at least two years, perhaps more', since it 'sent me back to my own proper effort, namely, towards using the living tongue (with younger men after me), though none of us has found a more natural language than Ford did'.[25]

'On Heaven', the War and later

Ford's *High Germany* (1912) includes 'Süssmund's Address to an Unknown God (Adapted from the High German)', a 'translation' from a fictional poet, showing a vigorous humour and satirical force with which Ford is not often credited:

> Dear God of mine
> Who've tortured me in many pleasant ways

Anecdotage of Ford Madox Ford', in Christopher Meredith (ed.), *Moment of Earth: Poems and Essays in Honour of Jeremy Hooker* (Aberystwyth: Celtic Studies, 2007), pp. 106–7.

[24]   Ezra Pound, 'Translations and Adaptations from Heine: VI', *Collected Shorter Poems* (London: Faber and Faber, 1968), p. 60.

[25]   Ezra Pound, 'Ford Madox (Hueffer) Ford: Obit', *Selected Prose*, ed. William Cookson (London: Faber and Faber, 1973), pp. 431–2.

> I hope you've had some fun. And thank you, God!
> No doubt you'll keep your bargain in the end,
> No doubt I'll get my twopenny-halfpenny pay
> At the back door of some bright hued pavilion
> From a whore of Heaven. . . . (p. 66)

He was not yet done with the celestial world. His most famous single poem, certainly up to the outbreak of the First World War, was 'On Heaven', first published in June 1914 but not collected until *On Heaven and Poems Written on Active Service*, published in April 1918. Apparently written in response to a challenge from the novelist Violet Hunt, Ford's partner at the time ('You say you believe in a heaven; I wish you'd write one for me'),[26] it's a curious affair.

The poem's speaker has waited for nine years in 'a little town near Lyons' for his lover to arrive, which she does, eventually, in 'her swift red car':

> Royally she stepped down,
> Settling on one long foot and leaning back
> Amongst her russet furs. And she looked round . . .
> Of course it must be strange to come from England
> Straight into Heaven. (p. 102)

The speaker's being English will have resulted, it's implied, in a life 'spent in the craze to relinquish / What you want most'. So now he seems unable to express either his love or his desire. The two of them sit 'at a little table'; they remember pains as well as pleasures; they see a man 'of great stature', God, and a woman, 'our Lady'. Yet it remains an oddly secular poem, a hymn to Ford's beloved Provence and, perhaps, a waking dream of tranquility at a tumultuous time in his life. One source of strain here is that Ford ostensibly writes the poem for one woman, Violet Hunt, to whom it is dedicated, while loving another. As Max Saunders points out, while a major theme of the poem may be passion, the writing itself is not passionate. Yet, though 'On Heaven' may not look particularly modern now, Saunders adds that it remains important 'both for its explicitness about desire, and for its attempt to break loose from etiolated Georgian lyricism'.[27]

When war broke out in August 1914, Ford wrote two propaganda books before securing a commission, though over-age and in indifferent health, served in France and was invalided home in 1917. *On Heaven and Poems Written on Active Service*

---

[26] Violet Hunt, *The Flurried Years* (London: Hurst and Blackett, 1926), p. 216. For discussions of 'On Heaven', see particularly Sara Haslam, *Fragmenting Modernism: Ford Madox Ford, the Novel and the Great War* (Manchester: Manchester University Press, 2002), pp. 167–78; Max Saunders, *Ford Madox Ford: A Dual Life*, 2 vols (Oxford: Oxford University Press, 1996), I, pp. 395–9; Derek Stanford, '"The Best Poem Yet Written in the Twentieth-Century Fashion": A Discursive Note on Ford Madox Ford's "On Heaven"', *Agenda*, 27.4/28.1 (1989/1990), 110–19.

[27] Saunders, *Ford Madox Ford*, I, p. 398.

included several wartime pieces highly regarded by his contemporaries: *Antwerp*, '"When the World Was in Building . . ."' and 'Footsloggers':

> What is love of one's land? . . .
>   I don't know very well.
> It is something that sleeps
> For a year – or a day –
> For a month – something that keeps
> Very hidden and quiet and still
> And then takes
> The quiet heart like a wave,
> The quiet brain like a spell,
> The quiet will
> Like a tornado; and that shakes
> The whole of the soul. (p. 91)

Following his demobilisation, Ford suffered for several years from the effects of shell shock and memory loss. He lived with a new partner, the painter Stella Bowen, in a Sussex cottage, and their daughter was born in November 1920. Ford's poem *A House*, published in March 1921, reflected these new circumstances:

> *The House*. I am the House!
> I resemble
> The drawing of a child
> That draws 'just a house.' Two windows and two doors,
> Two chimney pots;
> Only two floors. (p. 126)

Max Saunders points out that the poem's deceptive simplicity distracts us from 'the originality of its masque-like or dream-like form, and the exquisite tonal effects created by the variations in line-lengths'.[28] And, on that basis of clarity and apparent plainness, Ford does build a long poem remarkable for the variety of its features, the internal rhymes, half-rhymes, lines whose shape and extent mime their content.

A very different production was Ford's long poem *Mister Bosphorus and the Muses: or a Short History of Poetry in Britain: Variety Entertainment in Four Acts: Words By Ford Madox Ford: Music By Several Popular Composers: With Harlequinade, Transformation Scene, Cinematograph Effects, and Many Other Novelties, As Well As Old and Tried Favourites* (1923). Finely embellished with woodcuts by Paul Nash, and boasting a title page that resembles 'an advertisement for an evening in a music hall',[29] the high spirits of the new work were immediately

---

[28]   Max Saunders, Introduction, *Selected Poems*, p. xiii.

[29]   Robert E. McDonough, '*Mister Bosphorus and the Muses*: History and Representation in Ford's Modern Poem', in Joseph Wiesenfarth (ed.), *History and Representation in Ford Madox Ford's Writings*, International Ford Madox Ford Studies

visible. Ford remarked in a letter that he had 'yielded to the temptation' of writing a *Dunciad* (1728; 1743), drawing a parallel between Alexander Pope's mock-epic satire on the minor poets of his day, an attack on dullness, and Ford's own satire on contemporary poetry and its critics, the timidity and formulaic or highly derivative writing that he saw as stifling and impoverishing the genuine poets.[30]

Mister Bosphorus responded to both T.S. Eliot's *The Waste Land* (1922) and Pound's early cantos. It highlighted and exaggerated the formal features of the leading modernists' work, including Joyce's *Ulysses* (1922), about which Ford had already published an appreciative essay,[31] querying their frequent recourse to mythology and copious referencing of earlier literary works. Several characters recur in other guises, underlining the theme of disguise and transformation, while the powerfully rendered contrast between the Northern and Southern Muses reflects what became a major opposition in Ford's later writing, the warm and life-giving south (primarily Provence) as against a north which he characterised as cold, militaristic and damagingly receptive to mass production and consumer capitalism.

The 1930s: America and Provence

From the mid-1920s, Ford split his time between America and Provence, more and more concerned with self-sufficiency, ecological questions and the benefits of the frugality he had learned in the war, a way of life voiced and celebrated in his later poetry:

> There will be nothing but this hot sun
> And no rain at all
> Till well into the Fall.
>
> Till then we must trust to the fruits
> Though their trees are dried down to the ends of their roots.
> The muscats are done.
> The bunch that hangs by the kitchen door is the last but one.
> But the wine-grapes and figs and quinces and gages will go on
> Nearly till September.
> (If you lay down some of the muscat wine-grapes
>   on paper on the garret floor
> They will shrink and grow sweeter till honey is acid beside them.) (p. 152)

---

3 (Amsterdam: Rodopi, 2004), p. 156. See also Colin Edwards, 'City Burlesque: The Pleasures of Paranoia in Ford's *Mister Bosphorus and the Muses*', in *Ford Madox Ford and the City*, pp. 93–109.

[30]   Ford to Joseph Conrad (8 Nov. 1923), *Letters of Ford Madox Ford*, p. 157. Ford in his letters of this time was eager for his long poem to 'annoy' people: see *Letters of Ford Madox Ford*, pp. 146, 150, 154.

[31]   Ford Madox Ford, '*Ulysses* and the Handling of Indecencies', *Critical Essays*, ed. Max Saunders and Richard Stang (Manchester: Carcanet Press, 2002), pp. 218–27.

But the poems in *Buckshee* (1931; 1936) also remember the recent war and imagine the destructive force of another. 'Coda' tells 'the story of lovers in Paris: a writer and a painter', but this is not simple autobiography. Ford traces the complexities not only of personal relationships but of relationships between 'makers' – of art, of food, of reciprocal human contacts – and the wider world in which negative forces – aggression, greed, militarism, selfishness – often seem to predominate.[32]

Buckshee, as a whole, and 'Coda' in particular, represent a climax, a culmination of more than thirty years as a published poet. The sequence could be seen almost as an anthology, a careful gathering of Fordian styles, forms and effects. What is new is the level of confidence, of assuredness, of sure-footedness:

> Yesterday I found a bee orchid
> But when I gave it to you you never raised your eyebrows
> – 'That a bee *orchid*? . . . It's like neither bee nor orchid!'
> Was all you said. And dropped it amongst the tea table dishes
> And went on gazing over the lake;
> As once you dropped my letters into a VI Avenue garbage can
> And went on gazing up West Ninth Street
> Towards Wanamakers. (p. 150)

But what is recognisable, still, from the first poem quoted in this chapter, 'In the Little Old Market-Place', is the sense of freedom and fluency. While that is the recurring caveat of modernist critics – that Ford's poetry is too loose, uses too many words, lacks Imagist concision and hardness – it would be churlish to deny the pleasure given by a poetry that *takes* such pleasure in its making and feels unencumbered by others' definitions of 'the modern'.

In the course of the sequence, Ford moves rapidly from long, languorous twenty-syllable lines to short, brisk, rhyming quatrains; from a cacophony of voices overheard at a party to a translation of Ronsard's famous sonnet 'Quand vous serez bien vieille';[33] from a dialogue for two voices, one constantly recurring to a sung chorus, to the remarkable 'Coda', a testament and summation:

> I suppose
> This is our final stamping ground.
> We may perhaps never leave it again.
> This mouldering triangle of streets mounting from the Seine
> Up to the Luxemburg mouldering on its mound . . . (p. 155)

---

32   See Joseph Wiesenfarth, 'Coda to the City', in *Ford Madox Ford and the City*, pp. 131–8.

33   Included in his *Sonnets pour Hélène*, II (1578). Ronsard's sonnet lies behind Yeats's 'When You are Old', written to Maud Gonne in 1891, and Ezra Pound quotes its first line in 'Canto 80'.

Ford Madox Ford's reputation over the last half-century has altered radically. His editorship of two short-lived but highly influential journals, the *English Review* and the *transatlantic review*, and his collaboration with Joseph Conrad are still closely studied;[34] but critical attention to the entire body of his work has broadened and deepened substantially. As a poet – and novelist – he is something of an enigma, never fitting entirely comfortably into any literary category, a 'misfit modern', as Rob Hawkes terms him.[35] Yet, as the 'twentieth-century fashion' proves progressively harder to identify, and as the modernist canon is endlessly enlarged and recalibrated, such misfits begin to look increasingly like paradigmatic figures. Certainly, Ford's claims in the field of modern poetry are no longer limited to his influence on others: recent scholarly writing has argued for the significance of some of the early lyrics, several of the wartime pieces, *Mister Bosphorus* and, perhaps above all, the late poems of *Buckshee*. Ford's poetry may not rank with that of Yeats or Eliot, yet, as a body of work produced by a major modernist *writer*, its power to intrigue and inform is unlikely to diminish.

[34] See Jason Harding (ed.), *Ford Madox Ford, Modernist Magazines and Editing*, International Ford Madox Ford Studies 9 (Amsterdam: Rodopi, 2010) and Chapter 2 in this volume.

[35] Rob Hawkes, *Ford Madox Ford and the Misfit Moderns: Edwardian Fiction and the First World War* (Basingstoke: Palgrave Macmillan, 2012).

Chapter 9

Ford and the First World War

Andrew Frayn

Ford Madox Ford occupied a distinctive and often ambivalent national, literary and intellectual position in response to the First World War. His version of the war was consequently out of step with many of his contemporaries, of which he was conscious: 'the only work that one does that is any good is always the work one does against the grain'.[1] Ford was a British subject with German ancestry, still known during the war as Ford Madox Hueffer, which made him a target for heightened scrutiny; he was also a committed Francophile.[2] For many early twentieth-century authors the war was their first major subject, and for some their only subject. By contrast, Ford had already published prodigiously for over twenty years in a variety of forms and genres. The war became an epoch-defining event for Ford not least because, as Trudi Tate bluntly puts it, 'being a soldier was Ford's first real job'.[3] However, it did not give Ford the taste for physical labour. Many poets of the war also later wrote memoirs or barely fictionalised novels about it, but Ford wrote about it in almost every conceivable form: propaganda, poems, short stories, novels, a novel sequence, and autobiographical works. This chapter surveys these writings, and illustrates Ford's unique position.

Ford immediately understood the war as a break from the past. The first part of *The Good Soldier* (1915) was serialised before the start of the war in *Blast* as 'The Saddest Story', a title which the publisher John Lane viewed not unreasonably as unsaleable in wartime.[4] The novel's second part, however, immediately takes account of the date on which the conflict started.[5] The 4th of August is mentioned

---

[1] Ford to Stella Bowen (early Sept. 1918), *The Correspondence of Ford Madox Ford and Stella Bowen*, ed. Sondra J. Stang and Karen Cochran (Bloomington: Indiana University Press, 1993), p. 11.

[2] Ford's ambivalent national identity is discussed by Christine Berberich in Chapter 13 of this volume. He satirises the heightened fear of the Germanic and its consequences in the short story 'The Scaremonger', which is reproduced in *War Prose*, ed. Max Saunders (Manchester: Carcanet Press, 1999), pp. 142–8.

[3] Trudi Tate, *Modernism, History and the First World War* (Manchester: Manchester University Press, 1998), p. 52.

[4] See Ford to John Lane (17 Dec. 1914), *The Ford Madox Ford Reader*, ed. Sondra J. Stang (Manchester: Carcanet Press, 1986), p. 477.

[5] See Max Saunders, *Ford Madox Ford: A Dual Life*, 2 vols (Oxford: Oxford University Press, 1996), I, pp. 436–7. Saunders discusses *The Good Soldier* at length in

five times in its first paragraph, as the narrator John Dowell tells us following the death of his wife Florence that:

> the thought that Mr. Bagshawe would almost certainly reveal to me that he had caught her coming out of Jimmy's bedroom at five o'clock in the morning on the 4th of August, 1900 – that was the determining influence in her suicide. And no doubt the effect of the date was too much for her superstitious personality. She had been born on the 4th of August; she had started to go round the world on the 4th of August; she had become a low fellow's mistress on the 4th of August. On the same day of the year she had married me; on that 4th she had lost Edward's love, and Bagshawe had appeared like a sinister omen – like a grin on the face of Fate. It was the last straw.[6]

Florence's persistent adultery, under the smokescreen of supposed physical frailty, precipitates the disintegration of the settled life of both the Dowells and the Ashburnhams, and this chain of events comes to an end with her suicide on 4 August 1913. This foreshadows the millions of deaths, and tens of millions of casualties, which were caused by the war that began a year later. The date recurs, unsurprisingly, in Ford's propaganda treatise *Between St. Dennis and St. George* (1915) to signal a change in his mentality: 'until August 4th, 1914, the idea of striking a created human being was as abhorrent to me as the idea of committing the sin against the Holy Ghost'.[7] The change was enacted on a personal and national level: 'any conception of war as a physical contact between large numbers of individual men is – or at any rate, was until August 1914 – abhorrent to the English mind' (p. 60). The date remained a red letter day for Ford after the war, and in *The Marsden Case* (1923) the protagonist 'George Heimann [...] left Froghole for Germany on the third of August, 1914; his father hanged himself on the fourth of that month, probably about three o'clock in the afternoon. George was arrested at about eleven o'clock of that night'.[8] The plot is driven by the war, but combatant experience is not the subject. The complex case of Heimann/Marsden's patrimony alludes to the German ancestry of the British monarchy, while George's father's suicide stands for the desired death of the ruling class.

'*The Good Soldier*: Desiring, Designing, Describing', *Ford Madox Ford*, I, pp. 402–60. See also Chapter 6 in this volume.

[6]   Ford Madox Ford, *The Good Soldier*, second edition, ed. Martin Stannard (New York: Norton, 2012), p. 85. See also p. 59, the start of Part II.

[7]   Ford Madox Ford, *Between St. Dennis and St. George: A Sketch of Three Civilisations* (London: Hodder and Stoughton, 1915), p. 60. All further references are to this edition.

[8]   Ford Madox Ford, *The Marsden Case: A Romance* (London: Duckworth, 1923), p. 261. All further references are to this edition.

Antwerp

Antwerp (1915) is an evocative early response to the war, written after the city's surrender in October 1914. It was lauded by T.S. Eliot as 'the only good poem I have met with on the subject of the war'.[9] *Antwerp* still has in mind the reasons for going to war, the defence of Belgium's honour implicit in the title. The Allied action is divinely sanctioned: 'In the name of God, / How could they do it?'[10] The moral importance of the conflict is balanced with Ford's early realisation that 'you cannot praise it with words / Compounded of lyres and swords' (p. 83). The jarring sight-rhyme highlights the inappropriateness in modern warfare of what Ernest Hemingway called the 'abstract words such as glory, honor, courage, or hallow',[11] at a time when poets such as Siegfried Sassoon and Robert Graves were still writing in the rousing, patriotic diction now usually associated with Rupert Brooke. Sassoon later describes his fictionalised self, George Sherston, as having 'serious aspirations to heroism in the field', and his initial view that 'they are fortunate, who fight' endured well into the war.[12] Dominic Hibberd summarises tersely that Graves's 'later reputation as an opponent of the war has little basis in anything he wrote at the time'.[13] Ford allies the camaraderie of the war, upheld in popular books about the training camp such as Ian Hay's *The First Hundred Thousand* (1915), with a disdain for empty rhetoric, a position that was not popularly accepted until the late 1920s.

This vocabulary was often used within metaphors of sport which emphasised loyalty, teamwork and fair play, epitomised in Henry Newbolt's 'Vitaï Lampada' by the refrain 'Play up! Play up! and play the game!'[14] These values were inculcated by the public school system, which filtered down into state education. However, Ford uses the metaphor differently in *Antwerp*. The second exclamation

---

[9]   T.S. Eliot, 'Reflections on Contemporary Poetry', *Egoist*, 4.10 (Nov. 1917), 151. *Antwerp* was first published as 'In October 1914', *Outlook*, 34 (24 Oct. 1914), 523. On the development of the poem, see Ashley Chantler, 'Editing Ford Madox Ford's Poetry', in Jason Harding (ed.), *Ford Madox Ford, Modernist Magazines and Editing*, International Ford Madox Ford Studies 9 (Amsterdam: Rodopi, 2010), pp. 253–65.

[10]   Ford Madox Ford, 'In October 1914 [Antwerp]', *Selected Poems*, ed. Max Saunders (Manchester: Carcanet Press, 1997), p. 83.

[11]   Ernest Hemingway, *A Farewell to Arms* (London: Arrow, 1994), p. 165. See Sara Haslam, *Fragmenting Modernism: Ford Madox Ford, the novel and the Great War* (Manchester: Manchester University Press, 2002), pp. 84–7.

[12]   Siegfried Sassoon, *Memoirs of a Fox-Hunting Man* (London: Faber and Gwyer, 1928), p. 307; Sassoon, 'France', *Collected Poems 1908–1956* (London: Faber and Faber, 1982), p. 13.

[13]   Dominic Hibberd, *Wilfred Owen: A New Biography* (London: Weidenfeld and Nicolson, 2002), p. 278.

[14]   Henry Newbolt, 'Vitaï Lampada', *Collected Poems 1897–1907* (London: Thomas Nelson, 1910), pp. 131–3.

of 'doom!' signals the death of a Belgian man who stands in for Antwerp and, in turn, the Belgian nation:

> He finds that in a sudden scrimmage,
> And lies, an unsightly lump on the sodden grass . . .
> An image that shall take long to pass![15]

The analogy with rugby is recast as the man's downfall, the 'scrimmage' (now more usually 'scrum') an appropriate image as it comprises of two closely-matched packs of men pushing against each other to gain a (usually small) territorial advantage. There is no break into open play or quick movement in this case: the man is dead, a blot on the landscape saturated by:

> the swift outpouring of the blood,
> Till the trench of grey mud
> Is turned to a brown purple drain by it.[16]

Blood is added to the familiar browns and greens of Flanders and the fought-over land becomes a drain taking away the remains of the dead, an image seared on the speaker's mind. The 'image that shall take long to pass' also invokes Ford's association with Imagism: Jörg Rademacher describes Ford as 'the craftsman who echoed both the event he's dealing with and the poetical movements of the day'.[17] Ford's early perception of the war's impact and his distaste for jingoism meant that he could put forward a more nuanced view than many other authors.

Ford's Propaganda

Ford wrote two books of propaganda for his friend C.F.G. Masterman, who was in charge of the War Propaganda Bureau at Wellington House.[18] *Between St. Dennis and St. George* and *When Blood is Their Argument* (1915) take their titles from Shakespeare's *Henry V*, famed for the King's rousing speech ('We few,

---

[15]   Ford, 'In October 1914 [Antwerp]', p. 83.

[16]   Ford, 'In October 1914 [Antwerp]', pp. 82–3.

[17]   Jörg Rademacher, 'Images of the First World War: Ford's "In October 1914" Read in the Context of Contemporary German Writers', in Paul Skinner (ed.), *Ford Madox Ford's Literary Contacts*, International Ford Madox Ford Studies 6 (Amsterdam: Rodopi, 2007), p. 179. For more on Ford and Imagism, see Chapter 7 in this volume.

[18]   See Mark Wollaeger, *Modernism, Media, and Propaganda: British Narrative from 1900 to 1945* (Princeton: Princeton University Press, 2006), pp. 13–22, for details about the workings of Wellington House through the war. Anurag Jain discusses Ford's propaganda within the wider frameworks for distribution and dissemination in: 'When Propaganda is Your Argument: Ford and First World War Propaganda', in Dennis Brown and Jenny Plastow (eds), *Ford Madox Ford and Englishness*, International Ford Madox Ford Studies 5 (Amsterdam: Rodopi, 2006), pp. 163–75.

we happy few, we band of brothers'), but also the tale of a sick and dispirited army in France.[19] Ford's propaganda shows little sign of seductive flag-waving or social pressure, a contrast with recruiting posters and works such as George Bernard Shaw's anti-war polemic *Common Sense About the War* (1914), to which *Between St. Dennis and St. George* responds. Here, Ford subtly signifies his ambivalent national identity by placing himself in 'Berwick which is neither England nor Scotland, but just Berwick' (p. 41). He asserts his position between nations, but also implies that he is unopposed in principle to warfare: Berwick was apocryphally still at war with Russia due to its non-inclusion on Crimean War peace treaties. However, war-making must be a response to an attack; militarism and its rhetoric is unacceptable and Ford builds to an idiosyncratic but increasingly strong denunciation of Germany, which 'is always [...] absolutely wrong; it is always only Germany that accepts with inevitable voracity every phrase that is bombastic and imbecile' (pp. 68–9).

As in *Antwerp* Ford validates England's cause, but he refuses easy stereotypes and hatemongering. He states in his preface to *When Blood is Their Argument* that 'my attack [...] is not upon German learning [but] is simply on the paucity of the products of German learning'.[20] These subtleties might seem lacking in force, but are central to Ford's argument in both works. He praises French culture and separates Germany from Prussia, building on his pre-war preface to Violet Hunt's *The Desirable Alien* (1913) and silently putting his Münster ancestry on the correct side of the divide.[21] Sara Haslam argues that: '*Between St. Dennis and St. George* often becomes a near riot of alternative voices, opinions, languages (including German and French) and discourses'.[22] In *Between St. Dennis and St. George*, Ford states that 'militarism must be fought in the home of militarism' (p. 12). Prussianism is literally inconceivable: 'how entirely different is the Prussian political point of view from the British. It is a difference not of degree, but of species; it is a difference not similar to, but as great as that which separates men from angels'.[23] The enemy is othered using the language of race and eugenics,[24]

---

[19]   William Shakespeare, *The Life of Henry the Fifth*, *Complete Works*, ed. Stanley Wells and Gary Taylor (Oxford: Clarendon Press, 1986), 4.3.60.

[20]   Ford Madox Ford, *When Blood is Their Argument: An Analysis of Prussian Culture* (London: Hodder and Stoughton, 1915), p. xvii.

[21]   Ford Madox Ford, Preface, Violet Hunt, *The Desirable Alien: At Home in Germany*, with preface and two additional chapters by Ford Madox Hueffer (London: Chatto and Windus, 1913), pp. vii–xii. See also Wollaeger, *Modernism, Media, and Propaganda*, p. 150.

[22]   Sara Haslam, 'Making a Text the Fordian Way: *Between St. Dennis and St. George*, Propaganda and the First World War', in Mary Hammond and Shafquat Towheed (eds), *Publishing the First World War: Essays in Book History* (Basingstoke: Palgrave Macmillan, 2007), p. 209. See also Saunders, *Ford Madox Ford*, I, pp. 471–6.

[23]   Ford, *When Blood is Their Argument*, p. 42.

[24]   On Ford and race, see Max Saunders, '"All these fellows are ourselves": Ford Madox Ford, Race and Europe', in Len Platt (ed.), *Modernism and Race* (Cambridge:

and Englishness is aligned with godliness, anticipating Mark Tietjens' suggestion in *Last Post* (1928) that 'Christ was a sort of an Englishman'.[25] In *Between St. Dennis and St. George*, Ford presents his case in legal terms before summing up: 'one may be patriotically elated to observe [that] the English put up infinitely a better case. The poor Germans have absolutely nothing to say – nothing in the world' (p. 157). The enemy is rendered dumb, mobilising a rhetoric associated with modernist reactions against an idea of 'the masses' such as Masterman's *The Condition of England* (1909).[26] Like the best barristers, Ford's appeal to objectivity only strengthens his case; Wollaeger asserts that 'Ford overwhelms his reader with a mixture of facts and opinions offered as facts – all disarmingly offered as mere impressions – that accumulate into a plausible picture'.[27] With Ford acting simultaneously as counsel for the prosecution and judge, the only possible verdict is 'that the attitude of Great Britain was absolutely correct'.[28] The weight of Ford's carefully-chosen evidence sends the balance thudding down on Britain's side.

Ford's Military Service

The subtleties of Ford's propaganda were not universally appreciated and he enlisted in 1915, claiming that he: 'had to give up literature and offer [him]self for service to George Five'.[29] He realised that: 'enlistment would silence those who misconstrued his writing as pro-German'.[30] Ford's age kept him out of the front line when he was posted to the Western Front during the Battle of the Somme. He became part of the First Line Transport for the 3rd Battalion of the Welch Regiment, operating: 'generally two or three miles behind the Front, within range of the big guns'. Ford was injured in a blast, which left him with: 'a damaged mouth and loosened teeth', concussed and shell-shocked.[31] The suggestion that he might 'give up literature' could not hold. He wrote poems throughout the war, evidenced by his careful dating of the poems in *On Heaven and Poems Written on Active Service* (1918). Ford knew that he was writing against patriotic poets such as Jessie Pope, and the pathos of dead soldier-poets such as Brooke and Julian Grenfell. He wrote

Cambridge University Press, 2011), pp. 49–51. Marius Turda, *Modernism and Eugenics* (Basingstoke: Palgrave Macmillan, 2010), discusses the subject more generally.

25   Ford Madox Ford, *Last Post*, ed. Paul Skinner (Manchester: Carcanet Press, 2011), p. 91.

26   On a similar trait in Ford's own writing, see John Attridge, 'Steadily and Whole: Ford Madox Ford and Modernist Sociology', *Modernism/modernity*, 15.2 (2008), 297–316.

27   Wollaeger, *Modernism, Media, and Propaganda*, pp. 145–6.

28   Ford, *Between St. Dennis and St. George*, p. 189.

29   Ford to John Lane (12 Aug. 1915), *Letters of Ford Madox Ford*, ed. Richard M. Ludwig (Princeton: Princeton University Press, 1965), p. 61.

30   Saunders, *Ford Madox Ford*, I, p. 478.

31   Saunders, *Ford Madox Ford*, II, p. 2. Ford was attached to the 9th Battalion during the Somme and Ypres attacks; see *War Prose*, p. 110, n. On shell shock in Ford's war fiction, see Haslam, *Fragmenting Modernism*, pp. 103–11.

in September 1917 that: 'I am trying to get together, languidly, a small volume – that no one, probably, will want to publish'.[32] Fortunately, Ford was wrong: John Lane brought out the volume in early 1918 to some critical acclaim.[33]

On Heaven charts the change in Ford's life and in his relationship with the army during the war. Enlistment was an escape for Ford, and he wrote to his mother that: 'I have never felt such an entire peace of mind as I have felt since I wore the King's uniform'.[34] Army life was all-consuming, and Violet Hunt reported in her diary that Ford told her: 'I am cold and I have one passion now, the Army and that England should win'.[35] Life away from military service is so distant as to be heavenly in a secular sense, and is a necessary motivation: 'We *must* have some such Heaven to make up for the deep mud and the bitter weather and the long lasting fears and the cruel hunger for light, for graciousness and for grace! . . .'.[36] The stress on *must* shows an attempt to remember a disappearing vision, also signified by the ellipsis after the desperate exclamation; current conditions are hellish by implicit contrast. In 'Footsloggers', Ford has become ambivalent towards life: 'we shall endure the swift, sharp torture of dying, / Or the humiliation of not dying'.[37] Death is torture, but also an escape from survivor guilt; that escape is to a Heaven which, the title poem of the collection asserts, contains both 'the joys and the toil'.[38] Pain is no longer obliterated by death as combatants die violent and untimely deaths:

> For that too is the quality of Heaven,
> That you are conscious always of great pain
> Only when it is over
> And shall not come again.[39]

Even in 'On Heaven', written before the war, death is an escape from the pain of quotidian experience. However, pain remains part of consciousness in Heaven, highlighted by the extreme contrast between the second and fourth lines of the above quotation. By the time the war finished, Ford was ready to be released from

---

[32]   Ford to Lucy Masterman (8 Sept. 1917), *Letters of Ford Madox Ford*, p. 84.

[33]   See Saunders, *Ford Madox Ford*, II, pp. 45–6 on the reception of *On Heaven*. Later US reviews by Conrad Aiken in *Dial* and Harriet Monroe in *Poetry* are in Frank MacShane (ed.), *Ford Madox Ford: The Critical Heritage* (London: Routledge and Kegan Paul, 1972).

[34]   Ford to Cathy Hueffer (18 Sept. 1915): quoted in Saunders, *Ford Madox Ford*, I, p. 479.

[35]   Robert Secor and Marie Secor, *The Return of the Good Soldier: Ford Madox Ford and Violet Hunt's 1917 Diary* (Victoria: English Literary Studies, University of Victoria, 1983), p. 52.

[36]   Ford Madox Ford, Preface, *On Heaven and Poems Written on Active Service* (London: John Lane, 1918), p. 8.

[37]   Ford Madox Ford, 'Footsloggers', *Selected Poems*, p. 97.

[38]   Ford Madox Ford, 'On Heaven', *Selected Poems*, p. 99.

[39]   Ford, 'On Heaven', p. 101.

the army, and wrote in January 1919 to Stella Bowen that: 'I haven't the patience to wait longer than I absolutely need, and time is slipping away'.[40]

Ford's return to civilian life was only heavenly release in its encompassing of both joys and toil. His relationship with Hunt was finally over and he rented a smallholding with Bowen. Following demobilisation, he struggled to write creatively and composed, or part-composed, several works about the war immediately afterwards. He started 'True Love & a GCM' before the war had finished, although it remained unpublished until 1999.[41] A novel, 'Mr Croyd', was completed in 1920, and probably offered to and rejected by John Lane at the time.[42] Ford's take on the war was out of key in a reception climate in which heroic novels such as Ernest Raymond's *Tell England* (1922) were the bestselling norm. He wrote a memoir, *Thus to Revisit* (1921), which mentions the war but pointedly reveals nothing of his own experience. *The Marsden Case* does not depict combatant life but the war is present from the very first sentence and impacts on the principal characters' domestic and professional conflicts. However *No Enemy*, the most personal of his war writings, was written mostly in 1919 but not published until ten years later, and then only in the USA, its appearance just three weeks after the Wall Street Crash of 1929 hindering its sales dramatically.

No Enemy

No Enemy brings together previously-written discursive essays within a fictional framework.[43] It is an experimental text which shows Ford's struggle to find a form in which to represent the war. Its composition from fragments was a similar process to C.E. Montague's influential *Disenchantment* (1922), which adapted Montague's leader articles for the *Manchester Guardian*.[44] *No Enemy* is 'A Tale of Reconstruction', the reconstruction of Ford himself in the two protagonists, set against larger post-war reconstructions exemplified in Britain by Lloyd George's promise 'to make Britain a fit country for heroes to live in'.[45] Cornelia Cook states that: '"Reconstruction" was a wartime political buzzword which became

---

[40] Ford to Stella Bowen (6 Jan. 1919), *The Correspondence of Ford Madox Ford and Stella Bowen*, p. 53; Ford wrote the next day that he 'was gazetted out of the Army this morning' (p. 53).

[41] Saunders, *Ford Madox Ford*, II, p. 47. 'True Love & a GCM' was finally published in *War Prose*, pp. 77–139.

[42] On 'Mr Croyd', see Saunders, *Ford Madox Ford*, II, pp. 92–4.

[43] See Paul Skinner, Introduction, Ford Madox Ford, *No Enemy: A Tale of Reconstruction*, ed. Paul Skinner (Manchester: Carcanet Press, 2002), pp. xi–xiv. All further references are to this edition.

[44] The *Manchester Guardian* is today titled simply as the *Guardian*.

[45] Lloyd George's speech was given in Wolverhampton on 23 November 1918 and reported in most newspapers one or two days later. See, for example, 'Mr. Lloyd George on His Task', *The Times*, 25 Nov. 1918, 13; and the leader comment 'The Election: Prime Minister on the Issues', 9.

a post-war political agenda'.[46] Despite the continuities with the pre-war world, authors often saw the war as rupture. Soldiers claimed that they were lost for words about the war, and that the experience of being under fire was so profound that it could not be expressed to civilians. This claim was repeated so often that it became a narrative of the war in itself. The Compiler in *No Enemy* tells us that Gringoire's testimony:

> present[s] a picture of the poet under fire – a matter as to which he here refuses to say anything elsewhere under the plea that to talk about actual fighting disturbs his subsequent sleep with nightmares and also that he intends to treat of fighting subsequently himself when both the public bitterness and his own emotions shall have diminished. (p. 67)

The psychological effects of the war are highlighted as well as a prescient realisation that a literature of disenchantment could not yet succeed. *The Marsden Case* also shows the impact of war on authors as Ernest Jessop describes how his pen was in 'disuse during the war', and that he now has to 'grope [...] after expression' (p. 40). He states that 'This is not a war novel', describing the desire to leave the war behind and the impossibility of doing so:

> I [...] would willingly wipe out of my mind every sight that I saw, every sound that I heard, every memory in my brain. But it is impossible, though there are non-participants who demand it, to write the lives of people to-day aged thirty or so, and leave out all mention of the fact that whilst those young people were aged, say, twenty-two to twenty-eight, there existed – Armageddon. (p. 143)

War is Armageddon, the final break from earthly life, and the object of a melancholic attachment not only for Gringoire. Even novels not about the war cannot avoid its shadow; Barbara Cartland's first novel, *Jig-saw* (1925), a typically glossy tale of debutantes and social mores, was marketed explicitly as an escape from thinking about the war, paradoxically bringing it into the reader's consciousness.

Ford denigrates the Regular Army and its officers in *No Enemy*, a criticism which was still taboo at the time of composition. This antagonism is often seen as a modernist reaction against Victorian values, but is as much a reaction of soldiers against non-combatant officers and administrators. Ford wrote in one of his first letters from the front line that 'the off[ice]rs here are a terrible lot',[47] and in *No Enemy* grumbles that the Regular Army:

> had every guile from a military point of view. They were adepts in absences, swingings of the lead, drunks, excuses, barrack-breakings, cheerful lies, and a

---

[46] Cornelia Cook, 'Constructions and Reconstructions: *No Enemy*', in Robert Hampson and Max Saunders (eds), *Ford Madox Ford's Modernity*, International Ford Madox Ford Studies 2 (Amsterdam: Rodopi, 2003), p. 191.

[47] Ford to Lucy Masterman (28 July 1916), *Letters of Ford Madox Ford*, p. 67.

> desperate determination not to exhibit any glimmerings of intelligence, let alone
> any proficiency in the use of any weapon. (p. 17)

Ford found his escape partly in the army's discipline, and he reasserts the value of
the camaraderie that it caused. Similarly, in *The Marsden Case* the narrator tacitly
criticises: 'the etiquette of the old regular army, when eighty per cent of the men
enlisted under false names and it was indecent to ask a question. And that officer
was quite incurious. The lives of too many men passed through his hands' (p. 201).
Many of the officers came from the professional Regular Army, which was often
criticised for not adapting quickly. Gringoire observes in *No Enemy* that:

> a battalion looks grim indeed when it has been hammered by artillery [...] owing
> to a blunder of a staff officer. They had, I think, 160 men killed in one company –
> pretty well the whole strength as battalions were in those days. I don't like to
> think of it, much. (p. 118)

Tennyson's 'The Charge of the Light Brigade' (1855) is evoked, in which the
attack tragically fails because 'someone had blundered'.[48] Unlike the later writers
of disenchantment, Gringoire sympathises: 'I was actually bothering about the
wretched staff officer who had murdered all those men. I was worried about him.
You see, it would be such a trifling thing to do – as easy as forgetting – as every
human soul has done in its day – to post a letter' (p. 119). Mistakes are inevitable,
and officers are only human. There is none of Sassoon's terse condemnation in
'The General' (1918): 'But he did for them both by his plan of attack'.[49] Ford's
later war experience in similar roles enables him to appreciate the difficulties of
organisation; indeed, *On Heaven* is dedicated to Lieutenant-Colonel G.R. Powell
of the Welch Regiment.[50] Ford's variety of roles both on the Western Front and
the Home Front gave him an unusually wide experience on which to draw in
representing the war.

Parade's End and the Armistice

Ford's definitive treatment of the war is his great tetralogy *Parade's End*, discussed
at length by Isabelle Brasme in the following chapter.[51] In *A Man Could Stand
Up –* (1926) and *Last Post* (1928), the third and fourth volumes of the series, any

---

[48]   Alfred Lord Tennyson, 'The Charge of the Light Brigade', *The Major Works*, ed.
Adam Roberts (Oxford: Oxford University Press, 2000), p. 302.

[49]   Sassoon, 'The General', *Collected Poems 1908–1956*, p. 75.

[50]   Ford, *On Heaven and Poems Written on Active Service*, p. 13.

[51]   See also Andrew Frayn, '"*This* battle was not over": *Parade's End* as a Transitional
Text in the Development of Disenchanted First World War Literature', in Andrzej
Gąsiorek and Daniel Moore (eds), *Ford Madox Ford: Literary Networks and Cultural
Transformations*, International Ford Madox Ford Studies 7 (Amsterdam: Rodopi, 2008),
pp. 201–16.

possible joy at the coming of the Armistice is tempered. Ford wrote to Bowen in October 1918 that: 'I suppose the war is drawing to a close. But it's rather a fizzle out, isn't it?'[52] For Christopher Tietjens the Armistice is a pyrrhic victory, no longer the glorious victory of the fight for civilisation but the weary end to an overlong conflict. As the countdown to the Armistice continues, Tietjens observes that:

> The trouble was that *this* battle was not over. By no means over. There would be a hundred and eleven years, nine months and twenty seven days of it still. . . . No, you could not get the effect of that endless monotony of effort by numbers. Nor yet by saying 'Endless monotony of effort'. . . .[53]

Ford emphasises the monotony of the conflict throughout his writings about the war: time drags even in the first stanza of *Antwerp*. The length of the First World War is equated with the Hundred Years War, an appropriate comparison both for the apparent duration of the war and for the repeated analogy with the army of Henry V. This also invites a comparison with previous ideas of chivalry and honour in warfare, and suggests the impossibility of those values on the Western Front. Ford wrote to Bowen on Armistice Day that he felt 'inexpressibly sad',[54] and recalled later in the 1920s that 'the original Armistice Day was a sort of fever. For myself, I remember Armistice Day very well because I was kept so busy with military duties that I was on my feet all day until I fell into bed stone sober, at 4 next morning'.[55] For soldiers, the Armistice was not an end to their service; although Bullitt Lowry argues that it 'became a preliminary peace', he states that 'in their eyes it by no means assured an early German surrender'.[56] It was an end to immediate danger, but it was also the beginning of what for many was a long process of demobilisation, readjustment and reintegration.

Even the civilian experience of the Armistice is not celebratory. Valentine Wannop, the mistress of Tietjens, is interrupted on 11 November by a telephone call. The telephone means both communication and confusion, as in Ford's earlier novel *A Call* (1910),[57] and, in *A Man Could Stand Up –*, brings Valentine a 'tantalisingly half-remembered voice' which utters 'improbable sounding pieces of information half-extinguished by the external sounds' of the school's children celebrating (p. 8). The call leads Valentine to miss the moment of the Armistice, and she fears her future exclusion from commemoration: 'Then. . . . For the rest

---

[52] Ford to Stella Bowen (31 Oct. 1918), *The Correspondence of Ford Madox Ford and Stella Bowen*, p. 27.

[53] Ford Madox Ford, *A Man Could Stand Up –*, ed. Sara Haslam (Manchester: Carcanet Press, 2011), p. 68. All further references are to this edition.

[54] Ford to Stella Bowen (11 Nov. 1918), *The Correspondence of Ford Madox Ford and Stella Bowen*, p. 32.

[55] Ford, 'Preparedness', *War Prose*, p. 72.

[56] Bullitt Lowry, *Armistice 1918* (Kent: Kent State University Press, 1996), pp. xii, 11.

[57] See Philip Horne, 'Absent-Mindedness: Ford on the Phone', in *Ford Madox Ford's Modernity*, pp. 17–34.

of her life she was never able to remember the greatest stab of joy that had ever been known by waiting millions. There would be no one but she who would not be able to remember that. . . .' (p. 10). The confusion caused by the telephone call overpowers any celebration as the significance of the date forces her to look back. She contemplates the summer of 1912 before returning to the present: 'Now it was Eleven Eleven. . . . What? Oh, Eighteen, of course!' (p. 33). The return of the past into the present is embodied in Tietjens' reappearance on Armistice Day – this was the purpose of the call, it transpires eventually. While the past can reappear, revised, there can be no return to the pre-war. Valentine fears the war's effect on Tietjens, that 'she was to become the cold nurse of a shell-shock case' (p. 183), and concludes that:

> She was going to pass her day beside a madman; her night, too. . . . Armistice Night! That night would be remembered down unnumbered generations. Whilst one lived that had seen it the question would be asked: What did you do on Armistice Night? My beloved is mine and I am his! (p. 185)

Valentine tries to prepare for peacetime life, but she becomes convinced that Tietjens will return homicidal: 'What did you do on Armistice Night? "I was murdered in an empty house!"' (p. 186). While troops are 'murdered' in *No Enemy* by the non-fighting staff officers, here they become potential murderers, feared as trained fighting men who had changed radically from their pre-war selves by training and the experience of armed combat.

The war is commemorated in *Parade's End* by silence, by the inability to hear, by the inability to speak, or by the inability to interpret sounds. This draws on the codification during the 1920s of silence as an integral part of the Armistice Day ceremony.[58] In *A Man Could Stand Up –*, Valentine moves rapidly from uncertainty to an appreciation of silence:

> She didn't even know whether what they had let off had been maroons or aircraft guns or sirens. It had happened – the noise, whatever it was – whilst she had been coming through the underground passage from the playground to the schoolroom to answer this wicked telephone. So she had not heard the sound. She had missed the sound for which the ears of a world had waited for years, for a generation. For an eternity. No sound. When she had left the playground there had been dead silence. All waiting: girls rubbing one ankle with the other rubber sole. . . . (p. 10)

Although she misses the alert, in the school's own communication trench, her silent Armistice became the dominant commemorative experience; the silence before the celebrations of 11 November 1918 was reversed in memorialisation. Silent recollection provides the narrative for *Last Post*, which is the stream of Mark Tietjens' consciousness. He is mute almost for the whole novel, and John Coyle

---

[58]   See Adrian Gregory, *The Silence of Memory: Armistice Day, 1919–1946* (Oxford: Berg, 1994).

states that he is 'reduced to little more than a pair of eyes and a memory'.[59] His wife Marie Léonie conjectures that 'the terms of the armistice were of such a nature as to make a person of Mark's determination and idiosyncrasies resolve to withdraw himself for ever from all human contacts'.[60] He apparently takes his commemoration of the war to its extreme: the Armistice has a more profound effect on him than it does on Christopher, the combatant. However, Max Saunders observes that whether his silence is 'out of obstinate principle because he disapproves of the peace terms, or because of a stroke, or both, is left wonderfully uncertain'.[61] Eve Sorum argues that Mark's inability to communicate reflects the 'national desire to ignore the returning soldiers'.[62] Returning soldiers were a public concern, but there was as much welcome as wariness. Sorum's argument that the muteness of Mark Tietjens draws on the Armistice Day silence is more persuasive.[63] The title of the novel states that it is an elegy both for Mark Tietjens and for the war dead. It mourns actively, and focuses on moving forward: representatives and representations of the past, and tradition, are removed throughout the novel. Mark represents the death of the Victorian era, and the wished-for death of the government and official classes who had initiated and controlled the war, and who had failed to bring it to a timely conclusion.[64]

Ford's writing about the First World War is consistently out of step with popular narratives and representations. He does not get caught up in patriotic fervour in the early part of the war, either in poetry or propaganda. In his later writing, after he has felt the impact of war, he rethinks understandings of life and death, his relationship with the establishment, and his relationship with England, reflected in his reaction against the officer class and the reshaping of the sporting metaphor which epitomises the values of that class. Ford was even out of place as a modernist although he is now acknowledged as a major and influential early twentieth-century author, particularly for *The Good Soldier* and *Parade's End*. He straddled the nineteenth and twentieth centuries, and was a parental presence within the avant-garde. His prose and poetry effectively combines the old and the new: of the generation that Pound implored to 'Make it new',[65] only Ford, the elder statesman with a wealth of literary experience, was able to use his experience of and response to the war to make his own previous style new.

---

[59]   John Coyle, 'Mourning and Rumour in Ford and Proust', in *Ford Madox Ford's Literary Contacts*, p. 119.

[60]   Ford, *Last Post*, p. 26.

[61]   Saunders, *Ford Madox Ford*, II, p. 251.

[62]   Eve Sorum, 'Mourning and Moving On: Life After War in Ford Madox Ford's *The Last Post*', in Patricia Rae (ed.), *Modernism and Mourning* (Lewisburg: Bucknell University Press, 2007), p. 160.

[63]   Sorum, 'Mourning and Moving On', pp. 160–61.

[64]   For a penetrating discussion of this topic, see Andrzej Gąsiorek, 'The Politics of Cultural Nostalgia: History and Tradition in Ford Madox Ford's *Parade's End*', *Literature and History*, 3rd series, 11.2 (2002), 52–77.

[65]   Ezra Pound, 'XCVIII', *The Cantos of Ezra Pound* (New York: New Directions, 1993), p. 704.

Chapter 10
Parade's End

Isabelle Brasme

Parade's End – the tetralogy comprising *Some Do Not . . .* (1924), *No More Parades* (1925), *A Man Could Stand Up –* (1926) and *Last Post* (1928) – depicts the end of an era, the decay of a society and of its values, which the First World War both exposed and deepened. *Parade's End* may be construed at least partly as a portrayal of Englishness put to the test of war. Using characters from the upper and upper-middle classes, Ford explores their multifarious responses to the ideological changes correlated with the war.[1] However, whilst the war stands very much at the core of the tetralogy, *Parade's End* cannot be considered merely as a war novel. The war reveals rather than triggers the ideological, aesthetic, psychological and ontological upheavals that inform the four novels.

This chapter will first briefly mention the genesis of *Parade's End*. We shall then move on to Ford's choice of characterisation and to the organisation of the characters along a spectrum of various ideological stances. The narrative technique developed in the tetralogy will prove particularly rich and telling of the way in which Ford's art reaches new heights in this text. Finally, we shall see how, through its persistent and deliberate instability, the text is constantly moving towards an aesthetics whose contours are merely suggested, and which, while being undoubtedly modernist in its aim and spirit, seems to reach beyond the conventional boundaries of the modernist canon.

Genesis

As is argued by Andrew Frayn in the previous chapter, *Parade's End* is very much the offshoot of Ford's direct experience of war and of his acute sense of the changes it wreaked upon humanity, individually and collectively; it is also the product of Ford's private struggles and achievements in the late 1910s and early twenties. As Max Saunders posits in his chapter on 'Ford's Lives', Ford brought a lot of himself and his own relationships into his novels. Some parallels between Ford's

---

[1]   An ideology is a set of ideas and beliefs shared by a group. The concept of ideology implies that our grasp of and opinion on the world can never be immediate and unbiased: it is unavoidably filtered by a whole set of views that are conditioned by the social group we belong to. For further reading on the notion of ideology, see David Hawkes, *Ideology* (London: Routledge, 2003).

life before and during World War I and the novels are very transparent in *Parade's End*, by Ford's own account. Many elements in the narration may hint at Ford's own predicaments in the 1910s; much has been said in particular to compare Sylvia to Violet Hunt and Valentine to Stella Bowen, Ford's companion as he was writing *Parade's End*. A cross-reading of *Parade's End* with Ford's correspondence with Stella Bowen during and after the war is quite enlightening of the extent to which *Parade's End* owes to their relationship; as Sondra Stang states, 'the letters reveal, in their detail, much of the raw material of *Parade's End*'.[2]

Furthermore, many of the paradigms that are prevalent in *Parade's End* can also be linked back to some of his earlier novels. *The Fifth Queen* (1906–08) centres on a man endowed with an all-encompassing mind and loaded with immense responsibilities (Henry VIII), caught between his dead first wife (an earlier version of Sylvia Tietjens) and the hope brought about by a young, educated, nurturing woman (Katherine Howard, to whom Valentine Wannop bears a strong resemblance). *The Good Soldier* (1915) likewise deals with a man trapped in a dysfunctional marriage with an impostor (Dowell and Florence) and with a man perhaps unjustly condemned for his adulterous tendencies, misunderstood by society, steeped in a feudal ideology, and apparently unfit for twentieth-century modes of conduct (Ashburnham). Christopher Tietjens may to some extent appear as a combined study of Dowell and Ashburnham, as a further exploration on the part of Ford of the potentialities already at work in the cast of *The Good Soldier*. To a large extent, therefore, *Parade's End* may appear to crystallise many of Ford's deep-seated concerns as well as his own inner struggles.

Characterisation and Ideological Stances

Characters in *Parade's End*, however, are more than mere avatars of previous characters or actual persons in Ford's life. On a larger and less personal scope, they are organised along a range of varied and contrasted responses to what can be considered as Ford's vision of the Edwardian mindset. References to Englishness will be purposefully limited here, as this notion is covered in Chapter 13; I will focus instead on the characters' varied relationships to tradition and modernity.

The notion of heritage plays a crucial role for the characters as it allows them to be connected to what precedes their own existence, and thus to insert themselves within a reassuring continuity. The importance of descent is made clear from the opening pages of the first volume: the protagonists are first and foremost presented through their lineage. This is clear in the initial description of the main character, Tietjens: 'The youngest son of a Yorkshire gentleman, Tietjens himself was entitled to the best – the best that first-class offices and first-class people could

---

    [2]   Sondra J. Stang, Introduction, Ford Madox Ford, *The Correspondence of Ford Madox Ford and Stella Bowen*, ed. Sondra J. Stang and Karen Cochran (Bloomington: Indiana University Press, 1994), p. xii.

afford'.[3] The word 'entitled' is redolent of a feudal system that still seems to be ruling most social relations in *Parade's End*. The syntax of this sentence is also telling: lineage transcends identity since it is mentioned before the character's own name; this initial descriptive clause conditions the entire ensuing portrait of Christopher in this opening chapter of the tetralogy. The omnipresence of lineage as the prominent way to determine characters is highlighted by Valentine Wannop, in the final volume:

> It was astonishing the descents they all had! She herself was descended from the surgeon-butler to Henry VII – Henry the Somethingth. And of course from the great Professor Wannop [...]. . . . And Christopher was eleventh Tietjens of Groby with an eventual burgomaster of Scheveningen or somewhere in some century or other: time of Alva. Number one came over with Dutch William, the Protestant Hero![4]

Individuals are thus first and foremost defined backwards, as it were – by what predates them. Characters in the narration indeed aspire to define their identity thanks to landmarks that are issued from the past, as these seem to warrant more stability. This need to ensure one's identity may be ascribed to the far-reaching social and economic changes of the late nineteenth and early twentieth centuries: these challenged the individual's ability to position himself or herself within the mutating society.

The Ritual of Tradition: The Duchemins and the Macmasters

Faced with these changes, the characters representing the Establishment harden their ideological stance and practice, in order to reassert their differences from the lower classes. The Duchemins and later the Macmasters display a stable ideological discourse and *praxis* throughout the tetralogy; they may be considered as embodying the dominant ideology within the society depicted in *Parade's End*, one that is being shared by most characters in the novels. Etymologically, 'identity' means permanence of the same (*idem*); the individual's attempt to define himself in a world that is characterised by change and flux since at least the eighteenth century is a recurring trait in English literature.

However, in *Parade's End* – and as the title suggests – a shift occurs: rather than identity itself, most characters strive to define and maintain its semblance. This is illustrated to the point of caricature by Vincent and Edith Macmaster. Valentine realises that their relationship is solely built on appearances: 'it was a sort of parade of circumspection and rightness' (*Some Do Not . . .*, p. 293). This 'parade' involves above all an ostentatious respect of tradition. Yet the 'sort of'

---

[3]   Ford Madox Ford, *Some Do Not . . .*, ed. Max Saunders (Manchester: Carcanet Press, 2010), p. 6. All further references are to this edition.

[4]   Ford Madox Ford, *Last Post*, ed. Paul Skinner (Manchester: Carcanet Press, 2011), pp. 174–5. All further references are to this edition.

qualifier used by Valentine signals that the *parade* is no longer quite functional – it is indeed already at an *end*. The Duchemins' environment, as is later that of the Macmasters', is a ritualised replication of the past: it is no coincidence that Mr Duchemin is a clergyman and lives in a parsonage, which is presented as a sanctuary of conventions. The Duchemins' Saturday breakfast may be construed as a replacement of the Sunday mass – as a rite saluted in the pre-war English elite as glorifying tradition. This corresponds to what Eric Hobsbawm called 'the invention of tradition'. Hobsbawm differentiates between genuinely ancient traditions – 'customs' – and 'invented traditions', which are generated in modern times to recreate landmarks in a world threatened by instability, when the continuity with the past is broken:

> The very appearance of movements for the defence of or revival of traditions, 'traditionalist' or otherwise, indicates such a break. Such movements, common among intellectuals since the Romantics, can never develop or even preserve a living past (except conceivably by setting up human natural sanctuaries for isolated corners of archaic life), but must become 'invented tradition'. [...] Where the old ways are alive, traditions need neither be revived nor invented.[5]

The ostensibly celebrated traditions at the Duchemins' and the Macmasters' are thus a construct. Their flaunted continuity with the past reveals precisely that the link with the latter is in fact broken.

The Macmasters' and their circle's response to the outbreak of the war is to close in upon themselves and remain impervious to the rest of the world, in the name of the preservation of culture – or more rightly, of their ideal of a fossilised culture. One of them thus asserts, in *Some Do Not . . .*: 'it's one's sole duty to preserve the beauty of things that's preservable' (p. 285). The polyptoton[6] of the words 'preserve' and 'preservable' illustrates and pinpoints a circular, solipsist mode of thinking. The satirical mode grows more acute in the mention of the letters sent by 'men of genius' to Mrs Duchemin during the war: they are 'written, as a rule, from the Continent or most distant and peaceful climates, for most of them believed it their duty in these hideous times to keep alive in the world the only glimmering spark of beauty' (p. 294). Satire is palpable in the clichéd phrases and the hackneyed metaphor of beauty as light.

The environment thus contrived by the Macmasters is utopian:[7] in their attempt to abolish the line between past and present, the Macmasters, leading in their wake the mainstream elite depicted in the novel, inhabit a world that exists neither in the past – since it is inescapably over and can never be fully reconstituted –

---

    5   Eric Hobsbawm, 'Introduction: Inventing Traditions', in Eric Hobsbawm and Terence Ranger (eds), *The Invention of Tradition* (Cambridge: Cambridge University Press, 2007), pp. 7–8.
    6   A polyptoton is a stylistic device where various words derived from the same root are being used, thus creating an effect of repetition.
    7   The etymological meaning of 'utopia' is 'non-place': οὐ ('no') + τόπος ('place').

nor in the present, since it is denied existence. The theatrical dimension of the Macmasters' mode of existence is patent: their seemingly stable sense of identity is sheer performance. A clear instance of this is Mrs Duchemin dressing up in Pre-Raphaelite attire: 'her dress [...] had certainly been dark blue – and certainly of silk [...]. And it contrived to be at once artistic – absolutely in the tradition! And yet well cut! Very large sleeves, of course, but still with a certain fit' (p. 70–71). This dress bears an unmistakable resemblance to that painted by Dante Gabriel Rossetti in *Jane Morris (The Blue Silk Dress)* (1868).[8] The tension between the 'artistic' feel of the dress and its up-to-dateness, contrived by the cut and the 'certain fit', encapsulates the pretence of Edith's whole lifestyle.

An Equivocal Champion of Modernity: Valentine

While I won't tackle specifically the question of gender as it is dealt with in Chapter 12, it is worth pondering to what extent the complex opposition between the two main female protagonists, Valentine Wannop and Sylvia Tietjens, crystallises the ideological ambivalences of the Edwardian and post-war era.

Within the community staged in *Parade's End*, Valentine is the character most openly opposed to conventions. This is made obvious from her very first appearance in *Some Do Not . . .*, as a suffragette defying patriarchal order by trespassing on an eminently male territory, the golf course. Her active stance, emphasised by her confronting men 'in [...] the bright open' (p. 82) as opposed to the traditionally feminine indoors, is articulated in her long, peremptory speeches. Valentine's opposition to established order is made even more blatant in the third volume, when Armistice is announced in London. The first part of *A Man Could Stand Up –* consists entirely of an interior monologue on the part of Valentine, which is itself a token of her will to have a voice in the world. The recurrence in this part of negative phrases such as 'no more respect', or indeed 'no more parades', demonstrates the deliberate and even programmatic nature of Valentine's irreverence: 'She was not going to show respect for any Lady anything ever again. [...] She was never going to show respect for anyone ever again. She had been through the mill: the whole world had been through the mill! No more respect!'[9] Besides the recurrence of negative terms that bespeak Valentine's will to do away with rules, the anaphora of 'she' as a subject emphasises Valentine's feeling of empowerment; so does the continuous tense, which lays the emphasis on the subject's intentions. There is a plethora of such passages in *A Man Could Stand Up –*. Valentine believes it her intellectual duty to relentlessly question the validity

---

8   For more on the connections between Duchemin and Rossetti's work, see Isabelle Brasme, 'Articulations of Femininity in *Parade's End*', in Ashley Chantler and Rob Hawkes (eds), *Ford Madox Ford's Parade's End: The First World War, Culture, and Modernity*, International Ford Madox Ford Studies 13 (Amsterdam: Rodopi, 2014), pp. 173–85.

9   Ford Madox Ford, *A Man Could Stand Up –*, ed. Sara Haslam (Manchester: Carcanet Press, 2011), p. 12. All further references are to this edition.

of the social, political and cultural *status quo*. Such a questioning is inseparable in her mind from feminist claims:

> If, at this parting of the ways, at this crack across the table of History, the School – the World, the future mothers of Europe – got out of hand, would they ever come back? The Authorities – Authority all over the world – was afraid of that; more afraid of that than of any other thing. Wasn't it a possibility that there was to be no more Respect? None for constituted Authority and consecrated Experience? [...] No more respect. . . . For the Equator! For the Metric system. For Sir Walter Scott! Or George Washington! Or Abraham Lincoln! Or the Seventh Commandment! (pp. 17–18)

The accumulation of capitalised words is ironic, since the notions thus highlighted are being challenged precisely as they are given this semblance of importance. The incongruous juxtaposition of notions, historical people and places, all placed on the same level, generates a feeling of meaninglessness: each of these words appears as interchangeable and therefore valueless. As this passage makes clear, Valentine believes that the collapse of established order to do away with the mistakes that led to World War I rests upon the rebellion of women – 'the future mothers of Europe' – against a patriarchal order: all the historical figures Valentine mentions are men, and the Seventh Commandment, dealing with adultery, may be construed as the basis of patriarchal order, relying on the exclusive possession of one woman by one man.

However, Valentine's view is itself an ideological construct that is based on prejudice. This is apparent in the following passage from *Some Do Not . . .*: 'She had an automatic feeling that all manly men were lust-filled devils, desiring nothing better than to stride over battlefields, stabbing the wounded with long daggers in frenzies of sadism' (p. 284). Valentine's conception of the masculine is itself fantasised. The phallic allusion through the 'long daggers' is so blatant that it exposes the hackneyed character of Valentine's vision. It seems that she fights a pre-established system of values only to replace it with another set of equally questionable constructs.

Besides, Valentine's advocacy of 'modernity' is itself relative. The feminist principles she defends, with her obsession with a physical as well as an intellectual education, come straight out of eighteenth-century feminist texts such as those of Mary Wollstonecraft.[10] Above all, the Valentine staged in *Last Post*, the final volume of *Parade's End*, is considerably less uncompromising towards established order. In spite of her formerly triumphant rejection of the Seventh Commandment, Valentine is in fact far from comfortable in her role as the adulterous woman, since she conceives of it as living 'in open sin' (p. 182). Furthermore, Valentine now considers herself an instrument in the preservation and continuity of patriarchal order. She is convinced that the child she is bearing is a boy, imagining him as

---

[10] See, for instance, Mary Wollstonecraft, *A Vindication of the Rights of Woman* (Oxford: Oxford University Press, 1999), p. 257.

a miniature replica of Christopher, with the same bulging blue eyes – 'spinning pebble-blue eyes' (p. 176); and she wants him to have the same name as his father, to perpetuate the Tietjens dynasty. Her obsession to see him born in an antique bed is particularly telling: 'She passionately desired little Chrissie to be born in that bed with the thin fine posts, his blond head with the thin, fine hair on those pillows' (p. 173). Interestingly, the same phrase, 'thin, fine', is used both to describe the ancient bed and the newborn child, which illustrates the fantasised continuity between present and past.

The discrepancy between Valentine's attitude here and that seen in the first three volumes is also blatant. One has to work hard to find traces of the assertive, independent woman previously portrayed: Valentine is now shut up indoors, locking herself inside her room, and expecting bitterly of Tietjens that he provides for his family. In a stark contrast with her first appearance as a suffragette beating a dozen men to a run in the open, Valentine is now voluntarily a recluse and absorbs herself in materialistic concerns.

Sylvia, or the New Woman

Sylvia Tietjens's relationship to conventions and to the dominant ideology is characterised by inconsistency and ambivalence. Sylvia resists any stable categorisation. On the one hand, and even though she outwardly professes to despise them, she can be associated to the Macmasters' circle insofar as she also adopts a reactionary stance during the war. In her will to escape the topicality of war, she removes herself from the world, in a convent, and focuses on pre-war literature: 'she spends nearly all her time in retreat in a convent reading novels of before the war' (*Some Do Not . . .*, p. 283). Her withdrawal from the world is thus both spatial and temporal. Yet her very handling of literature encapsulates her ambivalent relation to time. In contrast with this display of nostalgia, Sylvia confesses later to hating re-reading novels:

> almost always taking up with a man was like reading a book you had read when you had forgotten that you had read it. You had not been for ten minutes in any sort of intimacy with any man before you said: 'But I've read all this before. . . .' You knew the opening, you were already bored by the middle, and, especially, you knew the end. . . .[11]

A tension is thus at work within Sylvia between conservatism and the fear of monotony. Sylvia's yearning for newness corresponds to the newly-developed craze for disposable items, whose emergence coincides with the time of the story. Indeed, Sylvia is also portrayed as the embodiment of the New Woman. An avid consumer of fashion, she electrifies Tietjens's eighteenth-century home. During

---

[11]   Ford Madox Ford, *No More Parades*, ed. Joseph Wiesenfarth (Manchester: Carcanet Press, 2011), p. 128. All further references are to this edition.

the war, and in stark contrast with her convent retreat, Sylvia also becomes a major feature of fashion magazines, which reproduce photographs of her *ad infinitum*: through this, she turns her own image into a mass-produced, disposable object.[12]

Sylvia is thus split between two irreconcilable attitudes to modernity. Her son's description of her at the end of *Last Post* captures this ambivalence: 'His mother was splendid. Divinely beautiful; athletic as Atalanta or Betty Nuthall' (p. 56). Betty Nuthall was a popular tennis player after the war, and one of the first sportswomen to be given heavy media coverage, standing therefore as an icon of the growing access of women to traditionally male fields. Sylvia thus combines both the figures of a mythical and intemporal athletic woman through Atalanta, and that of a woman anchored within the specific mores of the twenties.

The Case of Christopher Tietjens

Tietjens's stance requires a specific analysis; not only is his relationship to time deeply ambivalent, but it grows more and more complex as the narration unfolds. From the outset, Tietjens is consistently presented as a man of the past; in *Some Do Not . . .*, Valentine considers him a museum piece: 'I've never met a Cambridge Tory man before. I thought they were all in museums and you work them up again out of bones' (p. 169). Tietjens is indeed constantly shown as a fossil from another temporal strata that doesn't belong in the current times. More specifically, he is associated to eighteenth-century culture: 'Tietjens [was] an eighteenth-century figure of the Dr. Johnson type' (p. 188); like Johnson's multifarious influence on his times, which was intellectual, philosophical, political and moral, Tietjens's attachment to the eighteenth century is simultaneously intellectual (through, for instance, his corrections of the *Encyclopaedia Britannica*, an epitome of the Enlightenment)[13] and political, as when he asserts, in *No More Parades*: 'I've no politics that did not disappear in the eighteenth century' (p. 235). The two negations, strengthened by the negative prefix in the verb 'disappear', is telling: Tietjens has no business in the twentieth century. In this, his relationship to time and to contemporary ideology is fundamentally different from that of the Macmasters and their circle: their own cult of tradition is a shallow kowtow to a fashionable construct. With the Macmasters, 'what is lost is the pastness of the past';[14] conversely, Tietjens treasures the past for what it is – irretrievably gone. As Philip Davis writes, in an illuminating article on Tietjens's relation to the past:

> For such figures, history is something lost – the lost potential of a race's ancient thoughts – or something which, if retained, is retained only as hidden within the

---

[12]   See, for instance, *Some Do Not . . .*, p. 183.

[13]   See *Some Do Not . . .*, pp. 13–14.

[14]   Catherine Belsey, 'Reading Cultural History', in Tamsin Spargo (ed.), *Reading the Past* (Basingstoke: Palgrave, 2000), p. 106; much of Belsey's analysis can be applied to the handling of tradition in *Parade's End*.

individual's memory, in the latent mixed-up store of inherited things that seem nonetheless utterly and personally instinctive. Such half-buried retention means that, even so, there is the possibility of resonant things coming through to us, like half-recognised forward memories, demanding development, seeking re-incorporation and adaptation in the persons and times they find.[15]

Tietjens's self-imposed duty is to commemorate the past's lost virtues, to deliberately alienate himself from his contemporaries through a 'loyal oppositional memory';[16] in this respect, he embodies what Davis calls the 'saving remnant'.[17]

Nevertheless, Tietjens's view of tradition is far from idealistic. He 'despise[s] people who use [...] works of reference' such as the *Encyclopaedia Britannica* (*Some Do Not . . .*, p. 14); he also believes that the war is due to a surfeit of eighteenth-century values: 'It's the incidental degeneration of the heroic impulse: if the heroic impulse has too even a strain put on it the incidental degeneration gets the upper hand' (p. 200). Tietjens is thus aware of the absurdity of his attachment to eighteenth-century values.[18]

Additionally, Tietjens's viewpoint evolves throughout the first three novels. His tentative, questioning voice as regards traditional values, be it within inner speeches or to Valentine, may appear to constitute the main musical theme of the novel. Tietjens is constantly caught between the imperative to respect, and the impulse to reject, the codes issued from the past. This dilemma is of course encapsulated in the 'Some do'/'Some do not' alternative that is made explicit in the title of the first volume. Tietjens belongs to 'the sort that . . . *do not*' (p. 344), who refuse to act on their impulses; yet the negative turn implies a lack, a void that demands to be filled for the character to lead a satisfying life.

However, when this lack seems to be fulfilled when Tietjens lives with Valentine in *Last Post*, Tietjens is anything but a triumphant hero. More shall be said on this in the final section of this chapter.

Narrative Technique

A major aspect of narrative technique in *Parade's End* is of course related to literary Impressionism, which is tackled in Chapter 5 of this volume. Laura

---

[15]   Philip Davis, 'The Saving Remnant', in Dennis Brown and Jenny Plastow (eds), *Ford Madox Ford and Englishness*, International Ford Madox Ford Studies 5 (Amsterdam: Rodopi, 2006), p. 20.

[16]   Davis, 'The Saving Remnant', p. 22.

[17]   For an in-depth analysis on this topic, I strongly suggest reading the whole of Philip Davis's article.

[18]   For further discussion of *Parade's End* and the eighteenth century, see Sara Haslam, 'From Conversation to Humiliation: *Parade's End* and the Eighteenth Century', in Ashley Chantler and Rob Hawkes (eds), *Ford Madox Ford's Parade's End: The First World War, Culture, and Modernity*, International Ford Madox Ford Studies 13 (Amsterdam: Rodopi, 2014), pp. 37–51.

Colombino's analysis of Ford's Impressionist technique as a locus of tension between 'objectivity and visionariness, perception and memory' fits to some large degree the aesthetics at work in the tetralogy. Due to space constraints, I will not be able to deal with this notion at length here; I have argued previously that while *Parade's End* may appear at first to be an exercise in Impressionism akin to *The Good Soldier*, it seems on closer analysis to negotiate a transition between Impressionism and a more markedly modernist aesthetics.[19]

To my mind, Ford's aesthetic project in *Parade's End* deepens and exceeds his Impressionist theory. As Max Saunders makes clear in his indispensible critical biography of Ford:

> Part of the great achievement of *Parade's End* is to let order from confusion spring. Its palimpsest of plots and motives is always on the verge of incoherence; it perpetually appears about to repeat, to contradict itself, or to digress. Yet, as in the magisterial command of syntax, there is always an architectonic intelligence at work, holding together the glinting and jarring details, fusing clarities of detail into clarity of design.[20]

Since literary Impressionism does not directly narrate a story, but renders its reverberation upon the characters' consciousnesses, an Impressionist narration is necessarily retrospective: the event has always already taken place and the focus is on its effect. Ford in *Parade's End* (as in *The Good Soldier*) deepens this process by centring most often not on a direct impression but on its memory – or on the impression caused by the re-emergence of a memory. Narration in *Parade's End* is thus inevitably vectorised towards the past. This is most striking at the beginning of parts or volumes, when the reader is put *in medias res* and has to painstakingly reconstruct the ellipses. A telling instance is the beginning of Part II of *Some Do Not . . .*, because the reader's unearthing of past events follows that of Tietjens, as he gradually recovers his memory after being shell-shocked.

However, just as a perfect reflection of the past on the part of the characters eventually transpires to be sterile, similarly, from a narrative point of view, the ideal of a satisfactory reconstitution of past impressions turns out to be futile. The whole aesthetic direction of the novels may thus appear as mirroring the characters' own journeys within the story. *Parade's End* is marked by an aesthetic eclecticism that matches the constant oscillation between past and present: Ford both salutes past influences and demonstrates an openness to more innovative techniques, via a collage of miscellaneous aesthetics. Narratively speaking, analepses find a

――――――

[19] Isabelle Brasme, 'Between Impressionism and Modernism: *Some Do Not . . .*, a Poetics of the *Entre-deux*', in Andrzej Gąsiorek and Daniel Moore (eds), *Ford Madox Ford: Literary Networks and Cultural Transformations*, International Ford Madox Ford Studies 7 (Amsterdam: Rodopi, 2008), pp. 189–99.

[20] Max Saunders, *Ford Madox Ford: A Dual Life*, 2 vols (Oxford: Oxford University Press, 1996), II, pp. 220–21.

counterpoint in the many prolepses scattered throughout the text.[21] They involve two main motifs: that of the relationship between Christopher and Valentine, and that of the war. Soon after her appearance in *Some Do Not . . .*, Valentine asserts: 'the right man for me [...] will be a married man' (p. 106), which initiates a series of utterances heralding the upcoming denouement. Proleptic speeches are also supported by visual scenes; on the same day, Valentine and Tietjens are caught in a kissing-gate:

> They were jammed in together: face to face, panting! An occasion on which sweethearts kiss in Kent: the gate being made in three, the inner flange of the V moving on hinges. It stops cattle getting through, but this great lout of a Yorkshireman didn't know, trying to push through like a mad bullock! (p. 137)

The situation is proleptic on multiple levels; lexically, first, through the choice of 'kissing-gate', which heralds the forthcoming relationship between the characters. The ambivalence of 'kissing-gate', whose usual and trivial meaning refers to cattle but whose literal meaning is sentimental, mirrors the characters' position, in a seemingly loving or even sexual posture: 'face to face, panting'; yet we are also acutely aware of the grotesqueness of the situation, through Valentine's likening of Tietjens to a 'mad bullock' (perhaps a periphrasis for 'mad ox', and a tongue-in-cheek hint at the author's middle name?). This kaleidoscope of meanings prefigures the complex relationship between Tietjens and Valentine, which is until the end characterised by a mixture of attraction and derision.

The same is true of the many hints foreshadowing the war in the first part of *Some Do Not . . ..* The narration is thus far from merely retrospective; the reader constantly needs to anticipate fragments of the narration as much as relate others back to past events. The narration is thus built as a network, with elements being interwoven in opposite directions. This corresponds to what Peter Nicholls considers as typical of 'high modernism': 'This strand of modernism casts the self as the bearer of a troubled history and makes writing a medium in which different temporalities intersect'.[22] David Lodge similarly associates this 'cross-reference backwards and forwards across the chronological span of the action' to modernist aesthetics.[23]

This endless vibration between past and future, however, may eventually appear to petrify narrative time. We can find a metatextual metaphor for this when Tietjens and Valentine's cart collides with Campion's car at the end of Part I of *Some Do Not . . .*: the shock between the horse-drawn vehicle, belonging to the

---

[21] Analepsis is the narrative device through which narration goes back in time, through a 'flashback' effect; prolepsis is the opposite device, heralding events that have not yet occurred at the time of the narration.

[22] Peter Nicholls, *Modernisms: A Literary Guide* (Berkeley: University of California Press, 1995), p. 252.

[23] David Lodge, *The Modes of Modern Writing: Metaphor, Metonymy, and the Typology of Modern Literature* (London: Edward Arnold, 1977), p. 46.

past, and the car, an epitome of modernity, provokes a suspension of temporality: 'The cart turned up, the horse emerged from the mist, head and shoulders, pawing. A stone sea-horse from the fountain of Versailles! Exactly that! Hanging in air for an eternity' (p. 174). The horse, frozen into a statue, acts as a metatextual comment both on the characters' predicament of being caught between two eras and on the narration's constantly contradictory directions. Prolepses and analepses in *Parade's End* are not mere stylistic devices: they act as the main structuring agent of the novels. Linearity is merely adumbrated and present only sporadically; it is constantly broken by these relentless leaps into the past or into the future. Narration in *Parade's End* is a collage of fragments.[24]

A Deliberate Indecision

Yet these fragments never fully add up; though the time-shifts act as the only structural frame for the narration, they turn out to be unsatisfactory. Similarly, the various perspectives offered through Impressionism never meet up, so that we are left with an unbridgeable gap between the characters' various impressions.[25] This needs to be related to the kaleidoscope paradigm, explored in depth by Sara Haslam: 'A key Fordian modernist image is that of the kaleidoscope. "You carry away from [a train]", he writes in 1905, a "vague kaleidoscope picture – lights in clusters, the bare shoulder of women, white flannel on green turf in the sunlight, darkened drawing rooms"'.[26] In a conversation with Valentine in *Some Do Not . . .*, Tietjens comments on the innovative use of advertisements at the time to illustrate the absence of convergence between the characters' perspectives:

> Do you know these soap advertisements signs that read differently from different angles? As you come up to them you read 'Monkey's Soap'; if you look back when you've passed it's 'Needs no Rinsing.' . . . You and I are standing at different angles and though we both look at the same thing we read different messages. Perhaps if we stood side by side we should see yet a third. (pp. 284–5)

Tietjens here describes a process of anamorphosis, according to which there is no single stable truth; ultimately, this very instability constitutes the only system at work in *Parade's End* – certainly paradoxical, but for this very reason, in keeping with the tetralogy's vibrations and instabilities. The process of anamorphosis, of

---

[24]   On the notion of collage in Ford, see Todd Bender, *Literary Impressionism in Jean Rhys, Ford Madox Ford, Joseph Conrad, and Charlotte Brontë* (New York : Garland, 1997), particularly Chapter 2, 'Impressionist Verbal Collage'.

[25]   This is discussed in detail in Brasme, 'Between Impressionism and Modernism'.

[26]   Sara Haslam, *Fragmenting Modernism: Ford Madox Ford, the Novel and the Great War* (Manchester: Manchester University Press, 2002), p. 7. Quotation from Ford is from *The Soul of London: A Survey of a Modern City* (London: Alston Rivers, 1905), p. 120. Chapter 2 of *Fragmenting Modernism* is particularly relevant to the kaleidoscopic narrative mode in *Parade's End*.

which Holbein's *The Ambassadors* (1533) is the best-known example,[27] is also relevant to Ford's aesthetic eclecticism – from the Renaissance to Cubism, from the Pre-Raphaelite[28] influence of his grandfather to cinematic montage.

In this respect, Ford's writing is certainly akin to high modernism, but it also appears to go beyond it. In high modernist works such as those by Joyce and Woolf, crisis is usually followed and redeemed by an ultimate epiphany of form coalescing with meaning. Patricia Waugh explains the importance of metatextuality in high modernism when she mentions:

> the modernist concern with the mind as itself the basis of an aesthetic, ordered at a profound level and revealed to consciousness at isolated 'epiphanic' moments. At the end of Virginia Woolf's *To the Lighthouse* (1927), for example, Lily Briscoe suddenly perceives a higher (or deeper) order in things as she watches the boat return. Her realisation is translated, directly and overtly, into aesthetic terms. Returning to her canvas, with intensity she draws the final line: 'It was finished. Yes she thought laying down her brush in extreme fatigue, I have had my vision'.[29]

Conversely, *Parade's End* does not conclude on any satisfying epiphany, either of form or of meaning. *Last Post* appears as an ironic and burlesque counterpoint to the first three volumes, especially to the brilliant ending of *A Man Could Stand Up –*. From a metatextual standpoint, the upcoming birth of Valentine and Tietjens's son, seemingly the result of a union between a modern woman and a man steeped in tradition, may appear an ideal symbol of reconciliation between the contrasting ideologies and aesthetics at work in the tetralogy. Yet Valentine is shown as everything but happy about her state; besides, as seen earlier, her stance as a modern woman is deeply questioned by her own choices and attitude in this volume. Another potential epiphany of meaning that is ultimately debunked is the image of Tietjens flying over the scene during most of this last volume. Max Saunders highlights this symbolism: 'Christopher is doing more than standing on a hill: he is flying over one having attained a god-like (or novelist-like) omniscient perspective'.[30] Yet Christopher is useless to the action because of this very position, as is decried by every other character. He is therefore a mere grotesque and impotent avatar of Christ or the novelist. In this last volume, any possibility of an aesthetic resolution is undermined by excess and irony.[31] The redemption through form that we find in other canonical modernist works is here denied to

---

[27]   See Ford Madox Ford, *Hans Holbein the Younger: A Critical Monograph* (London: Duckworth; New York: Dutton, 1905).

[28]   See Ford Madox Ford, *The Pre-Raphaelite Brotherhood: A Critical Monograph* (London: Duckworth, 1907).

[29]   Patricia Waugh, *Metafiction: The Theory and Practice of Self-Conscious Fiction* (London: Routledge, 1996), p. 23.

[30]   Saunders, *Ford Madox Ford*, II, p. 252.

[31]   For more on the ways in which *Last Post* derides and debunks the first three volumes, see Isabelle Brasme, '"A caricature of his own voice": Ford and Self-Editing

us; something is reached that goes beyond – or runs deliberately parallel to – high modernism.

Conclusion

With *Parade's End*, Ford is searching for a way to face and articulate the crisis of meaning inherent in the First World War. Simultaneously, he invites the reader to come to terms with the loss of our usual horizon of expectation and of an omniscient, objective narration; the only way to make sense of chaos in *Parade's End*, both on the characters' and on the reader's part, is a patient and hopeful reconstitution of fragments, while remaining forever aware that these will never fully make sense along a linear, stable organisation.

What ultimately differentiates *Parade's End* from a work of high modernism is a stance of humility on the part of Ford. Far from pretending to reach an epiphany, the text constantly defuses any possibility of a stable and satisfying form. At the end of a reading process that endlessly adumbrates potential answers, yet never fully unveils them, it behoves the reader to embrace the tensions of the text and to relinquish the temptation of flattening out the inconsistencies. The promise contained in the reading of *Parade's End* never falls short, since it is never exhausted.

in *Parade's End'*, in Jason Harding (ed.), *Ford Madox Ford, Modernist Magazines and Editing*, International Ford Madox Ford Studies 9 (Amsterdam: Rodopi, 2010), pp. 243–52.

Chapter 11

Ford and the City

Angus Wrenn

Cities, and the idea of the city, pervade much of Ford Madox Ford's work and yet are, at certain key stages in his career, markedly absent from it. Ford is of particular interest as a writer on the city in that he deals with the city not only as a prose writer in both the novel and non-fiction, but additionally as a poet. Ford is also of significance, as a writer on the city, in that he bridges the nineteenth and twentieth centuries. Furthermore, where some of the leading figures in European modernism were émigré Americans responding variously to London or Paris, Ford, besides writing on both places, also writes about New York as early as 1907 and later in the 1920s and 1930s. This chapter will attempt, by examining Ford's non-fiction on various cities, to identify whether Ford put forward any coherent theory of the city as a phenomenon. His fiction and poetry which deal with cities will then be considered, to establish to what extent they bear out his theories of the urban experience.

Between the turn of the twentieth century and his death in 1939 Ford wrote a variety of non-fiction descriptive pieces on a number of cities. These varied in length from the posthumously published short prose impressions of the American cities of Boston, Denver and Nashville to the rather more extended 'The Future in London' (1909), and the full-length *The Soul of London* (1905) and *New York Is Not America* (1927). *The Soul of London* has perhaps become Ford's most widely read non-fiction work, and is also a key example of literary Impressionism at the beginning of the twentieth century. It attempts to evoke the sense of what it is to inhabit London, as capital of the British Empire, arguably the most important world metropolis at this date. It is sometimes forgotten that the phrase 'Heart of Darkness', made famous by Ford's collaborator Joseph Conrad in the novella of that name, had signified London itself (the tale is related in the Thames Estuary, on the approach to the East End docks) every bit as much as the centre of the African continent. The title 'Soul of London' was almost certainly not Ford's own inspiration, but it is nevertheless telling that the animate metaphor is extended into the second volume of the trilogy finally published as *England and the English* (1907): *The Heart of the Country* (1906). Ford, by contrast, associates the word 'heart' not with the city but with the countryside in a volume devoted to rural England. Both titles imply the human and the personal.

In the opening pages of *The Soul of London*, Ford consistently emphasises the idea of the individual enjoying an almost personal relationship with the city inhabited:

Most of us love places very much as we may love what, for us, are the distinguished men of our social lives. Paying a visit to such a man we give, in one form or another, our impressions to our friends: since it is human to desire to leave some memorial that shall record our view of the man at the stage he has reached. We describe his manners, his shape, his utterances: we moralise a little about his associates, his ethics, the cut of his clothes; we relate gossip about his past before we knew him, or we predict his future when we shall be no more with him. We are, all of us who are Londoners, paying visits of greater or less duration to a Personality that, whether we love it or very cordially hate it, fascinates us all.[1]

Yet Ford, a notoriously unreliable memoirist, soon proves no more consistent here than in other more overtly 'autobiographical' works, by the end of the opening chapter saying: 'For, sooner or later, the sense of the impersonality, of the abstraction that London is, will become one of the most intimate factors of his daily life. And sooner rather than later it will become one for the young provincial' (p. 8). What Ford is at pains to stress is that facts and statistics have little to do with the experience of the city which he is concerned to convey:

A really ideal book of the kind would not contain 'writing about' a town: it would throw a personal image of the place on to the paper. It would not contain such a sentence as: 'There are in the city of —— 720 firms of hat manufacturers employing 19,000 operatives.' Instead there would be a picture of one, or two, or three hat factories, peopled with human beings, where slow and clinging veils of steam waver over vats and over the warm felt on cutters' slabs. And there would be conveyed the idea that all these human beings melt, as it were, into the tide of humanity as all these vapours melt into the overcast skies.

Similarly, in touching upon moral ideas, a book about places must be passionate in its attempt after truth of rendering; it must be passionless in the deductions that it draws. It must let neither pity for the poor nor liking for established reputations and clean floors, warp its presentations where they bear, say, upon the Housing Question. Its business is to give a picture of the place as its author sees it. (pp. 3–4)

Nevertheless, it would be wrong to suggest that this work sees Ford giving an entirely subjective account. Much is also made of the ways in which a metropolitan modern city is experienced by the individual, and this leads to consideration of the means of transport by which a city may be approached. This in turn gives rise to an emphasis upon the ways in which the individual in a modern city such as London is both privileged and at a disadvantage. Approaching the city most commonly by rail, the individual both enjoys a raised point of view – able to look down into private backyards – and is likely to be given only a fragmentary glimpse of what is seen before the train, strictly out of the individual's control, continues on its

---

[1]   Ford Madox Ford, *The Soul of London, England and the English*, ed. Sara Haslam (Manchester: Carcanet Press, 2002), p. 3. All further references are to this edition.

way. And Ford completes the emphasis upon modernity by revealing that it is not from direct conversation but by reference to the mass media – the popular newspapers in which, ironically, Ford received his first significant publicity – that the individual may seek to make sense of the tantalising fragments afforded him or her. Thus, the individual in the modern city is both put at an advantage previously rare in history (prior to the General Education Act of 1870 a large number of its inhabitants would still have been unable to read) and alienated – the individual is powerless to engage directly with what he or she can see, as it is at once snatched away. Ford says that:

> Perhaps the comparative quiet fosters one's melancholy. One is behind glass as if one were gazing into the hush of a museum; one hears no street cries, no children's calls. And for me at least it is melancholy to think that hardly one of all these lives, of all these men, will leave any trace in the world. One sees, too, so many little bits of uncompleted life. (p. 40)

The key distinguishing factors are both visual – the privileged angle of elevation where the train or the omnibus are concerned – and aural – the fact that what can be seen is behind glass, akin to a silent film, and the combination provokes a mood of melancholy. Yet Ford is far from simply lamenting the loss of a more connected, glamorised past – he is quick to admit that the lives of the majority were just as beleaguered and beset in previous eras (if for different reasons):

> He must not only sniff at the 'Suburbs' as a place of small houses and dreary lives; he must remember that the thatched, mud-hovels that crowded round the Tower of original London, were just as dull, just as ordinary, just as commonplace; that men in them lived lives, according to their scale, just as squalid and just as unromantic – or just as alert and just as tragic. (p. 5)

Ford's emphasis upon modes of transport is not peculiar to his response to London, but is intimately bound up with the question of what makes any city become great and what accounts for its location in a particular place. In a piece produced a couple of years after the *England and the English* trilogy, 'The Future in London' of 1909, Ford extends the point about modes of transport to all cities: 'For a city is not so much a place in which to dwell; it is what the Orientals call a bazaar, a place to which you can carry merchandise, a place in which you must run, from point to point to make your bargains'.[2] He concludes that accessibility is more important for the sustained development of a city than its ability to defend itself in the military sense:

---

[2]   Ford Madox Ford, 'The Future in London', in W.W. Hutchings, *London Town Past and Present*, 2 vols (London: Cassell, 1909), II, p. 1096. See also the 'Modernity and the City' section in Michael H. Whitworth (ed.), *Modernism* (Oxford: Blackwell, 2007), pp. 181–215.

> It is the roads, it is the accessibility of the city, that have caused London to arise. It lay always defenceless in the low plain of a river valley. Considering the violent thing that History was, it appears marvellous that London should have survived. But it is the inaccessible cities that have perished – all the little towns upon crags and pinnacles, with citadels, capitols, walls running between rock and inaccessible rock.[3]

To become pivotal for a city, 'accessibility' must surely be linked to making 'your bargains', and thus here, considering the city as a phenomenon, Ford anticipates nearly thirty years earlier the ideas that are amplified in *Provence* (1935) and *Great Trade Route* (1937). Once the city wall of the purely defensive settlement has been superseded, the next question which arises is what exactly constitutes a city, and where exactly a city's limits are to be found. Ford regards the city as being more than just a physical location, albeit the terrain and topography, its 'accessibility', lie behind its original development in a particular location. Ford seems to suggest that London is an 'abstraction' and an idea, an 'atmosphere'. In *The Soul of London* he cites both the far-flung developing suburb and also colonial communities as being effectively an extension of the city, so that it transcends formal geography: 'Deep in the New Forest you will find red brick houses trying to look like London villas; deep in the swamps of coastal Africa you will find lay white men trying to remain Londoners, and religious white men trying to turn negroes into suburban chapel worshippers' (p. 12). He adds that 'the stores and the circulating library make London extend to Jubbulpore and to the married officers' bungalows on the Irawaddy' (p. 24), concluding:

> Speaking a little arbitrarily, we may say that there are three Londons. There is the psychological London, where the London spirit is the note of life, there is the Administrative County, and there is the London of natural causes, the assembly of houses in the basin of the lower Thames. (p. 24)

Overall, Ford's response to the growing modern city, in 1905, is positive. He neither romanticises and sentimentalises the past nor rules the future out, though there is none of the fetishisation of a future, utopian city as found in, say, H.G. Wells. Perhaps that is linked to Ford's early rejection of Fabianism. Ford does not shy away from a vision of an expanded London to come, as shown in his imagining a London in 'The Future in London' extending from the south midlands to the Channel coast, with the central area of London given over to public buildings and residential districts confined to vast suburbs which Ford prefers to call 'foretowns'.

That was not a vision of the city with which Ford remained content. Within his own lifetime he came to abhor the development of London out into the suburbs. This is shown in his late essay 'London Re-visited', published in the *London Mercury* in December 1936. Here Ford execrates the suburbanisation:

---

[3]   Ford, 'The Future in London', pp. 1095–6.

London for me is a stretch of territory beginning, say, at Kew in the West and gradually broadening out into a triangular shaft contained by Folkestone on the SE and Newhaven on the SW. I am aware that that is not all in the administrative county of London, thank you. But in all that territory you cannot stand up on a hillock without seeing a red-brick villa, and eighty per cent of the food eaten come out of cans, or is borne to the market in refrigerators and 'treated' with preservatives mostly of pheno-phenyl origins. It differs physically from NY or Greater NY in that all its villas have, on each side the slopes of their gables, white veilettes of painted deal – I don't know the architectural name for these devices. Otherwise, if you were dropped in one or other of the Oranges or Bronx Park there would be nothing to show you were not in Greater London, or if you were dropped in the residential portions of Croydon, Sevenoaks, or Three Bridges there would be nothing to show you were not in Greater New York.[4]

With his 1927 non-fiction work *New York Is Not America*, Ford developed his ideas on the city in the American context. Here he again focuses on transport and its effect upon life in the city. For all that it may be more modern in date, Ford does not view New York as a place more straightforward to get around in than older, less planned cities such as London. Transport, whether below ground level, on the subway, or at street level by car or bus and even on foot, Ford argues, is made impossibly slow thanks to the overcrowding. And that overcrowding is effectively attributable to the urban design. The preponderance of skyscrapers on the very small land mass of Manhattan leads to intractable traffic jams and congested trains. And the traffic is not only horizontal, but, as Ford brilliantly observes, vertical:

Now fourteen stories is no extravagant altitude as altitudes go, nevertheless it took me eleven minutes before I was on the sidewalk [...]. There stood in the monumental corridor, beside me, alike waiting for means of descent, one of the remorseless-jawed, clean-shaven, grey tweed-suited representatives of the Big Business of this country. When we had waited seven and a half minutes he said 'Damn' several times between his teeth; at the ninth minute he said that if he had back all the hours he had wasted in waiting for these contraptions he would have time to write a book.[5]

Ford has earlier said that he finds it all but impossible to write creatively in New York because of the demands upon his time. The New Yorker, no creative artist, observes that he could have written a book, although of course, as a 'remorseless-jawed' businessman, he never will.

Yet writing later – in 1936 – in 'London Re-visited' Ford draws little distinction between New York and London, finding both equally alienating:

And that, for Londoners, is the real note of London – that we never see her. We go engrossed from Balham to the Strand and, thinking our own thoughts, we have no glances to spare for the landscape.

4   Ford Madox Ford, 'London Re-Visited', *London Mercury*, 35 (Dec. 1936), 177.
5   Ford Madox Ford, *New York Is Not America* (London: Duckworth, 1927), p. 62.

So that when you ask me what outward changes I observe in a London that I have not seen for twenty years after three months of her, I answer, rather offensively, that there aren't any.[6]

Although Ford does emphasise the aspects of the city which persist and the personal dimension by use of pronouns:

And Shepherd's Bush Green is still there; and Brook Green; and the Goldhawk Road . . . and I . . . and Whitehall and Palace Green and Lambeth Palace and St. Bartholomew's the Great and Blackfriars Bridge . . . and you . . . and he . . . and she . . . and the bootblacks in Charing Cross Station Yard and Hampstead Pond. . . . Well, then, what more do you want?[7]

There is here a hint of that stress upon personal city lives found at the beginning of *The Soul of London*, with the reference to 'and I', 'and you...and he ...and she' yet by now Ford seems disenchanted with both cities in equal measure.

Fiction

Without doubt certain of Ford's novels are in some degree dependent on the city as both a setting and an idea: *A Call* (1910) and *An English Girl* (1907) are two which come especially to mind. In the former, Dudley Leicester, protégé and effectively surrogate for the wealthy Robert Grimshaw, who arranges his marriage and entrée into a political career, proves to be fatally paranoid about gossip concerning his former liaison with Etta Stackpole. An unexpected telephone call received in the night (later proving to have been made by Grimshaw) has the effect of convincing Dudley that he can be observed and that the whole of London is privy to the secrets of his private life. He is rendered dumb (an affliction which had affected Ford himself in the early 1900s)[8] by his fear and abandons London for the country. For Dudley, the whole of London becomes a source of paranoia: 'He had felt insane desires to ask strangers – perfect strangers in the street – whether they were the men who had rung up 4259 Mayfair'.[9] It is worth in this connexion noting that Alan Judd, writing of Ford's pre-World War I nervous breakdown of 1904, observes that Ford's specific complaint, agoraphobia, 'is apparently more commonly found in women and applies as much or more to busy city streets as to open spaces'.[10]

---

[6] Ford, 'London Re-Visited', p. 178.
[7] Ford, 'London Re-Visited', p. 179.
[8] Alan Judd, *Ford Madox Ford* (London: Collins, 1990), p. 128. See also Max Saunders, *Ford Madox Ford: A Dual Life*, 2 vols (Oxford: Oxford University Press, 1996), I, pp. 178–80, for a discussion of Ford's breakdown involving agoraphobia.
[9] Ford Madox Ford, *A Call: The Tale of Two Passions* (Manchester: Carcanet Press, 1984), p. 79.
[10] Judd, *Ford Madox Ford*, p. 128.

Among the early novels, it is in *An English Girl* that the city comes to play the most significant role in the outcome of the plot. Here, the city in question is not one of which Ford could claim any long-term experience. He wrote the novel in immediate response to his first trip to the United States in 1906. The city he visited, and which proves central to *An English Girl*, is New York. The novel's hero Don Kelleg is the son of an Englishman who made his fortune by unscrupulous means following emigration to the United States. Kelleg is long expatriated, having been educated in Britain, but on the death of his father returns to the United States, with his fiancée, Eleanor Greville, the English Girl of the title. Kelleg is deeply shocked by the squalor and poverty of much of New York and lays this at the door of his robber-baron father:

> it's worse for the poor over there. They've paid taxes to him – they're paying them to me – at this moment – on light, on house rent, on locomotion, on bread, on salt. There's hardly a thing that my father has not made the starving starve worse for need of. Ice now is a necessity in the slums of New York – and you don't know what slums there are in New York.[11]

The novel's overall message is hard to gauge. Kelleg attempts to renounce his father's ill-gotten fortune and eventually his engagement is broken off. He neither achieves his objective of making some improvement to what he sees as the commercial viciousness of contemporary American life nor succeeds in retaining the love of his fiancée (who proves far less shocked by the experience of New York than Kelleg himself).

By contrast, in Ford's most famous works in the genre, *The Good Soldier* (1915) and *Parade's End* (1924–28), the city is surely noticeable chiefly by virtue of its absence. It would surely be stretching a point to make much of the fact that it is Ashburnham's first showing a roving eye for girls in London's Bond Street which prompts his mother to express 'some alarm',[12] and write to Leonora's mother, thus leading to the Ashburnhams' eventual marriage. Likewise, though New York plays a role as the venue for the first meeting between Dowell and Florence, Dowell also says: 'I don't know why I had gone to New York'.[13] Thereafter, most of *The Good Soldier* is set in a continental spa town milieu, or on country estates. Critics such as Richard Cassell have described *The Good Soldier* as using 'the small group as a microcosm for society'.[14] And it is perhaps only to be expected that a story focused so determinedly upon the intimate relations of two couples should have little dependence upon any city in its telling.

---

[11] Ford Madox Ford, *An English Girl: A Romance* (London: Methuen, 1907), p. 14.
[12] Ford Madox Ford, *The Good Soldier*, second edition, ed. Martin Stannard (New York: Norton, 2012), p. 97.
[13] Ford, *The Good Soldier*, p. 17.
[14] Richard Cassell, *Ford Madox Ford: A Study of His Novels* (Baltimore: Johns Hopkins University Press, 1961), p. 77.

It might be tempting to suggest that the city is comparably absent from *Parade's End*. The crucial opening scenes of *Some Do Not . . .*, with Tietjens being first brought into contact with his lover-to-be Valentine Wannop, take place not in London but down at the golf links near Rye on Romney Marsh. Likewise large parts of *No More Parades* and *A Man Could Stand Up –* are set on the Western Front, and the final volume, *Last Post*, has a rural setting. That said, the reunion of Valentine and Tietjens and the important Armistice Day scene do take place in London, and the idea of London does at highly significant junctures have a pivotal importance. Thus in *Some Do Not . . .*, when Sylvia's suspicions about the possibility of a relationship are roused in Chapter IV, London comes into the equation:

> Valentine had felt a queer, queer sensation. She was not sure afterwards whether she had felt it before she had realised that Sylvia Tietjens was looking at them. She stood there, very erect, a queer smile on her face. Valentine could not be sure whether it was kind, cruel, or merely distantly ironic; but she was perfectly sure it showed, whatever was behind it, that its wearer knew all that there was to know of her, Valentine's, feelings for Tietjens and for Tietjens' feelings for her. . . . It was like being a woman taken in adultery in Trafalgar Square.[15]

This simile is revealing because it echoes the idea of Dudley Leicester's paranoid conviction that he will be exposed in *A Call*. The city here stands for the ultimate form of public exposure, something which, like Valentine, Tietjens is obsessed with avoiding. This is entirely consistent with the idea of Tietjens as the anachronistic feudal landowner who is profoundly out of his element in modern, urban society. As Tietjens puts it at the declaration of the Armistice, in *A Man Could Stand Up –*:

> What had he been before, God alone knew. A Younger Son? A Perpetual Second-in-Command? Who knew? But to-day the world changed. Feudalism was finished; its last vestiges were gone. It held no place for him. He was going – he was damn well going! – to make a place in it for. . . . A man could now stand up on a hill, so he and she could surely get into some hole together![16]

It is, then, hardly accidental that the city should be so absent (with perhaps the exception of *Some Do Not . . .*) from *Parade's End*. Ford's thesis in the non-fiction works dealing with cities had been that their basis lies in trade rather than feudalism. And here in *A Man Could Stand Up –* the end of feudalism is announced. Fittingly, the last volume of *Parade's End*, *Last Post*, is set in rural Sussex, or concerns the Tietjens estate at Groby (now let to an American tenant), and eschews the city altogether.

---

[15] Ford Madox Ford, *Some Do Not . . .*, ed. Max Saunders (Manchester: Carcanet Press, 2010), pp. 307–8.

[16] Ford Madox Ford, *A Man Could Stand Up –*, ed. Sara Haslam (Manchester: Carcanet Press, 2011), p. 210.

Tietjens has an abhorrence of his private life being exposed in public and is made to suffer for it. Within the scheme of the tetralogy, his insistence upon privacy is consistent with his adherence to the old forms of the rural, landed life. Having asserted in *The Soul of London* that the individual has a relation with a city as with a personality, there is little of this to be found in these two major works. Nowhere could London (or any other city) be said to figure almost as a character in the plot, as it does in Charles Dickens's *Bleak House* (1852) or *Great Expectations* (1860), or in other modernist works such as James Joyce's *Ulysses* (1922) or Virginia Woolf's *Mrs Dalloway* (1925).[17]

Poetry

If the city is central in only some of Ford's novels, and marginal in his most substantial work, what is its position in his poetry? Here it is possible to trace closer links to some of the theoretical principles which Ford had formulated in the non-fiction. Ford's poetry was first published in the nineteenth century, and Ford, born a good decade before most of the major modernist poets – T.S. Eliot, Ezra Pound and William Carlos Williams – exhibits a style ranging from a sort of Victorian faux mediaevalism, with persistent use of 'thy' and 'thine' as well as 'doth' (the equivalent of Ford Madox Brown's pictorial mediaevalism), to, at the other extreme, writing free verse in rigorously contemporary language. The city had provided a setting even in Ford's earliest phase in *The Questions at the Well* (1893) and features significantly from around the turn of the twentieth century, very much the period in which Ford was at work on *The Soul of London*. In 'Castles in the Fog' (1907), Ford creates images contrasting a 'tiny town' and a mediaeval world with a vision of contemporary London (italicised by Ford so that the distinction cannot be escaped):

> You should be a Queen – or a Duchess rather,
> Reigning in place of a warlike father,
> In peaceful times, in a tiny town,
> With crooked streets all winding down
> From your little palace – a small, old place
> Where every little soul should know your face
> And love you well.
> [...]
> In your small Great Hall, 'neath a firelit dais
> You'd sit with me at your feet, your jester.[18]

---

[17]   See the 'A Geography of Modernism' section in Malcolm Bradbury and James McFarlane (eds), *Modernism: A Guide to European Literature 1890–1930* (London: Penguin, 1991), pp. 95–190.

[18]   Ford Madox Ford, 'Castles in the Fog [Finchley Road]', *Selected Poems*, ed. Max Saunders (Manchester: Carcanet Press, 1997), p. 47. Ford changed the title of the poem to

This after having opened the poem:

> *As we come up from Bow Street,*
> *Where Tubes and Trains and 'Buses meet,*
> *There's a touch of frost and a touch of sleet*
> *And mist and mud up Hampstead way*
> *Towards the shutting in of day. . . .* (p. 46)

Ford also concludes in the present, ending the mediaeval idyll:

> *But here we are at Finchley Road,*
> *With a drizzling rain and a skidding 'bus*
> *And the twilight settling down on us.* (p. 47)

As in *The Soul of London*, there is an emphasis upon modern means of transport, but also the persistence of the idea of the 'feudal' which was to be seen as doomed in *Parade's End*.[19] Here, himself brought up in Hammersmith, Ford is writing of the known. It is interesting that in a contemporary poem, 'Views' (1910), Ford deals with a city of which he had minimal personal experience as an inhabitant, Rome, albeit a city which had for him, as an adoptive Roman Catholic since 1892, great symbolic and ideological significance. Ford speaks of Rome, and perhaps cities more generally, in terms which are charged with the idea of fragmentation and the distinction between the personal and the collective:

> I have that Rome; and you, you have a Me,
> You have a Rome and I, I have my You;
> Oh passing lonely souls we sons of men!
> My Rome is not your Rome: my you, not you. (p. 45)

There is a strong recollection here of the idea of a personal relationship with the city, elsewhere enunciated in *The Soul of London*, with its insistence upon Impressionism:

> Where the pavements gleam
> I have you alway with me: and grey dawns
> In the far skies bring you more near – more near
> Than City sounds can interpenetrate.

'Finchley Road' for publication in *Songs from London* (1910). All poems by Ford quoted in this chapter are from *Selected Poems*.

[19] On 'Finchley Road' and Ford's urban poetics, see Max Saunders, 'Ford, the City, Impressionism and Modernism', in Sara Haslam (ed.), *Ford Madox Ford and the City*, International Ford Madox Ford Studies 4 (Amsterdam: Rodopi, 2005), pp. 74–6. This volume contains a wide range of useful essays on Ford. See also Peter Nicholls, 'The Poetics of Modernism', in Alex Davis and Lee M. Jenkins (eds), *The Cambridge Companion to Modernist Poetry* (Cambridge: Cambridge University Press, 2007), pp. 51–67.

All vapours form a background for your face
In this unreal town of real things,
My you doth stand beside me and make glad
All my imagined cities and doth walk
Beside me towards yet unimagined hills. . . . (p. 46)

The language still incorporates archaisms – 'alway' and 'doth' – but with the phrase 'in this unreal town of real things' Ford claims that a city, the Eternal City, can be said to exist every bit as much in the words of those who have never lived there, perhaps never will live there, as in those of its actual denizens. The phrase also anticipates Eliot's refrain 'unreal city' in *The Waste Land* (1922). He speaks of a city the idea of which rivals in importance, perhaps far outweighs, its mere physical reality. Ford likens the relationship to that city with the reciprocal subjectivity of lovers. Again, this takes up the idea expressed in *The Soul of London*, that the city is 'illimitable' and an 'abstraction' (p. 15), and also the idea of a personal relationship. By 1913, with the publication of his *Collected Poems*, Ford was asserting in the preface to that volume that poetry need not be concerned exclusively with 'love in country lanes, the song of birds, moonlight [...] because we [poets] live in cities', indeed such safe, traditional themes would run the risk of amounting to sentimentalist escapism. Rather, Ford argues, proclaiming himself a Futurist, poetry should now just as readily take 'the emotions and environment of a Goodge Street anarchist' as its subject matter.[20]

In two poems written during the First World War, the city figures significantly. In 'The Old Houses of Flanders' (first published in *Blast* in July 1915), the houses, personified, are said to have 'eyes that have watched the ways of men for generations', but now aerial bombing means that they 'close forever' (p. 89) The personal relationship enjoyed by individuals with cities, suggested in *The Soul of London*, is extended to include bereavement.[21] Somewhat differently, in 'Footsloggers' (1918) Ford gives a sordid, unflattering description of London consistent with the *fin-de-siècle* 'realist' urban poetry of Ernest Dowson, W.E. Henley, Arthur Symons and others:[22]

But I ask you this:
About the middle of my first Last Leave,
I stood on a kerb in the pitch of the night

---

[20] Ford Madox Ford, Preface, *Collected Poems* (London: Max Goschen, 1914), pp. 16, 19. On the collection's date of publication, see Chapter 8 in this volume.

[21] For a further discussion of the poem, see Joseph Wiesenfarth, 'Death in the Wasteland: Ford, Wells, and Waugh', in Ashley Chantler and Rob Hawkes (eds), *Ford Madox Ford's Parade's End: The First World War, Culture, and Modernity*, International Ford Madox Ford Studies 13 (Amsterdam: Rodopi, 2014), pp. 204–5.

[22] See R.K.R. Thornton (ed.), *Poetry of the 'Nineties* (Harmondsworth: Penguin, 1970). On Ford's urban realism in his poetry, see Ashley Chantler, 'Ford's Pre-War Poetry and the "Rotting City"', in *Ford Madox Ford and the City*, pp. 111–29.

> Waiting for buses that didn't come
> To take me home.
>   That was in Paddington.
> The soot-black night was over one like velvet:
> And one was very alone – so very alone
> In the velvet cloak of the night.
>   Like a lady's skirt,
> A dim, diaphanous cone of white, the rays
> Of a shaded street lamp close at hand, existed,
> And there was nothing but vileness it could show,
> Vile pallid faces drilled through chalk white;
> Vile alcoholic voices on the ear, vile fumes
> From the filthy pavements . . . vileness!
>   And one thought:
> 'In three days' time we enter the unknown:
> And this is what we die for!' (pp. 91–2)

The bifurcation of experience between the Trenches of Flanders and day to day life of civilians on the Home Front (no more than 600 were killed by German bombing raids, compared to over 40,000 in World War II, and in the Battle of the Somme alone, where Ford was wounded, over 600,000 Allied troops were killed) seems to provoke his highly polarised view of everyday London. Furthermore, the references to London pollution, which had also figured pre-war in *The Soul of London* ('Roads into London'), where Ford mentioned the 'zone of blackened trunks' (p.25), denoting the perimeter of outer London), are here almost allowed to take on a figurative charge. The 'vileness' of the urban scene is what all the sacrifice on the Front is being made for. The purely physical vileness which is conveyed here is, later in the same poem (Section V), extended to the vileness of attitude towards the troops which Ford ascribes to civilians, when he speaks of 'Our Land, with its burden of civilians, / Who take it out of us as little dogs' (p. 93).

Finally, at the end of his career, Ford produced one of his most extended and substantial poems, 'Latin Quarter' (1936),[23] and once again it is the city – this time Paris, where Ford was resident with the painter Janice Biala – which is key. The Paris described is simultaneously in the twentieth century, a place of 'taxis' which:

> Glide
> Noiseless and slow
> Through the dark streets below (p. 157)

And yet the chiming of Richelieu's clock – an urban feature – reminds Ford of the passing of time but also leads to consideration of the other poets before him

---

[23]   After its first publication, Ford changed the title of the poem to 'Coda' and added it as a conclusion to his final poetic masterpiece, *Buckshee* (1931, 1936). On *Buckshee*, see Chapter 8 in this volume.

associated with the same city: Dante, Heloise and Abelard, and Heine. This calls into question the concept of time as merely measured by the clock, and introduces the idea of timelessness by way of literature: 'For you can't measure time or thought by the time-piece. / It can't be done' (p. 159).

> It is obvious that we must have patina and dust.
> We are the sort that must, since our brain
> Will not work in the atmosphere of the perfect Drain
> And Cellophane. And we must
> Live in irregular perspectives drawn in crumbling stone
> Running upwards into times long gone
> And yet so passionately here. . . . We must
> Hear Names and Affairs and old passions by which to adjust
> The mind and get into perspective
> Our era of plumbing and planes,
> And maniacal passion of invective,
> Of execration between nation and nation
> In a gigantic monotone. (pp. 155–6)

In this late poem, Ford both includes the modern – 'the perfect Drain / And Cellophane' – and 1930s political realities – the 'execration between nation and nation' – yet he also insists upon the past, speaking of 'irregular perspectives drawn in crumbling stone / Running upwards into times long gone / And yet so passionately here'. The personal relations between poet and painter are enabled by the city as 'haven' and yet they contrive to transcend the mere city of the present day.

While in his most lasting fiction Ford is seen often failing to bear out the continued fascination with the city which is announced in his non-fiction, by contrast in the poetry, be it from the pre-First World War period or the last years, Ford makes cities central to his most urgent concerns.

Chapter 12
Ford and Gender

Sara Haslam

What is our subject when discussing Ford and gender? It certainly includes the ways in which Ford deploys those basic, but shape-shifting, aspects of character and behaviour that can be critically tied to ideas about masculinity and femininity: from the weeping, golden-haired Princess Ismara of *The Brown Owl* (1891) through the intimate 'four-square coterie'[1] of protagonists in *The Good Soldier* (1915) to the partnered masculine 'doubles', androgynous rich girls, New York lesbians and capitalist powerhouses of his 1930s fiction.[2] As I have approached the subject in this chapter, it also includes exploration of some of the influences on Ford's evolving thinking about gender.

From the outset it is important to be clear that the categories with which we shall be dealing are not, in the main, biological ones (regarding which 'male' and 'female' would be appropriate terminology). 'Gender' describes a series of associated behaviours or attitudes that are constructed within a particular society and culture, often displaying, cumulatively, an implicit or explicit drive towards 'coherence'. The 'effect of gender', writes Judith Butler, 'is produced through the stylization of the body', including bodily gestures, movements, clothes and so on.[3] Thus it is the masculine/feminine binary which will be of more concern here than any notion of (relatively) essentialist, biological principles. This binary can sometimes itself be perceived as fixed. Critic Alan Sinfield describes the 'masculine/feminine binary structure' as the 'villain of the piece' in his preface to *The Wilde Century: Effeminacy, Oscar Wilde and the Queer Moment*, arguing that masculinity and femininity are not 'normative properties of men and women respectively'.[4] Ford might well have agreed. In his book *Women & Men*, published

---

[1]   Ford Madox Ford, *The Good Soldier*, second edition, ed. Martin Stannard (New York: Norton, 2012), p. 11. All further references are to this edition. In *The Brown Owl*, the Princess weeps early on as her father dies – from grief but also at the 'overwhelming prospect' of the power she will inherit on his death: Ford Madox Ford, *The Brown Owl: A Fairy Story* (London: T. Fisher Unwin, 1891), p. 8.

[2]   For Henry Martin's remarks about how New York 'swarmed' with lesbians, see Ford Madox Ford, *The Rash Act* (Manchester: Carcanet Press, 1992), p. 117.

[3]   Judith Butler, 'Bodily Inscriptions, Performative Subversions', *The Judith Butler Reader*, ed. Sarah Salih (Oxford: Blackwell, 2004), p. 114.

[4]   Alan Sinfield, *The Wilde Century: Effeminacy, Oscar Wilde and the Queer Moment* (London: Cassell, 1994), p. vii.

in Paris in 1923, Ford claimed that, in preparation for writing, he tried to eradicate his own preconceptions as to the differences between the sexes, pointing out that he had personally experienced most tenderness and tactfulness (those supposedly feminine attributes) from 'one or two men' in his life, and highlighting his belief in the role of social forces in shaping gendered behaviour.[5] It is certainly the case that what Ford put into his characters' performance of masculinity and femininity changed over time, as has been suggested above, and as we shall see in more detail over the course of this chapter.

While sexual behaviour must undoubtedly be considered an important part of any gender debate, for reasons of space it will feature in a limited fashion in this discussion. But it is worth briefly noting that, while sexual intrigues fuel many of his plots, desire and marriage rarely go together in Ford. And marriages rarely produce children. There is, in fact, a conspicuous lack of progeny in Ford's writing. It cannot all be down to biological ignorance – of the kind displayed by Edward Ashburnham in *The Good Soldier*, say, who apparently does not know how children are conceived even after his marriage (p. 99); or of Alice and Henry Martin in *The Rash Act*, who do know enough to try and avoid conception, but give this up out of fatalistic 'listlessness', accepting their later infertility, not really knowing whether they want to have children or not.[6] Sexuality undoubtedly fascinated Ford, as any reader of *The Good Soldier* will know. His characters are very limited as to its positive expression inside any marriage they undertake. In his representation of gendered behaviour, Ford is also more obviously interested in exploring the experience of being parented, than that of being a parent.

Finally, a related word of introduction about genre and its relation to gender. As will have become clear in this volume so far, Ford wrote prolifically, and in several genres. My focus in this chapter will be on his fiction, but gender politics were much on his mind in 1913, for example, when he wrote a pamphlet supporting women's suffrage – women's 'political equality' – for the Women's Freedom League.[7] And autobiography and memoir are acutely significant in any approach to Ford and gender. Trev Lynn Broughton's *Men of Letters, Writing Lives* points out that the late nineteenth century saw 'significant upheavals in what was understood by the "main story" of a life: upheavals in which issues of gender, sexuality and

---

[5]   Ford Madox Ford, *Women & Men* (Paris: Three Mountains Press, 1923), pp. 14, 21, 46. The book was originally conceived in 1911, under the title *Men and Women*. David Dow Harvey collects the relevant material on this early conception in *Ford Madox Ford: 1873–1939: A Bibliography of Works and Criticism* (Princeton: Princeton University Press, 1962), p. 56. See also Ford Madox Ford, *Letters of Ford Madox Ford*, ed. Richard M. Ludwig (Princeton: Princeton University Press, 1965), pp. 46–7.

[6]   Ford, *The Rash Act*, p. 107. Several pages later the protagonist wonders whether his wife is, in fact, a lesbian: p. 116.

[7]   See Ford Madox Ford, 'This Monstrous Regiment of Women', *The Ford Madox Ford Reader*, ed. Sondra J. Stang (Manchester: Carcanet Press, 1986), pp. 304–17.

literary authority were implicated'.[8] I say more about this process with specific reference to Ford in the section 'Gender and Creativity' below.

The chapter that follows is divided into sections which provide both an overview and some text-specific analysis of Ford and gender. It is also intended to provide suggestions for more sustained investigation of what is undoubtedly a rich and as yet under-explored subject in Ford's writing.

Context

Vita Sackville-West's novel *The Edwardians*, published in 1930 but set in England in 1905, opens as Sebastian, heir to the country estate of Chevron, climbs onto the great house's roof. His bird's eye view of the land which he will inherit grants him the satisfaction of a universe exquisitely ordered in particular ways:

> The whole community [...] was humming at its work. In the stables, men were grooming horses; in the 'shops', the carpenter's plane sent the wood-chips flying, the diamond of the glazier hissed upon the glass; in the forge, the hammer rang upon the anvil and the bellows windily sighed; in the slaughter-house, the keeper slung up a deer by its four feet tied together; in the shed, an old man chopped faggots. Sebastian heard the music and saw the vision.[9]

Both music and vision (which extends over subsequent paragraphs into the interior world of Chevron) are arranged with Sebastian in mind. He is 'the centre of all the life that hummed around him' (p. 52). That life emanates from its elevated male centre in gendered circles, beginning with the domestic interior, and stretching out to the slaughter-house. At 'luncheon' (p. 13), Sebastian's mother is shown to idolise her son, and acknowledges in turn the devotion of his 'dependents' (p. 52). His sister, one of those dependents, is 'always at home', and he thinks, as she enters his consciousness early on, that she was probably 'having her hair tweaked and frizzed, till, as her brother said, she could hardly shut her mouth' (p. 12).

Sackville-West's novel proceeds to chart some of the social changes in the period and, in its final pages, anticipates the First World War. However, its opening is a startlingly brash and simplistic representation of a life and culture based exclusively on clinically separate spheres – in class and gender terms. Sebastian is not only lord of all he surveys in the country; he has another life too, outside Chevron, as a student at Oxford. His sister, infantilised and tortured to project the required bodily version of coherent femininity – the perfect masculine equivalent of which Sebastian owns and exudes naturally – is cloistered by comparison. And yet, despite *The Edwardians*' assured perspective, broader understanding of the contemporary gendered 'vision' was far from this simple, or this predictable. With

---

[8]   Trev Lynn Broughton, *Men of Letters, Writing Lives: Masculinity and Literary Auto/Biography in the Late Victorian Period* (London: Routledge, 1999), p. 7.
[9]   Vita Sackville-West, *The Edwardians* (London: Virago, 2003), p. 50. All further references are to this edition.

Sackville-West's confection in mind, it seems astonishing to consider that by 1905 there had been talk of a crisis in masculinity for many years, as, to quote the social critic and self-styled 'Sage of Chelsea' Thomas Carlyle, 'the old ideal of Manhood' had 'grown obsolete'.[10] Patriarchal manhood, with landed wealth of the kind represented by Sebastian at the apex of the social structure, was one casualty of the re-ordering of society that took place as part of the industrial revolution. Many Victorian thinkers and writers – figures such Carlyle and John Ruskin, whose work Ford knew well – found themselves trying to establish new structures and 'scripts' for masculinity in its wake. Of most relevance to this chapter was the concurrent struggle to articulate intellectual endeavour as a part of nineteenth-century masculine identity. One critic of the period argues that the 1890s had 'unleashed uncertainty about masculinity',[11] but the issue was much older than that.

And Sebastian's sister, who was 'always at home' (an 'Angel in the House' in the making),[12] might have recognised the gendered world as she knew it in the art historian John Ruskin's influential series of lectures given in Manchester in 1864, published in *Sesame and Lilies* (1865). However, his belief that women had a sacred duty to devote themselves to the domestic sphere, making it a place of peace and safety, had also been under sustained attack long before Sebastian climbed up on that roof.[13] The 'New Woman' phenomenon had been culturally 'ubiquitous' since the mid-1890s; its first campaign was an explicit rejection of the 'home as woman's sphere' in favour of an active, educated and liberated lifestyle, in the public domain.[14] Sarah Grand published her essay 'The New Aspect of the Woman Question' (source of the phrase 'the new woman') in 1894; when the trials of Oscar Wilde began in 1895, focusing public attention on homosexuality, conservative commentators associated it with the contemporary 'liberation' of women. Writer and activist Edward Carpenter campaigned for women's rights and homosexuality at this time, publishing work that indicates the level of contemporary complexity in debates as to sex and gender (the Manchester Labour Press published a series of his pamphlets in 1894, beginning with 'Sex-Love and its Place in a Free Society').

We must read Ford's approach to masculinity and femininity with these contexts very much in mind. The inadequacy of the masculine/feminine binary itself is fundamental to the modernist challenge in his most famous novel, *The*

---

[10]   Thomas Carlyle, 'Characteristics' (1831): quoted in James Eli Adams, *Dandies and Desert Saints: Styles of Victorian Manhood* (Ithaca: Cornell University Press, 1995), p. 1.

[11]   Stephen Matthews, 'Gender and Sexuality', in Stephen Matthews (ed.), *Modernism: A Sourcebook* (Basingstoke: Palgrave Macmillan, 2008), p. 92.

[12]   A reference to the title of Coventry Patmore's famous serialised poem 'The Angel in the House' (1863).

[13]   For a longer analysis of these issues, see Adams, *Dandies and Desert Saints*, pp. 1–60. For the detail from Ruskin, see Josephine M. Guy (ed.), *The Victorian Age: An Anthology of Sources and Documents* (London: Routledge, 1998), pp. 505–19.

[14]   Carolyn Christensen, Introduction, in Carolyn Christensen (ed.), *A New Woman Reader* (Peterborough, Ontario: Broadview, 2001), p. ix.

Good Soldier. The infantile and conflicted 'soldier' (Edward Ashburnham); the 'greedy', wealthy male nurse (Dowell), self-identified as a 'sort of old maid' (pp. 81, 84); the secretive, confident, upwardly-mobile adulteress (Florence); and the suffering, methodical wife (Leonora): they form an intricately patterned quartet at its heart – varying immensely in the type of gendered behaviour they display depending on whom it is witnessing, or joining them in, the spectacle. But this was not Ford's first foray into such territory, as we shall see.

Ford's sensitivity to the potential richness and fluidity of the contemporary gender tapestry is evidence that he was an intelligent reader of cultural contexts. The historian John Tosh's work on changing masculinities in the Victorian period, and particularly the operation of male power in the domestic, professional and social arenas,[15] suggests that Ford's upbringing and early adulthood would also have shaped his awareness in notable ways. The 'male power' he most formatively experienced (through his father and grandfather) was narrated by him fictionally and autobiographically at various stages in his career. This power itself was relatively short-lived and unstable. Domestic and professional boundaries were fluid, especially in the Madox Brown household; patronage was necessary, and financial security impossible to arrange. Independence was a very messy business for Ford. (Ford Madox Brown had apparently threatened to turn Ford out of his house if he 'went in for any kind of commercial life'.[16]) When he eloped with Elsie Martindale in March 1894, he could not keep her financially. And yet, as one biography of the writer puts it, he never seemed to consider 'getting a job'.[17]

Gender and Creativity

In Joseph Conrad's *Heart of Darkness* (1899; 1902), Marlow muses at one point on professional labour:

> She [his battered steamboat] had given me a chance to come out a bit – to find out what I could do. No, I don't like work. I had rather laze about and think of all the fine things that can be done. I don't like work – no man does – but I like what is in the work, – the chance to find yourself.[18]

Marlow may not like work, but the matter is a simpler one for him than it was for Conrad – once he had left the sea. Conrad and Ford spent time battling poverty together as they tried to launch their writing careers, and the subject came up

---

[15] John Tosh, 'What Should Historians Do with Masculinity? Reflections on Nineteenth-Century Britain', *History Workshop Journal*, 38 (1994), 179–202. See also Broughton, *Men of Letters, Writing Lives*, pp. 37–9.

[16] Ford Madox Ford, *Ancient Lights and Certain New Reflections: Being the Memories of a Young Man* (London: Chapman and Hall, 1911), p. 157.

[17] Alan Judd, *Ford Madox Ford* (London: Collins, 1990), p. 45.

[18] Joseph Conrad, *Heart of Darkness and Other Tales*, ed. Cedric Watts (Oxford: Oxford University Press, 2002), p. 175.

in their own discussions.[19] Both men did 'like work', in fact (occasionally at least), but was it, in fact, 'work'? Ford often testified to the ambivalence about the relationship between 'manliness' and intellectual labour that was a key characteristic of the period. The 'thirst for applause' that Ruskin felt was properly fundamental to masculinity in the 1860s could be gratified, he suggests, by becoming a captain if one were a seaman, or a bishop, if one were a clergyman.[20] But Ruskin offers no examples using writers. Karl Pearson and other turn-of-the-century critics who focused on evolution and degeneration were similarly shy of locating the necessary vigour of the nation in its creative thinkers. 'If the national spirit', wrote Pearson in 1901, 'takes the form of a strong feeling of organizing the nation as a whole, of making its social and economic conditions such that it is able to do its work in the world and meet its fellows without hesitation in the field and in the market, then it seems to me a wholly good spirit'.[21] Earlier in *Heart of Darkness* there is a nod to Thomas Carlyle, as Marlow exults in his good fortune in securing (due, it must be noted, to the intercession of his aunt) his position in the Company.[22] Marlow reflects that 'it appeared, however, I was also one of the Workers, with a capital – you know' (p. 149). Carlyle's *Past and Present* (1843), for example, extravagantly praises such 'Workers', and though Marlow dismisses as 'rot' the idea that he might consider himself a 'lower sort of apostle' (p. 149) as a result of his appointment, both Conrad and Ford lacked any certainty that the later 'style of masculinity'[23] they were adopting, in becoming fiction writers, might also be positively encoded in print.

The year after *Heart of Darkness* was published in book form (1902), Ford's story 'The Baron (A Love Story)' appeared in *Macmillan's* magazine. This is a strange tale of national and emotional identity, madness, and love. Its first-person narrator shows himself to be a prototypical Dowell, conflicted as to his masculinity, when he asks himself at a key juncture: 'Where in the world did I stand?'[24] (He is asking himself: which is more important, his desire for Minne or his respect for the

---

[19]   Ford concentrates on Conrad's professional history in Part 1, Chapter VI of his memoir of Conrad, concluding that 'Conrad hated writing more than he hated the sea. . . . *Le vrai métier de chien!*': Ford Madox Ford, *Joseph Conrad: A Personal Remembrance* (London: Duckworth, 1924), p. 113.

[20]   John Ruskin, 'Of Kings' Treasuries', *Unto This Last and Other Writings*, ed. Clive Wilmer (Oxford: Oxford University Press, 1985), p. 256.

[21]   Karl Pearson, *National Life: From the Standpoint of Science* (1901): quoted in Mike Jay and Michael Neve (eds), *1900: A Fin-de-Siècle Reader* (Harmondsworth: Penguin, 1999), p. 39.

[22]   Despite this intercession, Marlow considers her, and the rest of her sex, to be 'out of touch with truth' regarding workers, and profit, and functioning capitalism. In an essentialist, 'separate spheres' remark, he describes how women 'live in a world of their own, and there had never been anything like it, and never can be. It is too beautiful altogether, and if they were to set it up it would go to pieces before the first sunset': p. 149.

[23]   Adams, *Dandies and Desert Saints*, p. 2.

[24]   Ford Madox Ford, 'The Baron (A Love Story)', *Macmillan's*, 87 (Feb. 1903), 314.

Baron, her father and his elder?) Perhaps more significantly, his question can be read autobiographically as well – as an example of Ford's deepening anxiety as to the progress between generations and what it meant to 'grow up' as a man. Where was Ford going to stand in the world and would he be rewarded for it? 'Ford worried that the better his work, the less likely he was to be famous',[25] writes Alan Judd as he debates the fruits of Ford's collaboration with Conrad – introducing notions of the 'commodity text'.[26] Arthur Mizener says something very similar in *The Saddest Story*.[27] Both biographers relate this worry to Ford's interpretation of his grandfather's ultimately unsuccessful career – subject of Ford's *Ford Madox Brown* of 1896. Mizener's chosen title reflects in part his interpretation of Ford's pervasive sense of anxiety and self-doubt.

Ford's parents and grandparents had instilled in him the belief that artists were the only serious people. In the social and economic context in which Ford found himself – including a personal need to make money – whether he could afford to be the kind of (serious) writer-artist that prioritised the 'right word' over the word which sold well took a great deal of thought. *Trilby* (1895), by George Du Maurier, was the best-seller which exploited the zeitgeist more effectively, perhaps, than any other book, though Conrad and Ford expressed more overt professional and financial jealousy of Arnold Bennett. Without a large readership, they were also excluded from the role of 'prophet' that was open, James Eli Adams argues, to the writers who felt estranged from ascendant models of Victorian 'manhood'.[28] In any case, Ford's early experiences helped to determine available courses of action in this respect too. Ford took the unusual step in what was a highly unusual first volume of autobiography to warn his own children off being such a prophet, because of the suffocating effect greatness had had on him: 'Do not, that is to say, desire to be Ruskins or Carlyles. Do not desire to be great figures', he says in the preface to *Ancient Lights* (1911).[29] The reader (daughters aside) is told in ingenious fashion that this will not be a typical Victorian 'Great Life', but will reinterpret and resist masculine authority as part of its narrative drive.

Working, at least in the early days, with one eye very much on that late Victorian world that had failed to reward Ford Madox Brown, Ford found himself

---

[25]   Judd, *Ford Madox Ford*, p. 71.

[26]   Nick Feltes gives a good account of the meaning of this term, and of what it meant for the relationship between author and publisher, in *Modes of Production of Victorian Novels* (Chicago: Chicago University Press, 1989), pp. 6–10. He describes that professional relationship as increasingly 'militant' in the nineteenth century, while 'the object of this new, necessary militancy was to be the literary text, newly defined as a commodity, newly available as the locus of surplus value': pp. 6–7.

[27]   Arthur Mizener, *The Saddest Story: A Biography of Ford Madox Ford* (London: Bodley Head, 1972), p. 465.

[28]   Adams, *Dandies and Desert Saints*, p. 26.

[29]   Ford, *Ancient Lights*, p. ix. See also Sara Haslam, 'The Prophet and the Sceptic: George Eliot and Ford Madox Ford', in Paul Skinner (ed.), *Ford Madox Ford's Literary Contacts*, International Ford Madox Ford Studies 6 (Amsterdam: Rodopi, 2007), pp. 49–62.

in the unenviable position of inheriting his antecedents' moral framework, but not the means to indulge it. His own masculinity was called into question as he strove to find and hold a readership, and therefore earn an income, in a world that in its dramatic re-organisation of the means of literary production had made the transition to the 'commodity text', but had failed, he thought, to leave a place for a writer like him. 'I don't feel certain that the game is worth the candle', Ford wrote to his agent in 1906, asking for some money.[30] He stuck it out, but when Dowell in *The Good Soldier* reflexively queries the nature of the 'proper man', had Ford himself answered he would undoubtedly have had something to say about the 'writer' before he even got to thinking about 'neighing after his neighbour's womenkind' (p. 15).

Gender and the City

As Angus Wrenn discusses in the previous chapter, Ford was often – though by no means exclusively – a novelist of the city. New York, Paris and London were all important contexts for him at different periods in his life, and, as with contemporaries such as James Joyce and Virginia Woolf, the modern city backdrop can be seen to encourage particularly focused attention to subjectivity, including gender, in his readers.[31] The turn-of-the-century city was the locus for many kinds of cultural investigation and experimentation. Georg Simmel, an influential German sociologist, regarded the metropolis as the site of a new kind of urban consciousness, inflected mainly by intimacy. The modern city, theorised by Simmel, offered the ideal situation for the linked figure of the *flâneur* (literally a stroller, a wanderer, but also an observer or 'perfect idler'), who can be found across a wide spectrum of literature of the period and was evoked in its prominent characters.[32] Decadents and Aesthetes, among others, made sure the social role of art was a prominent contemporary theme;[33] figures such as Oscar Wilde and Walter Pater meant that complex performances of gender became part of the same debate. Ford later recalled that the 'horrible occasion' of Wilde's libel action came at a time when the 'poets and painters of London' were, 'for the first time in the

---

[30]　Ford to James B. Pinker (Aug. 1906), *Letters of Ford Madox Ford*, p. 24.

[31]　For more on Ford's urban contexts and subjects, see Sara Haslam (ed.), *Ford Madox Ford and the City*, International Ford Madox Ford Studies 4 (Amsterdam: Rodopi, 2005).

[32]　For a useful extract from Simmel's 1903 essay 'The Metropolis and Mental Life', see Vassiliki Kolocotroni, Jane Goldman and Olga Taxidou (eds), *Modernism: An Anthology of Sources and Documents* (Edinburgh: Edinburgh University Press, 2008), pp. 51–9. In the same volume, there is an extract from Charles Baudelaire's famous article on modernity, 'The Painter of Modern Life' (1859–60), which in this translation includes his description of the artist as a 'passionate observer' and 'perfect idler' amid the urban crowd: p. 105.

[33]　See Chapter 5 in this volume.

history of the world', front-page news.[34] But there are no dandies, aesthetes or decadents in Ford's non-fictional metropolitan text *The Soul of London* (1905), dedicated though it is to representing the new, urban sensibility. Ford is interested in communicating in this text the immensity of the city, its 'internationalism' and its toleration for all 'types of mankind',[35] as well as in exploring, as one critic has put it, 'the inescapable connection between living in a metropolis and the loss of totality, objectivity, permanence'.[36] The opening pages of *The Soul of London* conspicuously lack 'swagger', grand gesture and confidence. They construct, instead, a mentally stimulated, enthralled, but also a disoriented male city subject, who, as he walks the streets, can neither escape the sense of fantastic perspectives (and so he is infantilised too),[37] or gain a clear view of the city:

> But the last thing that, even then, he will get is any picture, any impression of London as a whole, any idea to carry about with him – of a city, in a plain, dominated by a great building, bounded by a horizon, brought into composition by mists, great shadows, great clouds or a bright and stippled foreground. It is trite enough to say that the dominant note of his first impression will be that of his own alone-ness.[38]

There is no order in what he sees, in other words, and his own relation to it is equally opaque (how different from Sebastian's vision from his roof). This is also because urban 'intimacy' is strangely absent. Our 'man who knows his London' is thus given no opportunity either to grasp the big picture, or to display his masculinity.[39] Other contemporary city subjects are very different in each respect.

James Joyce published his only collection of short stories, *Dubliners*, in 1914. Dublin's wide and open streets provided an arena similar in some ways to the boulevards and department stores of bigger metropolitan cites, in which the *flâneur* was particularly susceptible to all the visual and aural stimuli the modern city could offer. Into this arena, in 'Two Gallants', Joyce drops two intensely, largely stereotypical, masculine protagonists. Lenehan and Corley are intimates. The physical detail Joyce treats us to – 'constant waves of expression break

---

[34] Ford Madox Ford, 'Memories of Oscar Wilde', *The Ford Madox Ford Reader*, p. 141.

[35] Ford Madox Ford, *The Soul of London, England and the English*, ed. Sara Haslam (Manchester, Carcanet Press, 2003), p. 11.

[36] Giovanni Cianci, 'Three Memories of a Night: Ford's Impressionism in the Great London Vortex', in Robert Hampson and Max Saunders (eds), *Ford Madox Ford's Modernity*, International Ford Madox Ford Studies 2 (Amsterdam: Rodopi, 2003), p. 49.

[37] If that subject, 'your man who knows his London', has known the city as a child, then 'there will remain to him always an odd sensation of being very little, of peering round the corners of grey and gigantic buildings': Ford, *The Soul of London*, pp. 7–8.

[38] Ford, *The Soul of London*, p. 9.

[39] Ford, *The Soul of London*, p. 7.

over [Lenehan's] face from the corners of his nose and eyes and mouth'[40] – is partly so we experience directly how closely they see each other. They work as a reinforcing team, amusing each other with stories as they prowl their urban environment, seeking the female prey whom they will dupe and seduce in the endless quest for petty sums of money. Despite their poverty, they are seen to own the streets, possessed of an existential certainty as to their permanence, their entitlement and their view of reality, all of which are rewarded, temporarily at least, at the conclusion of the tale. An explicitly gendered confidence is key, too, to the construction of Virginia Woolf's Mrs Dalloway who, in the opening of the novel of the same name, 'said she would buy the flowers herself'. Her feminine quest may be less a matter of life and death than Lenehan's and Corley's (she is a member of the political and financial elite, which explains what she enjoys of feminine 'freedom'), but what links the two texts, in terms of their representation of urban, gendered subjectivity, is that the characters are repeatedly reminded of their place in an ordered and densely populated universe. In the opening pages of Woolf's novel – even when thoughts of the recent war intrude – flowers, Society, sartorial elegance, marriages, mothers, 'the interminable talk of women's ailments' and jewellery lead to the climax of this first section in which Mrs Dalloway exults in the fact that 'Bond Street fascinated her' and she has a 'passion for gloves',[41] finally enjoying a quasi-orgasmic experience in the flower shop.

Robert Grimshaw, protagonist of Ford's Edwardian novel *A Call* (1910), walks the same streets as Mrs Dalloway. Like Joyce's and Woolf's urban characters in the examples above, Grimshaw is placed in tightly patterned encounters with other men, and with women, in the opening pages. Unlike the urban subject in *The Soul of London*, therefore, he experiences a great deal of intimacy, and this intimacy gives him the opportunity, we initially suppose, to perform his masculinity in a variety of ways. We are introduced to him as a character for whom the expression of quietly predatory masculinity is intensely important,[42] and the backstory is divulged quickly, with particular reference to his previous affairs, which then become the dominant theme. He is also a 'strong, silent man' (p. 13) to whom expansive knowledge is fundamental, and when he moves out of 'the ring', a 'very visible and circumscribed' arena in which the action takes place, it is only in favour of the spiritually-enhanced ability to stand on a little hill and look down into 'the misty affair' in which 'he was so deeply engaged' (p. 121). His far-reaching perspective seems as assured as his gendered identity.

---

[40]   James Joyce, *Dubliners* (London: Penguin, 2000), p. 43. I qualified 'stereotypical' with 'largely' two sentences ago because Corley prostitutes himself to the 'tarts' and 'slaveys' he and Lenehan hunt: p. 44.

[41]   Virginia Woolf, *Mrs Dalloway*, ed. David Bradshaw (Oxford: Oxford University Press, 2009), pp. 8, 9.

[42]   This is through the extraordinary presentation of Peter, his roving dachshund, who Grimshaw 'most nearly' resembles: Ford Madox Ford, *A Call: The Tale of Two Passions* (Manchester: Carcanet Press, 1988), p. 8. All further references are to this edition.

No scene in the book is as compelling, therefore, as the one in which Grimshaw undergoes an emotional collapse born of sexual jealousy, during which, far from standing on a hill, he is prone, sweating in his bed as many of the explicitly gendered structural aspects of his identity – his 'English public-school training' (p. 153), for example – are removed from his make-up, leaving him only with something he thinks he recognises as desire. But is it? Surely not. Grimshaw's expressed passion regarding Pauline Lucas, before as well as after this climactic episode, is to *watch* her, from a parent-like height, as she dances a 'gentle and *infantile* measure' (p. 14; my italics). He is very clear that he does not want to touch her. The twists of the plot situate him instead opposite his childhood sweetheart, the grimly professional Katya Lascarides, whereupon he makes himself her diminutive companion: 'It's you who are strong and who gets what you want, and I'm only a meddler who muddles and spoils' (p. 157). Grimshaw, despite the suggestiveness of the opening page, spends the entire novel symbolically separated from the kind of masculinity that Peter, his sausage dog, represents. His experience of intimacy does not lead to sexual satisfaction; his moments of vision do not lead to real understanding or processed, internalised experience. *A Call* plots its gendered points on the map of the masculine/feminine binary in such a way as to invite comparison with the yet more murkily, destructively gendered world of *The Good Soldier*.

Gender at War

H.G. Wells did not fight in the First World War; this fact helps to explain the approach he takes in *What is Coming?* (1916), in which he considers the war primarily as a catalyst for the redefinition of contemporary gendered behaviour. Despite the challenge many later readers would want to make to his assertion that 'the questions between men and women are far more important and far more incessant than the questions between Germans and the rest of mankind',[43] as well as to the fact that an account of the war's effect on notions of masculinity (the social and psychological impact of shell shock, for example[44]) is notably absent from his essay, I am going to take as my focus in this section Ford's representation of gender relations at war. The fact that, as Wells put it, the war was 'accentuating, developing, defining'[45] relations between men and women is born out in Ford's fiction, in which attention to gendered behaviour and how it might be changing is broadly concerned with a new kind of 'love'.

---

[43]   H.G. Wells, *What is Coming?: A Foretaste of Things After the War* (London: Cassell, 1916), p. 164.

[44]   Critical literature on the First World War deals with masculinity in detail. See, for example, Eric Leed, *No Man's Land: Combat and Identity in World War I* (Cambridge: Cambridge University Press, 1979); Fiona Reid, *Broken Men: Shell Shock, Treatment and Recovery in Britain 1914–30* (London: Continuum, 2010); and Trudi Tate, *Modernism, History and the First World War* (Manchester: Manchester University Press, 1998).

[45]   Wells, *What is Coming?*, p. 162.

This is not to say that the politics of gender is any more absent from Ford's fiction than it is from Wells's essay, in which the power of British 'feminine discontent' and 'feminine energy'[46] is most notably narrated as relied on by Germany to paralyse the war effort. Appropriately enough, therefore, the suffragette Valentine Wannop, a central consciousness in Ford's war tetralogy *Parade's End* (1924–28), is tasked with providing a general threat to 'constituted Authority',[47] including bourgeois marriage, the social hierarchy, senior civil servants, as well as the occasional game of golf. Indeed, in the first chapter of *A Man Could Stand Up –* (1926), she seems more than capable of representing on her own the 'World Turned Upside Down' (p. 19), before we encounter the men at the Front.

One might think that domestic scenes, of the kind that open *A Man Could Stand Up –*, or Armistice Day scenes would form the majority of the textual evidence to be consulted in the analysis of Ford and gender at war. Even on domestic turf, the state acted to control interaction between men and women in 1916, and local orders and curfews were in operation earlier in the war.[48] Suffragettes, or, at least, certain factions in the multi-faceted 'women's movement', as Wells accurately describes it, were instrumental in 'moral policing' around military camps, regulating the kind of employment and contact that might take place. Ford is not interested in this kind of policing, however, and nor is Valentine. The Armistice Day conclusion to the war is certainly notable in the confident way that Valentine takes her place among the celebrating soldiers; and the transition from club house misogyny to small-holding living between *Some Do Not . . .* (1924) and *Last Post* (1928) is demonstrated in part in gender terms. But the Front itself is the locus of a series of climactic exchanges as to gender – in terms of both masculinity and femininity – which must be read in terms of Ford's representation of character and autobiographical experience as well.

In the hut with which *No More Parades* (1925) opens, the men are pinned down as the heavy artillery 'said things of an intolerable intimacy'[49] to each of them. Such intolerable intimacy leads to blood and death. McKechnie, struggling with his nerves, asks Christopher Tietjens, 'Why isn't one a beastly girl and privileged to shriek?' Tietjens's reply is immediate, generous and ambiguous: 'Why not shriek? [...] You can, for me' (p. 23). Women physically find their way to the Front in *Parade's End*, and they also do so imaginatively or symbolically, as Ford re-constructs the gender paradigm through his experience of war. One of the strangest and most interesting aspects of the text with respect to gender is Tietjens's tendency to read his lover's androgyny in such a way as to confuse her psychologically with his Lance-Corporal, Duckett, when he is in front of him: 'he

---

46   Wells, *What is Coming?*, p. 165.

47   Ford Madox Ford, *A Man Could Stand Up –*, ed. Sara Haslam (Manchester: Carcanet Press, 2011), p. 18. All further references are to this edition.

48   See Cate Haste, *Rules of Desire: Sex in Britain: World War 1 to the Present* (London: Pimlico, 1992), pp. 31–5.

49   Ford Madox Ford, *No More Parades*, ed. Joseph Wiesenfarth (Manchester: Carcanet Press, 2011), p. 11. All further references are to this edition.

liked to think of the blond boy resembling Valentine Wannop dressed all in slim white' (*A Man Could Stand Up –*, pp. 168–9).

Sylvia Tietjens, Christopher's wife, fights her testosterone-fuelled way to the Front in order to display the most extreme versions of her sadistic sexual cruelty through the humiliation of her husband. (In *No More Parades* she whips a bulldog to death because it reminds her of Tietjens.[50]) Some readers – Tom Stoppard included from the evidence offered by the BBC/HBO adaptation of the novel – interpret her actions once there rather as a representation of the complexity of her desire for him, but either way Sylvia's 'feminine energy', to return to Wells, is of a completely different order from that posed by Valentine. It brings Tietjens up short, and, by extension, the army command as well. He wonders, 'what had his mind done in similar moments before?' (*No More Parades*, p. 223), as General Campion makes a decision to send him up the line to what is almost certain death, a direct result of the sexual and social havoc caused by Sylvia's presence. 'But there had never been a similar moment!' (p. 223). At times, therefore, Tietjens's 'masculine energy' can only seem compromised in comparison. And no wonder expression of it is problematical when, on the home front, Valentine is shown to be thinking about him thus:

> She could not afford – she could not bear! – to recall even his name or so much as to bring up before her mind, into which, nevertheless, they were continually forcing themselves, his grey-blond face, his clumsy, square, reliable feet; his humpish bulk; his calculatedly wooden expression; his perfectly overwhelming, but authentic omniscience. . . . His masculinity. His . . . his Frightfulness! (*A Man Could Stand Up –*, p. 28)

But the war makes a new man of Tietjens, and he survives the experience – he actively seeks the experience – of being reconstituted by and through his love for Valentine. This new man combines feminine as well as masculine qualities, and strength. Rescuing one of his men in the heat of battle, Tietjens feels 'tender, like a mother' (p. 176); several pages later he decides that he will live with his lover after the war because 'he wanted Valentine Wannop enough to take her away' (p. 207).[51] He stands up to face the post-war world.

What the new man finds there, as readers of Ford will discover, is focused less on English politics and class, and more on the New World, on America and on the cash nexus. Many of his 1930s texts are generated by an interest in the Wall Street Crash of October 1929 and its impact on social relations, including those between the sexes. As I have argued elsewhere, women keep Henry Martin

---

[50]   See Ford, *No More Parades*, Part II, Chapters 1 and 2, and p. 154.

[51]   I have written elsewhere on the way in which the climactic battle scene brings out what is most masculine about Tietjens (his 'enormous physical strength', for example), as well as what is most feminine. See Sara Haslam, *Fragmenting Modernism: Ford Madox Ford, the Novel and the Great War* (Manchester: Manchester University Press, 2009), pp. 99–101.

(for example) afloat, financially as well as emotionally in the end, even while the 'Crisis' provides Ford with a whole new metaphorical language for representing the dissolution of identity post-war.[52]

Conclusion

Ford's war-time experience left him wrestling above all, perhaps, with questions of perspective: of how to represent the war in narrative as he had seen and known it, if he was to do this at all. Two important essays written in 1916 and 1917, 'Arms and the Mind' and 'War and the Mind', offer some of the best evidence of this,[53] but there is, of course, also the question of the title of the third volume of *Parade's End*: *A Man Could Stand Up –*. One of the reasons a man wants to stand up is to combat the narrowness of vision inflicted by war. But a totalising view (Sebastian's view) is impermanent and elusive, more so after the war. It was never an Impressionist's natural perspective. As I hope I have shown in this chapter on Ford and gender, Ford's view of this matter close up was as unstable, complex and pluralist – and as provocatively interesting – as the other elements of his novelist's armoury.

---

[52]   On the function of the 'cash/emotion nexus' in Ford's 1930s novels, see Sara Haslam, '*The Rash Act* and *Henry for Hugh*: A Fordian History of Self-Construction', in Joseph Wiesenfarth (ed.), *History and Representation in Ford Madox Ford's Writings*, International Ford Madox Ford Studies 3 (Amsterdam: Rodopi, 2004). See also Rob Hawkes, 'Trusting in Provence: Financial Crisis in *The Rash Act* and *Henry for Hugh*', in Dominique Lemarchal and Claire Davison-Pégon (eds), *Ford Madox Ford, France and Provence*, International Ford Madox Ford Studies 10 (Amsterdam: Rodopi, 2011), pp. 229–42.

[53]   See Ford Madox Ford, *War Prose*, ed. Max Saunders (Manchester: Carcanet Press, 1999), pp. 36–48. See also Ashley Chantler and Rob Hawkes (eds), *War and the Mind: Ford Madox Ford's Parade's End, Modernism, and Psychology* (Edinburgh: Edinburgh University Press, 2015).

Chapter 13

Ford and National Identity

Christine Berberich

Ford Madox Ford has been referred to as 'that hybrid figure of paradoxes and disguises',[1] a statement that might be thought about in relation to Max Saunders's comment that Ford has 'often been a subject of controversy as a candidate for literary canonization'.[2] Opinions about Ford have always been divided, and this ambiguity is also present in the subject of this chapter: Ford and his attitude towards national identity, and here in particular to Englishness. Despite being, as Jenny Plastow highlights, a 'writer [who] particularly valued internationalism', Ford was also intrigued by the notion of national identity, whether it was something one was born into or something that could be acquired and changed.[3] This chapter argues that Ford's ideas about national identity in general and Englishness in particular are not only ambiguous but also often contradictory: on the one hand, Ford's love of England is deep-rooted and often takes recourse to countryside descriptions and imagery that is very traditional. On the other hand, however, Ford was also occasionally under the impression that national identity was something that could be assumed and discarded at will, and could, consequently, be changed whenever it was convenient. As such, Ford also held that there was not one single, unified and unchanging notion of national identity (and, for the sake of coherence of argument, I will here focus entirely on Ford's take on 'Englishness') but a variety of different interpretations, different forms of identity, different 'Englishnesses', so to speak, depending on outlook, background and individual situation. My argument will conclude that Ford simultaneously upheld a traditional view of England while also challenging and even ruthlessly dismantling it. In order to illustrate the above points I will focus on his trilogy *England and the English*, his First World War novel *No Enemy* (1929) and, in more detail, Ford's most challenging text as far as national identity is concerned, *The Good Soldier* (1915).

Ford's conflicting preoccupation with national identity has long been at the forefront of academic research. In 2004, the Ford Madox Ford Society dedicated an entire conference, held in Manchester, to the study of Ford and Englishness,

---

[1] Philip Davis, 'The Saving Remnant', in Dennis Brown and Jenny Plastow (eds), *Ford Madox Ford and Englishness*, International Ford Madox Ford Studies 5 (Amsterdam: Rodopi, 2006), p. 21.

[2] Max Saunders, General Editor's Preface, in *Ford Madox Ford and Englishness*, p. 9.

[3] Jenny Plastow, 'Englishness and Work', in *Ford Madox Ford and Englishness*, p. 177.

a debate that culminated in the publication of volume 5 in the International Ford Madox Ford Studies series, *Ford Madox Ford and Englishness* (2006). The editors, Dennis Brown and Jenny Plastow, argue in their introduction that 'the theme of Englishness permeates Ford Madox Ford's work overall'.[4] Their volume, accordingly, covers a variety of texts from Ford's *oeuvre*, ranging from his seminal early prose writing on England – the trilogy now known as *England and the English* comprising *The Soul of London* (1905), *The Heart of the Country* (1906) and *The Spirit of the People* (1907) – his historical trilogy *The Fifth Queen* (1906–08), his journalistic work in the *English Review*, his poetry, war propaganda writing, and his best-known fictional works, *The Good Soldier* and *Parade's End* (1924–28). The editors conclude that his consistent preoccupation with national identity shows that, for Ford, Englishness 'is not a stable and unitary concept but a changeable ideal', something he needs to engage with continuously.[5] In this respect, Ford showed considerable foresight: while, at the end of the nineteenth century, English national identity was very much something taken for granted, something that was prescribed and perpetuated through, say, literature and popular culture, he instead invited debate about it by suggesting that it was open to individual interpretations and, consequently, changed with time.[6] In contemporary Britain, there is now a renewed debate about the meaning of Englishness, with a suggestion that, instead of one unified Englishness, there might be a large variety of Englishnesses that are open to debate.[7]

The *England and the English* trilogy is Ford's first and most consistent engagement with Englishness – divided into individual books dedicated to London, the (traditional) countryside and English men and women. Sara Haslam, editor of the 2003 edition, explains that Ford's trilogy was: 'Part of a wave of such texts, [investigating] England and Englishness with originality, [and] in impressionist style'.[8] Written and published at the very beginning of the twentieth century, the three volumes represent a typical, centennial preoccupation with national identity – what would the new century bring for England? Further strength and influence as an imperial nation, or would that very power be on the wane and under threat from other nations? It was not only such wide-ranging political questions that much writing at the time tried to address, though, but also questions of cultural change: modernism, for example, was fast gaining influence and many writers

---

[4]   Dennis Brown and Jenny Plastow, Introduction, in *Ford Madox Ford and Englishness*, p. 13.

[5]   Brown and Plastow, Introduction, pp. 13, 18.

[6]   See, for example, Krishan Kumar's argument that, throughout the nineteenth century, English national identity was largely perpetuated through a newly formed canon of literary work: *The Making of English National Identity* (Cambridge: Cambridge University Press, 2003).

[7]   See, for example, Arthur Aughey and Christine Berberich (eds), *These Englands: A Conversation on National Identity* (Manchester: Manchester University Press, 2011).

[8]   Sara Haslam, Introduction, in Ford Madox Ford, *England and the English*, ed. Sara Haslam (Manchester: Carcanet Press, 2003), p. xiii.

used their work to express their fear of ongoing social and cultural changes in the wake of modernity: think only of E.M. Forster's fear of the city encroaching on the rural idyll of Howards End in the 1910 novel of the same name, or the feeling of displacement his character Margaret Schlegel experiences when travelling at the increased speed a motor car allows. In that context, Ford's detailed work on city and country life and English characteristics in general was typical for its time. What was not typical, however, was the style Ford chose, the very personal and rather literary Impressionist way of presenting his thoughts and findings; even more importantly, however, *England and the English* is seminal especially for its *critical* engagement with Englishness. Rather than presenting a backwards-looking, nostalgic assessment of English life and culture, Ford provides opinions and challenges to existing notions of Englishness that might also be explained by his own personal background: with an English mother and a German father, Ford would, throughout his life and at opportune moments, assume the role of the insider or outsider, the cultural observer who can assess the nation simultaneously from the inside, the margins or the outside, whichever position was the most constructive at the time. In *The Spirit of the People*, Ford famously referred to himself as 'a man of no race and few ties – or of many races and many ties':[9] when it was beneficial, Ford was ready to style himself as the perfect English gentleman – for example, recalling a discussion on the term 'gentleman' in his memoir *A Moveable Feast* (1964), Ernest Hemingway describes Ford as having quickly assumed the role of the benign country squire teaching a younger, and clearly *foreign*, man the basics of English life.[10] However, he also enjoyed challenging his readers' or audience's expectations, for example when giving a lecture on modernism at the Rebel Art Centre in 1914, dressed in a tailcoat – the new encountering the old, so to speak.[11] But Ford occasionally also took recourse to his German antecedents: when he planned setting up home with Violet Hunt after leaving his first wife, for instance, he considered taking German nationality to escape the stringent morality of Edwardian England.[12] Languages were important for Ford's assertion of national identity, and being able to effortlessly switch from one European language to another helped facilitate his shift in national identities. He showed himself aware of those chameleon-like qualities when he explained that 'whenever I have thought with *great* care of a prose paragraph, I have framed it in my mind in French, or more rarely in Latin, and have then translated it into English; whereas when it was a matter of such attempts at verse as I have made my thinking has been done in

---

[9]   Ford, *England and the English*, p. 325.

[10]   See Ernest Hemingway, *A Moveable Feast* (London: Arrow, 1996), pp. 73–4. See also Christine Berberich, 'A Modernist Elegy to the Gentleman? Englishness and the Idea of the Gentleman in Ford's *The Good Soldier*', in *Ford Madox Ford and Englishness*, pp. 195–209.

[11]   For full details on this incident, see Jeffrey Mathes McCarthy, '*The Good Soldier* and the War for British Modernism', *Modern Fiction Studies*, 45.2 (Summer 1999), 303–39.

[12]   See T.J. Henighan, '*The Desirable Alien*: A Source for Ford Madox Ford's *The Good Soldier*', *Twentieth Century Literature*, 11.1 (April 1965), 25.

colloquial English. When, on the other hand, it has been a matter of pleasures of the table, of wines and the like, I have been quite apt to think in German'.[13] For Ford, national identity was thus something he could easily switch and change, just like a language. But different national identities also represented different cultural frameworks and associations that he fitted himself into. Sarah Henstra writes that 'Ford insists on [national] identity as a citational practice',[14] while Patrick Parrinder asserts that 'for Ford, Englishness is (by and large [...]) a willed identity rather than a settled character. Anyone who wants can come to England and call himself English'.[15] With this attitude, Ford seemed to be considerably ahead of his time – and to some extent still is. In our contemporary society, where the process of naturalisation now comes hand in hand with an overly complex 'Citizenship' test and at increasing financial expense, Ford's extremely liberal attitude has still not found its match, and interestingly enough, a lot of contemporary debate about Englishness is still divided over whether or not Englishness is innate or something that can be adopted and adapted. Of the contributors to the website *What England Means to Me*, for example, a considerable number still believe Englishness to be something that a person has to be born into, not something that can be assumed (or shed).[16] At the beginning of the twentieth century, Ford thus raised questions that are still hotly debated at the beginning of the twenty-first.

For Ford, this 'flexible' attitude to national identity meant that Englishness itself was a diverse and much-encompassing concept – something to fit everybody, so to speak. He explained this idea with the help of the 'composite photograph'. In *The Spirit of the People* he elaborated that:

> A great number of photographs of individuals is taken, and one image being set upon another, a sort of common denominator results, one face blending into one another, lending salient points, toning down exaggerations. And, when one speaks of the 'Englishman' [...] one refers to a mental composite photograph of all the thousands and thousands of English [...] that one has met, seen, conversed with, liked, disliked, ill-used, or beaten at chess.[17]

---

13   Ford Madox Ford, *When Blood is Their Argument* (1915): quoted in Colm Tóibín, 'Outsiders in England and the Art of Being Found Out', in Andrzej Gąsiorek and Daniel Moore (eds), *Ford Madox Ford: Literary Networks and Cultural Transformations*, International Ford Madox Ford Studies 7 (Amsterdam: Rodopi, 2008), p. 69.

14   Sarah Henstra, 'Ford and the Cost of Englishness: "Good Soldiering" as Performative Practice', *Studies in the Novel*, 39.2 (Summer 2007), 178.

15   Patrick Parrinder, '"All that is solid melts into air": Ford and the Spirit of Edwardian England', in Joseph Wiesenfarth (ed.), *History and Representation in Ford Madox Ford's Writings*, International Ford Madox Ford Studies 3 (Amsterdam: Rodopi, 2004), p. 7.

16   See http://whatenglandmeanstome.co.uk: a contemporary 'Domesday Book' of Englishness, canvassing public opinion on what, exactly, it means now to be English. Contributors include critics, writers, politicians and bloggers.

17   Ford, *England and the English*, p. 232.

What Ford used in association with people can be seamlessly extended to images of the country as a whole: landscape images, for example, that overlap and merge into one another in one's mind and so make up one's very own version of England, one's very own affective landscape. And with this we have the explanation why for Ford national identity was not a static but an ever-changing dynamic concept: because it should be a personal one, with different meanings for each and everyone; not an Englishness that can be learnt faithfully from a book but one that is acquired throughout life and that changes with every new impression and experience. Ford's England is a palimpsest of images, ideas and impressions and his attitude to national identity is rhizomatic in its very multi-layeredness, different strands of meaning that overlap and interlock and come to form a meaningful whole.[18] Parrinder writes that, *'The Spirit of the People* [in particular] is [...] a frontal assault on the conception of national character as a stable and unchanging inheritance'.[19] Ford's take on Englishness instead seems to foreshadow that of the contemporary postcolonial novelist Andrea Levy, who succinctly stated: 'If Englishness does not define me, then redefine Englishness'.[20] Overall, national identity for Ford was no longer a stifling, backwards-looking, reactionary concept but a truly personal and welcoming one that really turns a nation into, in Benedict Anderson's words, an 'imagined community', not only inviting but actively encouraging individual contributions.[21]

However, and despite this liberal and truly forward-looking attitude towards national identity and Englishness, some of Ford's writing *does* hark back to traditional nineteenth-century conceptions of Englishness that were often characterised by clichéd landscape descriptions: in many cases, they are adulations of a stereotypical English landscape that echo Samuel Taylor Coleridge and William Wordsworth, or could have been inspired by a John Constable painting. In *No Enemy*, for example, the character Gringoire, who, despite his French-sounding name, is a British war veteran, explains that he had English landscape visions in the trenches, images that sustained him at a time of enormous peril and trauma and helped him survive:

> for I suddenly began to see bits of a landscape that has pursued me ever since [...]. Not quite a landscape; a nook, rather; the full extent of the view about one hundred seventy yards by two hundred seventy – the closed up end of a valley; closed up by trees – willows, silver birches, oaks, and Scotch pines;

---

[18]   'Palimpsest' means something with a number of layers that overlap and link into each other. 'Rhizomatic', a term often used by the cultural critics Gilles Deleuze and Félix Guattari, similarly refers to something multi-layered, interconnecting, overlapping.

[19]   Parrinder, 'Ford and the Spirit of Edwardian England', p. 7.

[20]   Quoted in Vera Nünning, 'The Importance of Being English: European Perspectives on Englishness', *European Journal of English Studies*, 8.2 (2004), 150.

[21]   Benedict Anderson, *Imagined Communities: Reflections on the Origin and Spread of Nationalism* (London: Verso, 1991).

deep, among banks; with a little stream, just a trickle, level with the grass of the
bottom. You understand the idea – a sanctuary.[22]

This preoccupation with a particular kind of (English) landscape as a safe haven is
typical of much writing produced by veterans several years after the war: Edmund
Blunden, in *Undertones of War* (1928), for example, conjured up images of himself
as 'a harmless young shepherd in a soldier's coat',[23] firmly locating himself, both
physically and metaphorically, in a pastoral tradition of writing that, at first glance,
seems to be far removed from a war narrative. Similarly, Siegfried Sassoon's
Memoirs of a Fox-Hunting Man (1928), the first volume in *The Complete Memoirs
of George Sherston*, dedicates 243 out of 313 pages to the detailed evocation of
pre-war rural England, an England that Sassoon, writing from the vantage point
of the late 1920s, recognises as a mythical England that probably never really
existed in this idyllic form.[24] Those three very different works all make the point
that trench soldiers constantly had to remind themselves of the land they were
actually fighting for – and by doing so they created their own mythical versions of
the English landscape; as Gringoire, in *No Enemy*, explains:

> the whole landscape [...] suddenly changed. It was as if the focus of the camera
> had suddenly clicked, readjusting itself – as if it grew – though before one hadn't
> known it for anything but all that was possible of tranquility, breath, security,
> and peace – grew quieter, calmer, broader, more utterly secure and inviolable.
> English country![25]

Ford's pre-war challenges to and liberties with national identity are forgotten in
his writing about the First World War: in times of national crises, Englishness,
for him, is inviolable, and his book is, in his own words, 'a perfect paean to the
English countryside [and] a true tribute to the country and my comrades in arms'.[26]

Similarly, and as Dennis Brown has admirably shown, Ford's early poetry
'invoke[s] and convoke[s] a communal consciousness as foundation of nationality
[...]. Figures tend to be typological – ploughman, townsman, pedlar, gipsy, parson
or auctioneer. There is a William Morris wishfulness as to social life [...]. The
poems mythologise more than describe, recycling familiar modes in the process'.[27]

---

[22]   Ford Madox Ford, *No Enemy: A Tale of Reconstruction*, ed. Paul Skinner
(Manchester: Carcanet Press, 2002), p. 33.

[23]   Edmund Blunden, *Undertones of War* (London: Cobden-Sanderson, 1950), p. 209.

[24]   On Sassoon's construction of Englishness in his Sherston trilogy, see Christine
Berberich, '"Isn't This Worth Fighting For?" The First World War and the (Ab)Uses of the
Pastoral Tradition', in Petra Rau (ed.), *Conflict, Nationhood and Corporeality in Modern
Literature* (Basingstoke: Palgrave Macmillan, 2010), pp. 26–45.

[25]   Ford, *No Enemy*, p. 22–3.

[26]   Ford to Hugh Walpole (2 Dec. 1929), *Letters of Ford Madox Ford*, ed. Richard
M. Ludwig (Princeton: Princeton University Press, 1965), p. 191.

[27]   Dennis Brown, '"But One is English": Ford's Poetry 1893–1921', in *Ford Madox
Ford and Englishness*, p. 256. Contrary to this, see Ashley Chantler, '"In This Dead-

In his early poetry and in his war-time writing, Ford thus takes recourse to a mythical Englishness that, he believes, everybody shares in because it uses common signifiers that need no explanation. This attitude can also be seen in his poem 'Footsloggers', included in his 1918 collection *On Heaven and Poems Written on Active Service*, which merits inclusion at some length here. It opens:

> What is love of one's land? . . .
>   I don't know very well.
> It is something that sleeps
> For a year – or a day –
> For a month – something that keeps
> Very hidden and quiet and still
> And then takes
> The quiet heart like a wave,
> The quiet brain like a spell,
> The quiet will
> Like a tornado; and that shakes
> The whole of the soul.

And it concludes:

> What is love of one's land?
>   Ah, we know very well.
> It is something that sleeps for a year, for a day,
> For a month, something that keeps
> Very hidden and quiet and still,
> And then takes
> The quiet heart like a wave,
> The quiet brain like a spell,
> The quiet will
> Like a tornado, and that shakes
> The whole being and soul . . .
> Aye, the whole of the soul.[28]

Throughout the course of the poem, Ford succeeds in turning the earlier uncertainty about national identity, exemplified by the first stanza's resigned 'I don't know very well', into something that requires no explanation, something that is innate after all and is recognised instinctively when needed – a far cry from his earlier attitude about the 'composite photograph' that makes up national characteristics and that, crucially, allows outsiders to make themselves at home, too. Instead,

---

Dawning Century": Ford Madox Ford's Edwardian Poetry', in Laura Colombino and Max Saunders (eds), *The Edwardian Ford Madox Ford*, International Ford Madox Ford Studies 12 (Amsterdam: Rodopi, 2013), pp. 91–103.

28 Ford Madox Ford, 'Footsloggers', *Selected Poems*, ed. Max Saunders (Manchester: Carcanet Press, 1997), pp. 91, 98.

Ford here evokes a quasi-mythical sense of 'one's land' that is secretly shared by all English men and women, and that requires no words at all, an emotion felt in the heart and in the head that provides a sense of belonging and security.

Here, then, we have the conflicted Ford, the fighter for a liberal, forward-looking, all-embracing and inviting national identity that moves with the times; and, at the same time, the reactionary celebrant of the bucolic, of the pastoral, of a traditional, rural Englishness that seems a far cry from his otherwise avowed internationalism. This conflict finds its apotheosis in *The Good Soldier*, a novel that simultaneously upholds and deconstructs traditional Englishness, a novel whose international setting both belies and reinforces the alleged English values it presents to its readers. Andrzej Gąsiorek refers to *The Good Soldier* as a 'Condition of England novel' in the same vein as H.G. Wells's *Tono-Bungay* (1909) and Forster's *Howards End* (1910) as it 'blurs the distinction between the psycho-sexual real and the social-national context'.[29] Published in 1915, in the early stages of the First World War, the novel is preoccupied with questions of national identity that reflect Ford's own conflicting attitudes towards it, but also his own unique position as both insider and outsider in English society. Following a few years after the publication of his *England and the English* trilogy, Ford seemed to be putting his theoretical discussions of Englishness into practice in this text – there are traces of the quintessential and traditional England as well as ideas about a more fluent Englishness. Above all, however, Ford wanted to open his readers' eyes to stereotypical conceptions of Englishness – and how misleading, if not downright wrong, they can occasionally be. Set predominantly in Germany, the novel is nevertheless closely associated with England, mainly through the discussion of its central character, the English gentleman Edward Ashburnham. However, the *American* narrator John Dowell brings in the outsider's perspective on Englishness – he wishes to belong, but, fundamentally, misunderstands what Englishness might denote. Additionally, and as Petra Rau has shown, the novel's settings also link it to the discussion of Englishness: on the one hand, we have the English location, the Ashburnhams' country estate of Branshaw Teleragh, a place denoting quintessential and traditional Englishness. The majority of the novel, however, is set in the German spa of Nauheim, a place popular with English travellers in the early twentieth century, where the Ashburnhams and Dowells regularly take up residence.[30]

The Englishness of *The Good Soldier* has been a topic for much academic discussion and research over recent years. Austin Riede, in an essay tellingly titled 'The Decline of English Discourse and the American Invasion in *The Good Soldier* and *Parade's End*' argues that Englishness in the novel eventually

---

²⁹   Andrzej Gąsiorek, '"Content to be Superseded"?: Ford in the Great London Vortex', in *Ford Madox Ford: Literary Networks and Cultural Transformations*, p. 97.

³⁰   Petra Rau, *English Modernism, National Identity and the Germans, 1890–1950* (Farnham: Ashgate, 2009), p. 108.

makes way for Americanness;[31] Colm Tóibín sees the conflict between Edward
Ashburnham and his Irish-born wife Leonora as the struggle between Englishness
and Irishness from which Irishness eventually emerges victorious;[32] and Rau
points out that early reviewers criticised the novel for its alleged 'foreignness'.[33]
However, I would contend that it is those very 'foreign' aspects that bring the issue
of Englishness further to the forefront of Ford's novel. The remarkable thing about
The Good Soldier is that Ford reinforces its Englishness – both in order to show
up the shortcomings of it and, yet, still to uphold it. Yes, Dowell, the American
narrator of the novel, does end up living in Branshaw Teleragh, the former home
of Ashburnham – the point that Riede considers to prove the American 'take over'
and English 'decline' apparent in the novel. It also foreshadows developments
later in the twentieth century, with many grand country estates being either broken
up, demolished, turned into schools or sold to American millionaires because their
English owners could no longer afford them.[34] However, we have to bear in mind
that, throughout the novel, Dowell paints Ashburnham as the epitome not only
of English masculinity but of mankind overall, and as someone he, in various
ways, tries to model himself on. In Dowell, we consequently do not have an
American consciously taking over a piece of England in a quasi-imperial bid, but
rather somebody who desperately tries to assert a stereotypical and quintessential
Englishness for himself. Although Ford has, throughout the novel, shown the
shortcomings of Englishness in Ashburnham, Dowell's refusal to see them and
his stubborn attempt to model himself on the quintessentially English gentleman
simultaneously dismantles and reinforces traditional English characteristics.

A similar case can be made against Tóibín's argument that the conflict between
Ashburnham and Leonora is symbolic of the wider political struggles between
England and Ireland. Tóibín argues that 'in Leonora [...] Ford created the most
significant Irish presence in an English novel since Trollope' and the fact that
Leonora can so easily 'read [Ashburnham] at all times' and see through his
pretences, suggests a simple Englishness much inferior to Leonora's Irishness.[35]
Ashburnham is clearly a far more problematical character than the narrator Dowell
allows for; however, the argument of Leonora's superior Irishness can be met with
the counter-argument that she herself assumes the role of the perfect *English* lady
of the manor, both at Branshaw Teleragh and later on with her second husband,
Rodney Bayham. What, ultimately, the use of those non-English characters achieves
is to pitch Englishness against everything else. And while Ford openly critiques
Englishness through the shortcomings of Ashburnham (who, instead of being the
chivalrous gentleman Dowell depicts, really is a serial womaniser), he suggests

---

[31]   Austin Riede, 'The Decline of English Discourse and the American Invasion in *The Good Soldier* and *Parade's End*', in *Ford Madox Ford and Englishness*, pp. 211–24.

[32]   Tóibín, 'Outsiders in England and the Art of Being Found Out', pp. 61–80.

[33]   Rau, *English Modernism, National Identity and the Germans, 1890–1950*, p. 92.

[34]   This, for example, is a topic at the heart of Kazuo Ishiguro's 1989 novel *The Remains of the Day*, which deals with the idea of Englishness in crisis.

[35]   Tóibín, 'Outsiders in England and the Art of Being Found Out', pp. 71, 77.

that, ultimately, it is the rest of the world that wants to uphold Englishness after all. Similarly, Samuel Hynes argued in 1961 that the main theme of *The Good Soldier* is the struggle between convention and passion.[36] Interestingly, it is Ashburnham, the supposedly reticent Englishman, who represents passion, whereas the 'foreign' characters of Dowell and Leonora desperately try to uphold allegedly traditional English conventions: keeping up appearances, as Leonora does throughout her marriage, or as Dowell ends up doing when taking over Branshaw to look after the mad Nancy. Expectations and stereotypes are thus subtly turned on their head, and this is particularly apparent when looking closely at Ashburnham.

Described by Dowell as 'the cleanest looking sort of chap; – an excellent magistrate, a first rate soldier, one of the best landlords, so they say, in Hampshire, England', a man who held a 'violent conviction of the duties of his station', who 'had the D.S.O.; and [whose] troop loved him beyond the love of men',[37] Ashburnham is, throughout the novel, depicted as the epitome of the English gentleman: loyal, decent, chivalrous, always putting the interests of others before his own. Or is he? Presented almost entirely through the eyes of the highly unreliable narrator John Dowell, the discerning reader might start seeing warning signs fairly early on (the novel demands close reading). Take, for example, one of the earliest descriptions he provides of Ashburnham:

> His face hitherto had, in the wonderful English fashion, expressed nothing whatsoever. Nothing. There was in it neither joy nor despair; neither hope nor fear; neither boredom nor satisfaction. He seemed to perceive no soul in the crowded room; he might have been walking in a jungle. I never came across such a perfect expression before and I never shall again. It was insolence and not insolence; it was modesty and not modesty. His hair was fair, extraordinarily, ordered in a wave, running from the left temple to the right; his face was a light brick-red, perfectly uniform in tint up to the roots of his hair itself; his yellow moustache was as stiff as a toothbrush and I verily believe that he had had his black smoking jacket thickened a little over the shoulder-blades so as to give himself the air of the slightest possible stoop. (p. 24)

This passage shows a variety of things. First of all, it quite clearly reveals Dowell's preconceptions of Englishness: what, exactly, does 'wonderful English fashion' imply? For him, it seems to include having an inscrutable expression – which taps into all the universally held stereotypes and clichés about the English stiff upper lip. Dowell describes Ashburnham as somebody who is always in command of every situation; not a hair is out of place in this carefully made-up man. But this is exactly where the problem for the reader lies. Ashburnham appears simply too good to be true. That suggests that Dowell does not really have a clear conception of what exactly Englishness means in the first place. He just strings together a

---

[36]   Samuel Hynes, 'The Epistemology of *The Good Soldier*', *Sewanee Review*, 69 (1961), 225–35.

[37]   Ford Madox Ford, *The Good Soldier*, second edition, ed. Martin Stannard (New York: Norton, 2012), pp. 14, 47, 70. All further references are to this edition.

series of clichés and stereotypes that, for him, represent perfection. Sarah Henstra writes that:

> Edward [...] serve[s] as living assurance for Dowell of the correspondence between sign and referent, appearance and reality. If identity can be that naturally born-and-bred and that unselfconsciously embodied, then other categorical certainties – like the difference between moral and immoral, right and wrong – must be buttressed by the same universal order. [...] Seeing Edward as archetypal of an Englishness that is natural and non-performative means that Dowell sees Edward's taste, refinement, and knowledge as almost supernatural or cosmically endowed [...].[38]

The question, however, that needs to be asked is whether or not Ashburnham's alleged Englishness really is that natural, and the passage from the novel quoted above is again quite revealing in that respect. With his inscrutable expression, Ashburnham seems to be wearing a mask behind which his real persona can hide. Telling, also, is the slight stoop Dowell remarks upon. That Ashburnham might feel the need to modify his attire to pretend to have a stoop again strongly suggests that he is a man putting on a façade, one that he might be aware is expected of him as an Englishman abroad. Instead of his Englishness being 'non-performative', it becomes, instead, highly performative – a man putting on an act to, if one wants to look at it positively, please and impress the people around him. More negatively, however, one could argue that Ashburnham wants to fool the people around him. The most important point in this context, however, is that Ford himself shows up Englishness as both a construct and as 'citational practice'[39] that Ashburnham can take recourse to whenever appropriate. Petra Rau, in a different context, writes that 'even being "in the landscape" is a form of disappearing',[40] and this statement can easily be applied to Ashburnham's performance as the perfect English gentleman. There is, after all, something rotten in the perfect world of the master of Branshaw Teleragh: beneath Ashburnham's suave and carefully styled exterior lurks a man who jeopardises not only his marriage and his and his family's financial security but, ultimately, his mind and life in the pursuit of his romantic infatuations. Pretending to be the perfect English gentleman is Edward's way of 'being in the landscape', blending in, meeting public expectations – and not attracting any unwanted attention. Though outwardly presenting, as Dowell says, 'all the virtues that are usually accounted English' (p. 101), Ashburnham, as Henstra argues, 'fails to embody the national-moral standards',[41] a fact the rest of the novel's cast try hard to ignore or deny (Dowell) or cover up (Leonora). Edward thus turns, quite clearly, into the 'composite photograph' of other people's expectations. Leonora

---

[38]   Henstra, 'Ford and the Costs of Englishness', p. 180.
[39]   Henstra, 'Ford and the Costs of Englishness', p. 178.
[40]   Rau, *English Modernism, National Identity and the Germans, 1890–1950*, p. 103.
[41]   Henstra, 'Ford and the Costs of Englishness', p. 178.

keeps up appearances much for her own sake. In the case of Dowell, however, Ashburnham's Englishness becomes a vested identity that he endows him with.

Throughout *The Good Soldier*, Dowell repeatedly asserts that the Ashburnhams are 'what in England it is the custom to call "quite good people"' (p. 10). What this term means precisely, he does not elaborate on – it is yet another example of his general vagueness where manifestations of English identity are concerned. Ford, however, leaves his readers in no doubt that those allegedly 'good people' are, in reality, deeply troubled characters, trying to keep up appearances and preserve a socially acceptable façade, and the high cost that they have to pay for it – in Edward's case, his mental health and, ultimately, his life. Critics have, in the past, read the novel as signifying an Englishness in deep crisis.[42] However, I believe that, more than highlighting a potential breakdown of Englishness, Ford wanted to show the pitfalls of taking so-called national-identity signifiers as a given, or of blindly believing in markers of national identity. At the very beginning of *The Good Soldier*, Dowell ponders the Ashburnhams: 'To have all that and to be all that!' (p. 13). Ford's moral lesson for his readers is rather that, even if all appears to be well, it could be a case of *not* to have, and *not* to be 'all that'.

---

[42]   See, for example, Rau, *English Modernism, National Identity and the Germans, 1890–1950*, p. 108.

Chapter 14

Ford and Politics

Andrzej Gąsiorek

Ford Madox Ford often described himself as a Catholic and a Tory. 'I write as a black Papist', he once observed, 'and, for what it is worth, a Tory mad about historic continuity'.[1] If we were to take these words at face value we would find ourselves puzzled by much else about Ford. For instance, that he was a literary innovator who wrote experimental fiction, poetry and reminiscences; a life-long advocate of the brash modernists he avuncularly called *les jeunes*; and an ardent supporter of Home Rule in Ireland and of the suffragette movement in Britain. If Ford was indeed a Tory, then he was a peculiar kind of Tory. This is, after all, a man who held that real Toryism was essentially the same thing as real socialism. How are we to make sense of such an assertion?

Ford's remark about the affinities between socialism and Toryism occurs in *England and the English* (1907). He argues that the Revolution of 1688 consolidated state power at the expense of the monarchy. Political centralisation gradually took hold, and in time this eroded the influence of the landed gentry. Maintaining that Robert Walpole's administration undermined 'the country interest', Ford suggests that when Walpole shifted power from the country to the state he 'did away with the true Toryism which is Socialism, and rendered possible Individualism'.[2] This observation helps us to understand Ford's political viewpoint. Toryism was for him a way of thinking and living that put the needs of the community before those of the individual. Ford aligns Toryism with socialism on the grounds that both political philosophies are communal in orientation and emphasise responsibilities rather than rights. This is an old-fashioned form of conservatism with roots in a long-standing tradition of Tory radicalism. Those who belonged to this tradition criticised industrialism for its destruction of settled ways of life and its impoverishment of working people; attacked capitalism for its utilitarian conception of political economy and its promotion of commercialism; stressed the importance of reciprocal social duties as opposed to individual civic rights; believed in a hierarchical society in which a responsible aristocracy was supposed to look after those less fortunate than itself; derided the rising middle classes for their materialism and complacence; and valued (rather nostalgically)

---

[1] Ford Madox Ford, *Henry James: A Critical Study* (London: Martin Secker, 1913), p. 103.

[2] Ford Madox Ford, *England and the English*, ed. Sara Haslam (Manchester: Carcanet Press, 2003), pp. 276, 277.

a pre-industrial agrarian way of life that was associated with a supposedly beneficent medieval period. This kind of Toryism was at once conservative and radical: it aimed to preserve certain social traditions and maintain continuity with the national past, while at the same time it sought to revolutionise a corrupt present by returning to values that were allegedly being eroded.

To what extent did Ford hold such beliefs? It seems pretty clear from everything he wrote on the subject of politics that he saw himself as a radical Tory humanist of some kind. In Alan Judd's words, Ford 'allied Catholicism with his favoured political attitude', which Judd describes as 'an imagined feudal Toryism that was really socialism without the state'.[3] It is important to acknowledge here that this is a strange kind of socialism, since it doesn't seek to overthrow the class system but aims to recall those who wield economic and political power to a proper sense of their civic responsibilities. Social hierarchies remain in place, in other words, but those who are in authority are expected to look after the less well off, not to take advantage of them. This is a political ideal rather than a practical prescription. And it's fair to say that although Ford knew a lot about politics and took a close interest in current affairs, he was not a programmatic thinker but a speculative one. Max Saunders suggests that Ford's Toryism should be seen as 'an impression rather than a political manifesto'.[4] So when Ford refers to himself as a 'sentimental Tory' (in an oft-repeated phrase) he is constructing what Benedict Anderson describes as an 'imagined community'.[5] His Toryism functions as a vision of how social life could look if the political order were reformed so that economic imperatives and the centralisation of power were no longer the state's *raison d'être*.

Holding such views meant that Ford was no died-in-the-wool reactionary. He was a democrat who sympathised with the plight of working people and grasped that they were frequently exploited. He believed that a new kind of conservatism, which was associated with *laisser faire* economics and Social Imperialism at the turn of the century, was disastrous for the body politic precisely because it ignored communal obligations. So it's wrong to suggest, as Robert Green has done, that Ford was in favour of right-wing individualism and its advocacy of property rights.[6] On the contrary, he tried to state the case for the bonds of community, and he attacked the new conservatism for its materialism, its implicit conception of human beings as self-serving egotists, and its failure to defend long established ways of life. Ford was himself a frugal man. He found it hard to understand why anyone would be motivated by a desire for material wealth. 'As for Bolshevism', he wrote in 1918, 'it is nothing to me. I never had or wanted great possessions – only I hate people to want other people's goods – or rather to grudge other people

---

   [3]   Alan Judd, *Ford Madox Ford* (London: Collins, 1990), p. 20.

   [4]   Max Saunders, *Ford Madox Ford: A Dual Life*, 2 vols (Oxford: Oxford University Press, 1996), II, p. 206.

   [5]   See Benedict Anderson, *Imagined Communities: Reflections on the Origin and Spread of Nationalism* (London: Verso, 1991).

   [6]   Robert Green, *Ford Madox Ford: Prose and Politics* (Cambridge: Cambridge University Press, 1981), pp. 13–14.

what they have. In the matter of Capital & Labour I am for Labour every time'. As far as he was concerned his view was: 'let the workman get *all* the profits of his labours, by all means & damn the manufacturer, who is always a sweating beast'.[7]

Ford also supported women's suffrage. He was appalled that women were denied the vote. It was a disgrace, he maintained, that women should be treated like 'children, criminals, lunatics', the only other groups who in England 'were refused the right of citizenship'.[8] When he was thinking about starting the *English Review*, a periodical that was dedicated above all to imaginative literature, he also had in mind that it would be a pro-suffrage paper. He despised the Boer War, which he saw as an imperialist venture, and he was disturbed by the crude nationalism of those who supported it; he wanted South Africa to be 'returned to its real owners, the natives, and Kruger and Mr Chamberlain hung on the same gallows'.[9] The same political logic ensured that he was also an advocate for Home Rule in Ireland. The Irish Catholic Leonora Ashburnham is described in *The Good Soldier* (1915) as coming from 'a family of small Irish landlords – that hostile garrison in a plundered country',[10] and in *Return to Yesterday* (1931) Ford described himself as a 'passionate Home Ruler', writing: 'I hate, I hate, I hate – three times – the idea of people of one race and religion being ruled over by people of alien race and another religion'.[11] A non-aligned figure, Ford was critical of Conservatives and Liberals alike. He claimed that he couldn't vote for the Conservatives because of their stance on Ireland and couldn't support the Liberals because of their failure to guarantee fair wages for working people.

Ford held to his radical Tory views consistently. But we can identify phases in his political thinking during which his preoccupations changed. In the years leading up to the First World War, he was concerned with the spread of various revolutionary and anarchist groups, the Boer War, nationalism in Ireland, and the suffrage movement. During the First World War he engaged in propaganda for C.F.G. Masterman's government unit, and he used this as an opportunity to write two books: *Between St. Dennis and St. George* (1915) and *When Blood is Their Argument* (1915). In these works he attacked the materialist and martial spirit of Prussian *kultur* and explained his own artistic and political commitments, which he presented as an alternative set of cultural values that could help to save a threatened civilisation. In the 1920s in several books – most notably in *Parade's End* (1924–28) – he explored different individuals' experience of the war; he also tried to understand its political implications, and he defended an ideal of international fraternity, which he hoped could be achieved by means of cultural exchange. (He conceived the *transatlantic review*, the literary periodical he edited in Paris in

---

[7]   Quoted in Saunders, *Ford Madox Ford*, II, p. 56.

[8]   Ford Madox Ford, *Return to Yesterday*, ed. Bill Hutchings (Manchester: Carcanet Press, 1999), p. 318.

[9]   Ford, *Return to Yesterday*, p. 65.

[10]   Ford Madox Ford, *The Good Soldier*, second edition, ed. Martin Stannard (New York: Norton, 2012), p. 102. All further references are to this edition.

[11]   Ford, *Return to Yesterday*, pp. 323–4.

1924, as an organ for fostering understanding between nations.) Finally, in the late 1920s and 1930s, Ford became more critical of industrialism and capitalism, which he had always actively disliked. During this period he outlined an agrarian ideal of self-sufficient and small-scale farming; attacked fascist totalitarianism; condemned anti-Semitism; argued in favour of an independent Jewish state in the Middle East; and articulated a modest form of quietist anarchism in such texts as *Provence* (1935) and *Great Trade Route* (1937).

It is striking how often in his pre-war writings Ford refers to a loss of cultural co-ordinates, which, he contends, makes it difficult for the critical observer to know what to think and how to act. Again and again, Ford refers to a generalised sense of bewilderment. In *Ancient Lights* (1911), for example, he is struck by the fragmentation of daily life and worries that people 'are losing more and more the sense of a whole, the feeling of a grand design, of the co-ordination of all Nature in one great architectonic scheme'.[12] In *The Critical Attitude* (1911) he writes plaintively: 'We have to watch modern life sweeping away the traditions that we love, the places that we consider hallowed; we have to consider that it is blowing away us ourselves as if we were no more than a little dust'.[13] For Ford, modernity was an unstoppable force; it transformed the fabric of everyday life and took away the signposts that enabled individuals to orientate themselves in social space. Literary Impressionism, unsurprisingly, was seen by Ford as the best technique for registering the subsequent sense of befuddlement. As Dowell tellingly puts it in *The Good Soldier*: 'the whole world for me is like spots of colour on an immense canvas. Perhaps if it weren't so I should have something to catch hold of now' (p. 17).

What particularly troubled Ford in the 1890s and early 1900s was the way in which human life seemed to be becoming more mechanised. The ongoing centralisation of power brought with it a host of specialists, professionals and bureaucrats, all of whom (though not always wittingly) conspired to make society increasingly commercial, materialistic, and standardised. In Ford's eyes, it seemed that human relations were becoming ever more atomised and that political life was being increasingly dominated by short-term pragmatic considerations. The Boer War was a kind of negative touchstone for Ford, in this respect, since it marked a break between two different social worlds. It was a 'never to be sufficiently accursed war', which set 'an iron door between the past and the present'.[14] Since the Boer War 'the whole tone of England' seemed 'to have entirely changed, principles having died out of politics, even as the spirit of artistry has died out amongst the practitioners of the arts'.[15] This is, of course, Impressionism at work. Ford isn't making a literal claim about the consequences of the Boer War but is

---

[12]   Ford Madox Ford, *Ancient Lights and Certain New Reflections: Being the Memories of a Young Man* (London: Chapman and Hall, 1911), p. 62.

[13]   Ford Madox Ford, *The Critical Attitude* (London: Duckworth, 1911), p. 9.

[14]   Ford, *Ancient Lights*, p. 175.

[15]   Ford, *Ancient Lights*, pp. 154–5.

giving us his sense of a major shift in the nature of English social and political life from the late 1890s onwards.

What, then, could be done? Ford was no politician, as he regularly insisted. Furthermore, his conviction that literature should not be used as a reformist tool meant that he wasn't about to invite writers to take up the cudgels against a nation-state that appeared unable to resist the social and political changes that disturbed him. His response, rather, was to argue that the 'critical attitude' (clear-sighted, dispassionate thought) and the arts could, by virtue of their non-partisan approach to contemporary problems, help people to make sense of the world that was falling into shape around them. This was a political argument. Ford was insisting on the importance of the arts to a society that was in his view becoming ever more technocratic. For Ford, 'life is a thing so complicated that only in the mirror of the arts can we have a crystallised view or any vicarious experience at all – if this be granted it must follow that only from the arts can any safety for the future of the State be found'.[16] Ford believed that the arts were inherently valuable, but he also maintained that they were socially useful since they helped individuals to understand the world they lived in. As he put it in his study *Henry James*: 'We stand today, in the matter of political theories, naked to the wind and blind to the sunlight'; the writer's task was 'to give us the very matter upon which we shall build the theories of the new body politic'.[17]

In the years before the war Ford wrote a number of satires in which he mocked those who believed they were capable of building a new body politic by elaborating abstract theories and then assuming they could be put into practice. Assorted Fabians, simple-lifers and garden city planners were mocked for thinking that they could transform society from their studies or offices. The artificial and degraded nature of English society was a major Fordian concern at this time. He was preoccupied with the numerous ways in which far-reaching changes were being concealed by a deceptive social facade. *Mr. Fleight* (1913), for example, registers Ford's anger at the corrupt nature of contemporary politics. Enraged by the ubiquity of the plutocrats whose rise Ford had identified in *Ancient Lights*, a disgusted onlooker creates a puppet-like proxy (Mr Fleight) in order to demonstrate how power can be gained through advertising and sloganeering, which package political candidates into commodities that are then 'bought' by a gullible populace. The public sphere in this novel is reduced to a 'giddy whirl of fashion and corruption and inquests and entertainments'.[18] Real politics cease to exist in this degraded environment.

The Good Soldier takes these ideas further. This text, Ford's greatest Impressionist *tour-de-force*, deals with adultery and repression among the upper classes, but it is also a 'Condition of England' novel that explores the social and political implications of the events it describes. The disaster that overtakes the

---

16   Ford, *The Critical Attitude*, p. 29.
17   Ford, *Henry James*, pp. 47, 48.
18   Ford Madox Ford, *Mr. Fleight* (London: Howard Latimer, 1913), pp. 124–5, 254.

novel's two couples is given a symbolic resonance when it is compared to 'the sack of a city or the falling to pieces of a people' (p. 11). But the people who are being destroyed are gradually shown to be deeply flawed. Far from being the perfect exemplars of their social class, they are revealed to be its damaged products. The novel registers a conflict between a practical, economising and efficient spirit associated with a rising bourgeoisie and an impractical, generous and philanthropic 'feudal' mentality associated with a disappearing Toryism. This is a battle between individualism and collectivism: on the one hand, we have the view that community depends on long-standing bonds and reciprocal duties, and on the other hand we have the belief that relationships are rights-based contracts between isolated monads. *The Good Soldier* explores the process of standardisation with which Ford was concerned in *The Critical Attitude* and *Ancient Lights*. As the novel's narrator puts it: 'Edward and Nancy found themselves steam-rollered out, and Leonora survives, the perfectly normal type, married to a man who is rather like a rabbit' (p. 158). All this, he observes bitterly, works out 'for the greatest good of the body politic' (p. 158).

Ford's two propaganda books are interesting responses to the First World War because, inasmuch as they are critical of Prussian *kultur*, they also call England to reform so that the country can, as it were, realise its best self. For Ford, Prussianism was opposed to true culture, which entailed a broad education, familiarity with the arts and sciences, knowledge of history, skill in the art of conversation, respect for the opinions of others, and belief in an affable spirit of amateurism, as opposed to a rigid attitude of hard-headed professionalism. All this went to make up the truly cultured individual – the person who was at once deeply informed about the world and gracefully tolerant of others. But Prussianism, Ford argued, extolled materialism, commerce, obedience to rules and authority, militarism, specialisation, and nationalism. The dominance of this way of thinking was for Ford the logical outcome of the Franco-Prussian War and of the rise of plutocracy on British soil. Thus Ford: 'The manners of the "Park Lane set" are of Prussian origin. The war of 1870, even more than the other great flail of humanity, the Great Exhibition of 1851, riveted on this country the worship of wealth, the cult of ostentation, and the never-ceasing restlessness in search of wealth'.[19] England isn't some kind of positive touchstone here; Ford is attacking his country for its apparent willingness to embrace 'Prussian' materialistic values. *When Blood is Their Argument* certainly offers a fierce indictment of Prussianism as Ford conceived it, but it is also an anti-English book insofar as it suggests that his own nation is more 'Prussian' than it realises. Ford thus countered Prussian monomania with civilised gentility. His desideratum was 'amateurism in politics, the arts, the universities, and every department of life', because he was convinced

---

[19]   Ford Madox Ford, *When Blood is Their Argument: An Analysis of Prussian Culture* (London: Hodder and Stoughton, 1915), p. 300.

that a choice had to be made between 'organised, materialist egoism' and 'the all-round sportsmanship of altruistic culture'.[20]

Parade's End considers what happens to an individual who upholds the values Ford espouses in *When Blood is Their Argument*. Some critics have read this novel sequence as a eulogy for an organic way of life and a quasi-feudal social order that is being crushed out of existence by post-war plutocracy. On this reading, Ford is a straightforward conservative whose politics can be aligned with those of his protagonist Christopher Tietjens – a landowning squire who describes himself as 'a Tory of such an extinct type' that he might be taken to be the 'last megatherium'.[21] Such readings of *Parade's End* ignore the ways in which Tietjens is ironised as a public-school-educated member of the governing classes who is trapped in a patriarchal view of male-female relations and a hierarchical conception of class. *Parade's End* in fact suggests that Tietjens's gentry politics are based on fantasy. His pre-war vision of 'God's England' as a pastoral idyll is, for example, immediately undermined by his recognition that the political reality of the nation is actually very different: '"By God," he said, "Church! State! Army! H.M. Ministry: H.M. Opposition: H.M. City Man. . . . All the governing class! All rotten! Thank God we've got a navy! . . . But perhaps that's rotten too!"'[22] The issue of governance displaces the question of inheritance here; *Parade's End* suggests that the ruling elite is corrupt and that the state is protected by military force.

Two lines of thought feed into Tietjens's negative view of the way his country is being run: firstly, he draws on the belief that society should be stratified according to class; secondly, he buys into organicist understandings of the relationship between class and the land. In a strict social hierarchy, all classes have a role to play in agriculture, from the landowners at the top to the lowliest peasants at the bottom; these classes – despite the obvious social and economic inequalities between them – are thought to co-exist in mutually beneficial relationships that are based on reciprocal duties. Tietjens's position, in other words, is that the social, economic and political changes associated with the early decades of the twentieth century must be reversed. But this longing to turn the clock back is destabilised in *Parade's End*. Taken as a whole, the novel sequence depicts the Tietjens family as isolated and out of touch; it's not just that their values have no purchase on modern life but also that they belong to an exhausted class that has been born out of time. A sense of fatigue hangs over this family; they symbolise the decay of an entire class. 'The lady had called them a corrupt and effete aristocracy', Mark Tietjens reflects. 'They were probably not corrupt but certainly, regarded as

---

[20]   Ford, *When Blood is Their Argument*, p. 318.

[21]   Ford Madox Ford, *No More Parades*, ed. Joseph Wiesenfarth (Manchester: Carcanet Press, 2011), p. 235.

[22]   Ford Madox Ford, *Some Do Not . . .*, ed. Max Saunders (Manchester: Carcanet Press, 2010), pp. 133–4.

landowners, they were effete [...]. They were simply bored at the contemplation of that terrific nuisance'.[23]

The Tietjens brothers repeatedly assert that though the times have changed, the land has not. In doing so, they draw on a long established language of national pastoral, which invokes the idea of a 'deep' England: 'The land had not changed. . . . There were still the deep beech-woods making groves beside the ploughlands and the rooks rising lazily as the plough came towards them. The land had not changed. . . . Well, the breed had not changed' (p. 115). But it is made clear in *Parade's End* that this vision is inseparable from the hierarchical social order that sustains the Tietjens's privileged way of life. Valentine Wannop muses to herself that 'England with its pleasant, green comeliness would go on breeding' men like Tietjens with loyal retainers 'to look after them' (p. 179). This rather gives the game away: it assumes that such men exist primarily to serve their masters but at the same time it acknowledges that the system of landed property that the Tietjens brothers want to maintain depends on such service. As one of the novel's working men puts it: 'It is all very well to say this is a land fit for whatever the word is that stands for simple folk. But they have the police and the keepers in their hands, and your cottages and [your] livings' (p. 51). *Parade's End* exposes Tietjens's quasi-feudal Toryism as a myth that seeks to preserve an inegalitarian society. This feudalism, moreover, is depicted as out of place in a plutocratic, oligarchical and rationalized post-war world. As Elliott B. Gose puts it, Tietjens himself eventually realises that all 'the rules which govern society' are 'being destroyed' and that 'a Tory gentleman is an anachronism in the twentieth century'.[24]

Ford published an essay titled 'The Passing of Toryism' in 1926, in the middle of the period in which he was writing *Parade's End*. The essay makes it clear that he didn't believe for one minute that Tietjens's politics were viable in the post-war world. Ford describes Toryism as above all 'a purely country frame of mind' that was 'at its best a very beautiful one'.[25] His sympathies for this mentality are obvious. But he argues that industrialism destroyed Toryism as a practical form of politics in the nineteenth century, with terrible consequences: 'When the direction of English affairs passed out of the hands of the Tory landowners into those of the big manufacturers, bankers, bill discounters, wire pullers, caucus leaders, labor leaders and the rest of the demagogues under whom the world suffers, the real disaster to the world – and not to England alone! – was that individualism became almost impossible and standardization almost inevitable'.[26] By invoking 'individualism' here Ford is emphasising the need for society to comprise a wide variety of persons (however eccentric they might be) if it wants to be truly

---

[23]   Ford Madox Ford, *Last Post*, ed. Paul Skinner (Manchester: Carcanet Press, 2011), p. 90. All further references are to this edition.

[24]   Elliott B. Gose, Jr., 'Reality to Romance: A Study of Ford's *Parade's End*', *College English*, 17.8 (May 1956), 447.

[25]   Ford Madox Ford, 'The Passing of Toryism', *McNaught's Monthly*, 5.6 (June 1926), 175.

[26]   Ford, 'The Passing of Toryism', p. 176.

cosmopolitan. Despite its cultural philistinism, Toryism in Ford's view was tolerant of human diversity because it didn't seek to mould human beings into standardised types. It 'does need all sorts to make a world', Ford argues, 'and now that Toryism is gone something will have to take its place'.[27]

In his own modest way, Ford tried to contribute to the creation of this 'something' through his writings in the 1920s. His brief editorship of the *transatlantic review* is particularly important in this respect. The *transatlantic review* lasted for twelve months – January 1924 to December 1924. In that period it approached the heights of the *English Review*, which Ford had edited in 1909 to great acclaim. Ford's announcement of the new journal's objectives reveals that the *transatlantic* was to have 'only two purposes, the major one, the purely literary, conducing to the minor, the disinterestedly social. The first is that of widening the field in which the younger writers of the day can find publication, the second that of introducing into international politics a note more genial than that which almost universally prevails'. There was a clear political agenda here. For in seeking to do away with national literatures – 'there will be only Literature' – Ford was looking to create 'a league of nations [that] no diplomatists shall destroy, for into its comity no representatives of commercial interests or delimitators of frontiers can break'.[28] He was suggesting that literature, and the arts more generally, had the capacity to transcend national boundaries and in doing so to foster international unity. He developed this view in his 'Stocktaking' articles in the *transatlantic*. These informal editorials advanced the argument that literature and the arts should contribute to the creation of an imagined international community that transcended political boundaries. As he had argued in *The Critical Attitude* and *Ancient Lights*, Ford maintained that more than any other form of human endeavour the arts enabled people to understand and to tolerate each other. The *transatlantic* didn't aim to promote any particular aesthetic line but to publish the best writing its editor could find, since he was convinced that all good literature (of whatever kind) worked as a cultural leaven. Revealingly, Ford observed in his closing editorial that he had sought 'to promote greater cordiality in international relationships so that the arts might work in a better atmosphere'.[29] The *transatlantic* had been engaged in a politically non-partisan project of cultural reconstruction.

As Ford approached the end of his life in the 1930s he became ever more troubled by the seemingly inexorable spread of capitalism. During this decade we find him mounting a passionate defence of small agrarian communities left free to organise themselves as they wished. Although there are links between his thinking in the 1930s and the Toryism he had long admired, works such as *Provence* and *Great Trade Route* suggest that he was distancing himself from Toryism's association with rigid social hierarchies. These works see him arguing in favour

---

[27]   Ford, 'The Passing of Toryism', p. 176.
[28]   Quoted in Bernard J. Poli, *Ford Madox Ford and the Transatlantic Review* (Syracuse: Syracuse University Press, 1967), pp. 38–9.
[29]   Ford Madox Ford, 'Stocktaking II', *transatlantic review*, 2 (Dec. 1924), 684.

of an ideal of social co-operation that, he hoped, might be realised through loosely federated but always independent communities devoted to small-scale farming. He explained his position in a 1935 letter: 'I live about the world with no politics at all except the belief – which I share with Lenin – that the only thing that can save the world is the abolition of all national feelings and the prevailing of the Small Producer – and the Latin tradition of clear-sightedness as to what one means oneself'.[30] Ford suggests in *Great Trade Route* that the 'best' kind of society is a form of feudal 'type-civilization'.[31] It becomes clear, however, that Ford isn't arguing in favour of a stratified society comprising rich landowners and poor peasants but is defending a distributist view of social organisation in which big landed estates are replaced by small farms. A key touchstone throughout the text is Thomas Jefferson. And Jefferson is important to Ford because he represents an ideal vision of citizenship that combines a belief in self-sufficient farming with a commitment to public service and civic duty. So when Ford extols the virtues of old Virginian farms he does so because he sees them as viable alternatives to industrialisation and to the mechanisation of agriculture; the latter, he argues, depends on an instrumental view of the relationship between land and labour, which alienates workers from what they produce.

Some of these ideas are indeed Jeffersonian. There are also connections here to the American Southern Agrarians, especially to those Agrarians who took inspiration from Jefferson. But Ford was no less strongly influenced by anarchist thought, and he was deeply sceptical about the Agrarian view of American history.[32] His emphasis on small, self-sufficient, and federated farming communities has affinities with the writings of Proudhon and Kropotkin. Ford's hatred of legal systems based on property rights was also anarchist in tenor. In *Great Trade Route*, he wrote: 'Customs are more satisfactory than laws because all the citizens or subjects of a political unit have had a hand in evolving them. Laws made by legislatures have the almost universal defect that they are inspired by the passion of property'. Ford also claimed that his politics were based on the principle of 'no-law' and, echoing Proudhon, he averred that 'property – above all the sense of, the passion for, impersonal property – is the source of all evil'.[33] What he wanted, Ford declared, was simply 'to belong to a nation of Small Producers, with some local, but no national feeling at all. Without boundaries, or armed forces, or customs, or government'.[34] Ford was combining radical Toryism with leftist anarchism, so it shouldn't surprise us that he invokes communism and conservatism together. 'I don't write as a communist – or that may possibly be reactionary', he claimed, before adding that 'if the Russian Soviet really puts its trust in hammers and

[30]   Ford to Julia Ford (11 Sept. 1935), *Letters of Ford Madox Ford*, ed. Richard M. Ludwig (Princeton: Princeton University Press, 1965), p. 238.

[31]   Ford Madox Ford, *Great Trade Route* (London: George Allen and Unwin, 1937), p. 320.

[32]   Saunders, *Ford Madox Ford*, II, p. 325.

[33]   Ford, *Great Trade Route*, pp. 206, 204, 225.

[34]   Ford, *Great Trade Route*, p. 86.

sickles I would willingly say that I was for the U.S.S.R. right or wrong and let it go at that. Since, putting its trust in the monstrous collections of wheels that are the Machine, it uses those tools merely as emblems on its banner [...] I don't say anything of the sort'.[35]

Great Trade Route is another of Ford's attempts to imagine an alternative politics, to posit a kind of counter-factual ideal as a way of encouraging his readers to look again at the way in which the world they live in is organised. As Saunders puts it, such texts seem 'to be offering radical political solutions while knowing quite well that they are a lost cause'.[36] This is true, but we need to ask why *Great Trade Route* operates in this way. It does so, I think, because Ford wants us to see that his unsystematic philosophy of quietist anarchism is the direct opposite of the despotisms that were dominating European political life in the mid-1930s. Hitler is a constant presence in *Great Trade Route*, and the threat of fascism is placed centre-stage at the end of the book when Ford refers to the Italian invasion of Abyssinia. Ford knows what he and his fellow Europeans are up against: '"We shall put up against a wall – and shoot – all Jews, all Catholics, all Communists" [...] The Nazi Professor, slim and dark, speaks in the smoking-room after midnight. . . . "Up against a wall. . . . All that Vermin!"'.[37] Ford's critique of fascism in *Great Trade Route* is inseparable from his attacks on slavery in the American south and on European imperialism, which he presents as the root cause of the First World War and, by implication, as the necessary back-story to the rise of Italian and German fascism.[38] Against fascism he pits an ethics of gentle persuasion. The very writing style of *Great Trade Route* offers a quiet rebuke to the monomaniacal ravings of the Fascist dictators who were on the verge of destroying the Europe Ford loved and which he had done so much to conserve.

In one of the last letters he wrote before he died Ford addressed himself to the plight of the Jews. He expressed his belief in the desperate need for 'a National Jewish Republic in Palestine' that would be 'represented at the League of Nations' and that would thereby provide Jewish people with a haven at a time when atrocities were being committed against them 'in every nation whose territory lies between the Baltic and the Black Seas'. Writing that the amelioration of 'the world condition of the Jews [...] must exist in the heart of every civilized man',[39] Ford denounced the British policy of appeasement. Chamberlain, he argued, was regarded by the American public as 'a dictator with no one to control him, who, at the bidding of the totalitarian dictators, has delivered infinite thousands of innocent humanity to a certain butchery'.[40] These were prophetic words. Ford sensed what was coming. He was perhaps fortunate not to live through the Second

---

[35] Ford, *Great Trade Route*, p. 225.

[36] Saunders, *Ford Madox Ford*, II, p. 505.

[37] Ford, *Great Trade Route*, p. 52.

[38] Ford, *Great Trade Route*, p. 132.

[39] Ford to The Rt. Hon. Malcolm MacDonald (27 Feb. 1939), *Letters of Ford Madox Ford*, pp. 311–12.

[40] Ford to The Rt. Hon. Malcolm MacDonald, p. 313.

World War. He had often been critical of England for its cultural philistinism, its materialism and its political dishonesty. But he was truly shocked by Munich, which he thought would isolate Britain in the conflict to come. More than this, Chamberlain's actions exposed his country to obloquy and threatened to place it, at a time of terrible historical crisis, outside that comity of nations that Ford had always tried to promote: 'If a nation earn the detestation and contempt of the public conscience of the world, it shall find no one to come to its assistance in the moment of extremity. And, living as I do amongst the class that forms public opinion in this country and in France, I am, I take the liberty to imagine, more aware than you how near we have already come to having earned the opprobrium and contempt of the civilized world'.[41]

---

[41]   Ford to The Rt. Hon. Malcolm MacDonald, p. 314.

Guide to Further Reading

Having now read *An Introduction to Ford Madox Ford*, you might want to do some further research into Ford's life and works.

This guide is split into three sections:

- 'Writing By Ford'
- 'Ford's Life'
- 'Writing On Ford'

I. Writing By Ford

Further to the works discussed in the previous chapters, there is an interesting and useful collection of Ford's articles, essays, literary portraits and reviews: *Critical Essays*, ed. Max Saunders and Richard Stang (Manchester: Carcanet Press, 2002). The earlier *Critical Writings of Ford Madox Ford*, ed. Frank MacShane (Lincoln: University of Nebraska Press, 1964), includes several major essays, particularly 'On Impressionism' (1914) and 'Techniques' (1935); for those two essays, see also *The Good Soldier*, second edition, ed. Martin Stannard (New York: Norton, 2012). *The Ford Madox Ford Reader*, ed. Sondra J. Stang (London: Paladin, 1987), includes selections from Ford's fiction, critical and other non-fictional writing, and letters. For a selection of Ford's writing about the First World War (reminiscences, short stories, prefaces and other pieces), see *War Prose*, ed. Max Saunders (Manchester: Carcanet Press, 1999).

If you are interested in Ford's letters, *Letters of Ford Madox Ford*, ed. Richard M. Ludwig (Princeton: Princeton University Press, 1965), is the collection scholars usually look at first because it covers the whole of Ford's life. There are also: *Pound/Ford: The Story of a Literary Friendship: The Correspondence Between Ezra Pound and Ford Madox Ford and Their Writings About Each Other*, ed. Brita Lindberg-Seyersted (New York: New Directions, 1982); *The Correspondence of Ford Madox Ford and Stella Bowen*, ed. Sondra J. Stang and Karen Cochran (Bloomington: Indiana University Press, 1993); and *A Literary Friendship: Correspondence Between Caroline Gordon and Ford Madox Ford*, ed. Brita Lindberg-Seyersted (Knoxville: University of Tennessee Press, 1999).

A full list of Ford's books can be found on the Ford Madox Ford Society's website: http://www.fordmadoxfordsociety.org/.

II. Ford's Life

As is probably now apparent, the most comprehensive biography is Max Saunders's *Ford Madox Ford: A Dual Life*, 2 volumes (Oxford: Oxford University Press, 1996); a paperback edition was published in 2012. But you still might find useful material in:

Goldring, Douglas, *The Last Pre-Raphaelite: A Record of the Life and Writings of Ford Madox Ford* (London: Macdonald, 1948); published in the USA as *Trained for Genius* (New York: Dutton, 1949).
Judd, Alan, *Ford Madox Ford* (London: Collins, 1990).
MacShane, Frank, *The Life and Work of Ford Madox Ford* (London: Routledge and Kegan Paul, 1965).
Mizener, Arthur, *The Saddest Story: A Biography of Ford Madox Ford* (New York: Harper and Row, 1971; London: Bodley Head, 1972).
Moser, Thomas C., *The Life in the Fiction of Ford Madox Ford* (Princeton: Princeton University Press, 1980).
Wiesenfarth, Joseph, *Ford Madox Ford and the Regiment of Women: Violet Hunt, Jean Rhys, Stella Bowen, Janice Biala* (Madison: University of Wisconsin Press, 2005).

III. Writing On Ford

Hundreds of articles, chapters, essays and books have been written on Ford. This list is a selection of the books and chapters that we think you will find particularly useful when beginning your research. Other secondary sources are listed in this volume's bibliography and a comprehensive list of works published from 2000 onwards can be found on the Ford Society's website: http://www.fordmadoxfordsociety.org/. Earlier works are listed in David Dow Harvey's *Ford Madox Ford: 1873–1939: A Bibliography of Works and Criticism* (Princeton: Princeton University Press, 1962) and Max Saunders's 'Ford Madox Ford: Further Bibliographies', *English Literature in Transition 1880–1920*, 43.2 (2000), 131–205.

Armstrong, Paul B., *The Challenge of Bewilderment: Understanding and Representation in James, Conrad, and Ford* (Ithaca: Cornell University Press, 1987).
Brown, Dennis, and Jenny Plastow (eds), *Ford Madox Ford and Englishness*, International Ford Madox Ford Studies 6 (Amsterdam: Rodopi, 2006).
Calderaro, Michela A., *A Silent New World: Ford Madox Ford's Parade's End* (Bologna: CLUEB, 1993).
Cassell, Richard A., *Ford Madox Ford: A Study of His Novels* (Baltimore: Johns Hopkins Press, 1962).
Cassell, Richard A. (ed.), *Ford Madox Ford: Modern Judgements* (Basingstoke: Macmillan, 1972).

Cassell, Richard A. (ed.), *Critical Essays on Ford Madox Ford* (Boston: G.K. Hall, 1987).

Chantler, Ashley, and Rob Hawkes (eds), *Ford's Madox Ford's Parade's End: The First World War, Culture, and Modernity*, International Ford Madox Ford Studies 13 (Amsterdam: Rodopi, 2014).

Chantler, Ashley, and Rob Hawkes (eds), *War and the Mind: Ford Madox Ford's Parade's End, Modernism, and Psychology* (Edinburgh: Edinburgh University Press, 2015).

Colombino, Laura, *Ford Madox Ford: Vision, Visuality and Writing* (Oxford: Peter Lang, 2008).

Colombino, Laura (ed.), *Ford Madox Ford and Visual Culture*, International Ford Madox Ford Studies 8 (Amsterdam: Rodopi, 2009).

Colombino, Laura, and Max Saunders (eds), *The Edwardian Ford Madox Ford*, International Ford Madox Ford Studies 12 (Amsterdam: Rodopi, 2009).

Fowles, Anthony, *Ford Madox Ford: The Principal Fiction* (London: Greenwich Exchange, 2002).

Frayn, Andrew, *Writing Disenchantment: British First World War Prose, 1914–30* (Manchester: Manchester University Press, 2014).

Gąsiorek, Andrzej, and Daniel Moore (eds), *Ford Madox Ford: Literary Networks and Cultural Transformations*, International Ford Madox Ford Studies 7 (Amsterdam: Rodopi, 2008).

Gordon, Ambrose, *The Invisible Tent: The War Novels of Ford Madox Ford* (Austin: University of Texas Press, 1964).

Green, Robert, *Ford Madox Ford: Prose and Politics* (Cambridge: Cambridge University Press, 1981).

Hampson, Robert, and Tony Davenport (eds), *Ford Madox Ford: A Reappraisal*, International Ford Madox Ford Studies 1 (Amsterdam: Rodopi, 2002).

Hampson, Robert, and Max Saunders (eds), *Ford Madox Ford's Modernity*, International Ford Madox Ford Studies 2 (Amsterdam: Rodopi, 2003).

Harding, Jason (ed.), *Ford Madox Ford, Modernist Magazines and Editing*, International Ford Madox Ford Studies 9 (Amsterdam: Rodopi, 2010).

Haslam, Sara, *Fragmenting Modernism: Ford Madox Ford, the Novel and the Great War* (Manchester: Manchester University Press, 2002).

Haslam, Sara (ed.), *Ford Madox Ford and the City*, International Ford Madox Ford Studies 4 (Amsterdam: Rodopi, 2005).

Haslam, Sara, and Seamus O'Malley (eds), *Ford Madox Ford and America*, International Ford Madox Ford Studies 11 (Amsterdam: Rodopi, 2012).

Hawkes, Rob, *Ford Madox Ford and the Misfit Moderns: Edwardian Fiction and the First World War* (Basingstoke: Palgrave Macmillan, 2012).

Lemarchal, Dominique, and Claire Davison-Pégon (eds), *Ford Madox Ford, France and Provence*, International Ford Madox Ford Studies 10 (Amsterdam: Rodopi, 2011).

MacShane, Frank (ed.), *Ford Madox Ford: The Critical Heritage* (London: Routledge and Kegan Paul, 1972).

Matz, Jesse, *Literary Impressionism and Modernist Aesthetics* (Cambridge: Cambridge University Press, 2001).

Meixner, John A., *Ford Madox Ford's Novels: A Critical Study* (Minneapolis: University of Minnesota Press, 1962).

O'Malley, Seamus, *Making History New: Modernism and Historical Narrative* (New York: Oxford University Press, 2014).

Saunders, Max, and Sara Haslam (eds), *Ford Madox Ford's The Good Soldier: Centenary Essays*, International Ford Madox Ford Studies 14 (Leiden: Brill / Rodopi, 2015).

Skinner, Paul (ed.), *Ford Madox Ford's Literary Contacts*, International Ford Madox Ford Studies 6 (Amsterdam: Rodopi, 2007).

Snitow, Ann Barr, *Ford Madox Ford and the Voice of Uncertainty* (Baton Rouge: Louisiana State University Press, 1984).

Stang, Sondra J., *Ford Madox Ford* (New York: Frederick Ungar, 1977).

Stang, Sondra J. (ed.), *The Presence of Ford Madox Ford* (Philadelphia: University of Pennsylvania Press, 1981).

Wiesenfarth, Joseph (ed.), *History and Representation in Ford Madox Ford's Writings*, International Ford Madox Ford Studies 3 (Amsterdam: Rodopi, 2004).

Bibliography

Adams, James Eli, *Dandies and Desert Saints: Styles of Victorian Manhood* (Ithaca: Cornell University Press, 1995).

Adorno, Theodor W., *Notes to Literature*, 2 vols, ed. Rolf Tiedeman, trans. Shierry Weber Nicholson (New York: Columbia University Press, 1991).

Anderson, Benedict, *Imagined Communities: Reflections on the Origin and Spread of Nationalism* (London: Verso, 1991).

Anon, [Untitled], *New York Times Book Review* (7 Mar. 1915), 86; reprinted in Ford Madox Ford, *The Good Soldier*, second edition, ed. Martin Stannard (New York: Norton, 2012), pp. 233–4.

Anon, [Untitled], *Boston Transcript*, 17 Mar. 1915, 24; reprinted in Ford Madox Ford, *The Good Soldier*, second edition, ed. Martin Stannard (New York: Norton, 2012), pp. 234–5.

Anon, [Untitled], *Independent* (US), 22 Mar. 1915, 432; reprinted in Ford Madox Ford, *The Good Soldier*, second edition, ed. Martin Stannard (New York: Norton, 2012), p. 235.

Anon, [Untitled], *Times Literary Supplement* (25 Mar. 1915), 103; reprinted in Ford Madox Ford, *The Good Soldier*, second edition, ed. Martin Stannard (New York: Norton, 2012), p. 235.

Anon, [Untitled], *Observer*, 28 Mar. 1915, 5; reprinted in Ford Madox Ford, *The Good Soldier*, second edition, ed. Martin Stannard (New York: Norton, 2012), p. 236.

Anon, 'The Election: Prime Minister on the Issues', *The Times*, 25 Nov. 1918, 9.

Anon, 'Mr. Lloyd George on His Task', *The Times*, 25 Nov. 1918, 13.

Antliff, Mark, and Vivien Greene (eds), *The Vorticists: Manifesto for a Modern World* (London: Tate, 2010).

Ardis, Ann, *Modernism and Cultural Conflict, 1880–1922* (Cambridge: Cambridge University Press, 2008).

Armstrong, Tim, *Modernism: A Cultural History* (Cambridge, MA: Polity, 2005).

Attridge, John, 'Steadily and Whole: Ford Madox Ford and Modernist Sociology', *Modernism/modernity*, 15.2 (2008), 297–316.

Aughey, Arthur, and Christine Berberich (eds), *These Englands: A Conversation on National Identity* (Manchester: Manchester University Press, 2011).

Bachner, Sally, '"The Seeing Eye": Detection, Perception and Erotic Knowledge in *The Good Soldier*', in Max Saunders and Robert Hampson (eds), *Ford Madox Ford's Modernity*, International Ford Madox Ford Studies 2 (Amsterdam: Rodopi, 2003), pp. 103–16.

Barnes, Julian, 'The Saddest Story', *Guardian Review*, 7 June 2008, 2–3; reprinted in Ford Madox Ford, *The Good Soldier*, second edition, ed. Martin Stannard (New York: Norton, 2012), pp. 418–21.

Barthes, Roland, *S/Z: An Essay*, trans. Richard Miller (New York: Hill and Wang, 1974).

Batchelor, John, *The Edwardian Novelists* (London: Duckworth, 1982).

Baudelaire, Charles, from 'The Painter of Modern Life', in Vassiliki Kolocotroni, Jane Goldman and Olga Taxidou (eds), *Modernism: An Anthology of Sources and Documents* (Edinburgh: Edinburgh University Press, 1998), pp. 102–8.

Baxter, Katherine Isobel, *Joseph Conrad and the Swan Song of Romance* (Aldershot: Ashgate, 2010).

Becquet, Alexandra, 'Modernity, Shock and Cinema: The Visual Aesthetics of Ford Madox Ford's *Parade's End*', in Laura Colombino (ed.), *Ford Madox Ford and Visual Culture*, International Ford Madox Ford Studies 8 (Amsterdam: Rodopi, 2009), pp. 191–204.

Belsey, Catherine, 'Reading Cultural History', in Tamsin Spargo (ed.), *Reading the Past* (Basingstoke: Palgrave, 2000), pp. 10–17.

Bender, Todd, *Literary Impressionism in Jean Rhys, Ford Madox Ford, Joseph Conrad, and Charlotte Brontë* (New York: Garland, 1997).

Benjamin, Walter, *Illuminations*, ed. Hannah Arendt, trans. Harry Zohn (New York: Harcourt, Brace and World, 1968).

Bennett, Arnold, *The Old Wives' Tale* (London: Penguin, 2007).

Berberich, Christine, 'A Modernist Elegy to the Gentleman? Englishness and the Idea of the Gentleman in Ford's *The Good Soldier*', in Dennis Brown and Jenny Plastow (eds), *Ford Madox Ford and Englishness*, International Ford Madox Ford Studies 5 (Amsterdam: Rodopi, 2006), pp. 195–209.

Berberich, Christine, '"Isn't This Worth Fighting For?" The First World War and the (Ab)Uses of the Pastoral Tradition', in Petra Rau (ed.), *Conflict, Nationhood and Corporeality in Modern Literature* (Basingstoke: Palgrave Macmillan, 2010), pp. 26–45.

Berman, Marshall, *All That is Solid Melts Into Air: The Experience of Modernity* (London: Verso, 2010).

Bertens, Hans, *Literary Theory: The Basics* (London: Routledge, 2010).

Blunden, Edmund, *Undertones of War* (London: Cobden-Sanderson, 1950).

Boulter, Jonathan, '"After . . . Armageddon": Trauma and History in Ford Madox Ford's *No Enemy*', in Joseph Weisenfarth (ed.), *History and Representation in Ford Madox Ford's Writings*, International Ford Madox Ford Studies 3 (Amsterdam: Rodopi, 2004), pp. 77–90.

Bowen, Stella, *Drawn from Life* (London: Virago, 1984).

Bradbury, Malcolm, and James McFarlane (eds), *Modernism: A Guide to European Literature 1890–1930* (Harmondsworth: Penguin, 1991).

Brasme, Isabelle, 'Between Impressionism and Modernism: *Some Do Not . . .*, a Poetics of the *Entre-deux*', in Andrzej Gąsiorek and Daniel Moore (eds), *Ford*

Madox Ford: Literary Networks and Cultural Transformations, International Ford Madox Ford Studies 7 (Amsterdam: Rodopi, 2008), pp. 189–99.

Brasme, Isabelle, '"A caricature of his own voice": Ford and Self-Editing in *Parade's End*', in Jason Harding (ed.), *Ford Madox Ford, Modernist Magazines and Editing*, International Ford Madox Ford Studies 9 (Amsterdam: Rodopi, 2010), pp. 243–52.

Brasme, Isabelle, 'Articulations of Femininity in *Parade's End*', in Ashley Chantler and Rob Hawkes (eds), *Ford Madox Ford's Parade's End: The First World War, Culture, and Modernity*, International Ford Madox Ford Studies 13 (Amsterdam: Rodopi, 2014), pp. 173–85.

Brebach, Raymond, *Joseph Conrad, Ford Madox Ford, and the Making of Romance* (Ann Arbor: UMI Research Press, 1985).

Brebach, Raymond, 'Ford's *Joseph Conrad: A Personal Remembrance*: A Reappraisal', *Conradian*, 12.2 (1987), 166–74.

Brice, Xavier, 'Ford Madox Ford and the Composition of *Nostromo*', *Conradian*, 29.2 (2004), 75–95.

Brooker, Peter, and Andrew Thacker (eds), *The Oxford Critical and Cultural History of Modernist Magazines: Volume II, North America 1894–1960* (Oxford: Oxford University Press, 2012).

Brooks, Peter, *Realist Vision* (New Haven: Yale University Press, 2005).

Broughton, Trev Lynn, *Men of Letters, Writing Lives: Masculinity and Literary Auto/Biography in the Late Victorian Period* (London: Routledge, 1999).

Brown, Dennis, 'But One is English: Ford's Poetry 1893–1921', in Dennis Brown and Jenny Plastow (eds), *Ford Madox Ford and Englishness*, International Ford Madox Ford Studies 5 (Amsterdam: Rodopi, 2006), pp. 255–74.

Brown, Dennis, and Jenny Plastow (eds), *Ford Madox Ford and Englishness*, International Ford Madox Ford Studies 5 (Amsterdam: Rodopi, 2006).

Brown, Dennis, and Jenny Plastow, Introduction, in Dennis Brown and Jenny Plastow (eds), *Ford Madox Ford and Englishness*, International Ford Madox Ford Studies 5 (Amsterdam: Rodopi, 2006), pp. 13–19.

Burgess, Anthony, *Earthly Powers* (Harmondsworth: Penguin, 1997).

Butler, Judith, 'Bodily Inscriptions, Performative Subversions', *The Judith Butler Reader*, ed. Sarah Salih (Oxford: Blackwell, 2004), pp. 90–118.

Byatt, A.S., Introduction, in Ford Madox Ford, *The Fifth Queen* (London: Penguin, 1999), pp. vii–xvi.

Cassell, Richard, *Ford Madox Ford: A Study of His Novels* (Baltimore: Johns Hopkins University Press, 1961).

Chantler, Ashley, 'Ford's Pre-War Poetry and the "Rotting City"', in Sara Haslam (ed.), *Ford Madox Ford and the City*, International Ford Madox Ford Studies 4 (Amsterdam: Rodopi, 2005), pp. 111–29.

Chantler, Ashley, 'Editing Ford Madox Ford's Poetry', in Jason Harding (ed.), *Ford Madox Ford, Modernist Magazines and Editing*, International Ford Madox Ford Studies 9 (Amsterdam: Rodopi, 2010), pp. 253–65.

Chantler, Ashley, '"In This Dead-Dawning Century": Ford Madox Ford's Edwardian Poetry', in Laura Colombino and Max Saunders (eds), *The Edwardian Ford Madox Ford*, International Ford Madox Ford Studies 12 (Amsterdam: Rodopi, 2013), pp. 91–103.

Cheng, Vincent J., 'English Behaviour and Repression: *A Call: The Tale of Two Passions*', in Robert Hampson and Tony Davenport (eds), *Ford Madox Ford: A Reappraisal*, International Ford Madox Ford Studies 1 (Amsterdam: Rodopi, 2002), pp. 105–31.

Cheng, Vincent J., 'A Chronology of *The Good Soldier*', *English Language Notes*, 24 (1986), 91–7; reprinted in Ford Madox Ford, *The Good Soldier*, second edition, ed. Martin Stannard (New York: Norton, 2012), pp. 391–5.

Childs, Peter, *Modernism* (London: Routledge, 2000).

Christensen, Carolyn, Introduction, in Carolyn Christensen (ed.), *A New Woman Reader* (Peterborough, Ontario: Broadview, 2001), pp. ix–xiv.

Cianci, Giovanni, 'Three Memories of a Night: Ford's Impressionism in the Great London Vortex', in Robert Hampson and Max Saunders (eds), *Ford Madox Ford's Modernity*, International Ford Madox Ford Studies 2 (Amsterdam: Rodopi, 2003), pp. 47–58.

Colombino, Laura, *Ford Madox Ford: Vision, Visuality and Writing* (Oxford: Peter Lang, 2008).

Colombino, Laura (ed.), *Ford Madox Ford and Visual Culture*, International Ford Madox Ford Studies 8 (Amsterdam: Rodopi, 2009).

Colombino, Laura, and Max Saunders (eds), *The Edwardian Ford Madox Ford*, International Ford Madox Ford Studies 12 (Amsterdam: Rodopi, 2013).

Connolly, Cyril, *The Evening Colonnade* (San Diego: Harcourt Jovanovich, 1975).

Conrad, Jessie, 'Correspondence', *Times Literary Supplement* (4 Dec. 1924), 826.

Conrad, Joseph, *Chance: A Tale in Two Parts* (London: Penguin, 1974).

Conrad, Joseph, *Within the Tides* (London: Penguin, 1978).

Conrad, Joseph, Preface, *The Nigger of the 'Narcissus'*, ed. Robert Kimbrough (New York: Norton, 1979), pp. 145–8.

Conrad, Joseph, *Lord Jim: A Tale* (London: Penguin, 1989).

Conrad, Joseph, *Under Western Eyes* (New York: Random House, 2001).

Conrad, Joseph, *Heart of Darkness and Other Tales*, ed. Cedric Watts (Oxford: Oxford University Press, 2002).

Conrad, Joseph, and Ford Madox Ford, *Romance: A Novel* (London: Smith, Elder, 1903).

Conrad, Joseph, and Ford Madox Ford, *The Inheritors: An Extravagant Story* (Garden City: Doubleday, Page, 1920).

Cook, Cornelia, 'Constructions and Reconstructions: *No Enemy*', in Robert Hampson and Max Saunders (eds), *Ford Madox Ford's Modernity*, International Ford Madox Ford Studies 2 (Amsterdam: Rodopi, 2003), pp. 191–205.

Coyle, John, 'Mourning and Rumour in Ford and Proust', in Paul Skinner (ed.), *Ford Madox Ford's Literary Contacts*, International Ford Madox Ford Studies 6 (Amsterdam: Rodopi, 2007), pp. 113–20.

Davie, Donald, *Ezra Pound* (Chicago: University of Chicago Press, 1982).

Davies, Laurence, and Gene M. Moore (eds), *The Collected Letters of Joseph Conrad: Volume 8, 1923–1924* (Cambridge: Cambridge University Press, 2008).

Davis, Philip, 'The Saving Remnant', in Dennis Brown and Jenny Plastow (eds), *Ford Madox Ford and Englishness*, International Ford Madox Ford Studies 5 (Amsterdam: Rodopi, 2006), pp. 21–35.

Edwards, Colin, 'City Burlesque: The Pleasures of Paranoia in Ford's *Mister Bosphorus and the Muses*', in Sara Haslam (ed.), *Ford Madox Ford and the City*, International Ford Madox Ford Studies 4 (Amsterdam: Rodopi, 2005), pp. 93–109.

Edwards, Colin, 'Dancing in the Mud: Bunting's Documentary Tradition and the Anecdotage of Ford Madox Ford', in Christopher Meredith (ed.), *Moment of Earth: Poems and Essays in Honour of Jeremy Hooker* (Aberystwyth: Celtic Studies, 2007), pp. 101–13.

Eliot, T.S., 'Reflections on Contemporary Poetry', *Egoist*, 4.10 (Nov. 1917), 151.

Eliot, T.S., *Selected Prose of T.S. Eliot*, ed. Frank Kermode (New York: Harvest, 1975).

Eliot, T.S., *Collected Poems: 1909–1962* (London: Faber and Faber, 2002).

Feltes, Nick, *Modes of Production of Victorian Novels* (Chicago: University of Chicago Press, 1989).

Ferber, Michael, *A Dictionary of Literary Symbols* (Cambridge: Cambridge University Press, 1999).

Ford, Ford Madox, *The Brown Owl: A Fairy Story* (London: T. Fisher Unwin, 1891).

Ford, Ford Madox, Preface, in Guy de Maupassant, *Stories from De Maupassant*, trans. E[lsie] M[artindale] (London: Duckworth, 1903), pp. vii–xxiii.

Ford, Ford Madox, 'The Baron (A Love Story)', *Macmillan's*, 87 (Feb. 1903), 304–20.

Ford, Ford Madox, *The Soul of London: A Survey of a Modern City* (London: Alston Rivers, 1905).

Ford, Ford Madox, *Hans Holbein the Younger: A Critical Monograph* (London: Duckworth; New York: Dutton, 1905).

Ford, Ford Madox, *An English Girl: A Romance* (London: Methuen, 1907).

Ford, Ford Madox, *The Pre-Raphaelite Brotherhood: A Critical Monograph* (London: Duckworth, 1907).

Ford, Ford Madox, *The Spirit of the People: An Analysis of the English Mind* (London: Alston Rivers, 1907).

Ford, Ford Madox, 'The Critical Attitude: English Literature of To-day II', *English Review*, 3 (1909), 655–72.

Ford, Ford Madox, 'The Future in London', in W.W. Hutchings (ed.), *London Town Past and Present*, 2 vols (London: Cassell, 1909).

Ford, Ford Madox, 'The Critical Attitude: Women's Suffrage – The Circulating Libraries – The Drama – Fine Arts, Etc.', *English Review*, 4 (1910), 329–46.

Ford, Ford Madox, *Ancients Lights and Certain New Reflections: Being the Memories of a Young Man* (London: Chapman and Hall, 1911).

Ford, Ford Madox, 'Joseph Conrad', *English Review,* 10 (1911), 68–83.

Ford, Ford Madox, *The Critical Attitude* (London: Duckworth, 1911).

Ford, Ford Madox, *Henry James: A Critical Study* (London: Martin Secker, 1913).

Ford, Ford Madox, *Mr. Fleight* (London: Howard Latimer, 1913).

Ford, Ford Madox, 'The Poet's Eye', *New Freewoman*, 1.6 (1 Sept. 1913), 107–110.

Ford, Ford Madox, *Collected Poems* (London: Max Goschen, 1914).

Ford, Madox Ford, 'Literary Portraits – XX: Mr. Gilbert Cannan and "Old Mole"', *Outlook*, 33 (24 Jan. 1914), 110–11.

Ford, Ford Madox, 'Literary Portraits – XXXIII. Mr. Sturge Moore and "The Sea is Kind"', *Outlook*, 33 (25 Apr. 1914), 560.

Ford, Ford Madox, 'On Impressionism', *Poetry and Drama*, 2 (June and Dec. 1914), 167–75, 323–4.

Ford, Ford Madox, 'In October 1914', *Outlook*, 34 (24 Oct. 1914), 523.

Ford, Ford Madox, *When Blood is Their Argument: An Analysis of Prussian Culture* (London: Hodder and Stoughton, 1915).

Ford, Ford Madox, *Between St. Dennis and St. George: A Sketch of Three Civilisations* (London: Hodder and Stoughton, 1915).

Ford, Ford Madox, *On Heaven and Poems Written on Active Service* (London: John Lane, 1918).

Ford, Ford Madox, *Thus to Revisit: Some Reminiscences* (London: Chapman and Hall, 1921).

Ford, Ford Madox, *The Marsden Case: A Romance* (London: Duckworth, 1923).

Ford, Ford Madox, *Women & Men* (Paris: Three Mountains Press, 1923).

Ford, Ford Madox, *Joseph Conrad: A Personal Remembrance* (London: Duckworth, 1924).

Ford, Ford Madox, 'Stocktaking II', *transatlantic review*, 2 (Dec. 1924), 684.

Ford, Ford Madox, 'The Passing of Toryism', *McNaught's Monthly*, 5.6 (June 1926), 175.

Ford, Ford Madox, *New York Is Not America* (London: Duckworth, 1927).

Ford, Madox Ford, 'Those Were the Days', in *Imagist Anthology 1930* (London: Chatto and Windus, 1930).

Ford, Ford Madox, 'Techniques', *Southern Review*, 1 (1935), 20–35.

Ford, Ford Madox, *Collected Poems* (New York: Oxford University Press, 1936).

Ford, Ford Madox, 'London Re-Visited', *London Mercury*, 35 (Dec. 1936), 177–84.

Ford, Ford Madox, *Great Trade Route* (London: George Allen and Unwin, 1937).

Ford, Ford Madox, *Mightier Than the Sword* (London: Allen and Unwin, 1938).

Ford, Ford Madox, *Critical Writings of Ford Madox Ford*, ed. Frank MacShane (Lincoln: University of Nebraska Press, 1964).

Ford, Ford Madox, *Letters of Ford Madox Ford*, ed. Richard M. Ludwig (Princeton: Princeton University Press, 1965).

Ford, Ford Madox, *A Call: The Tale of Two Passions* (Manchester: Carcanet Press, 1984).

Ford, Ford Madox, *The Ford Madox Ford Reader*, ed. Sondra J. Stang (Manchester: Carcanet Press, 1986).

Ford, Ford Madox, *Ladies Whose Bright Eyes* (Manchester: Carcanet Press, 1988).

Ford, Ford Madox, *A History of Our Own Times*, ed. Solon Beinfeld and Sondra J. Stang (Manchester: Carcanet Press, 1989).

Ford, Ford Madox, *The Rash Act* (Manchester: Carcanet Press, 1992).

Ford, Ford Madox, *The Correspondence of Ford Madox Ford and Stella Bowen*, ed. Sondra J. Stang and Karen Cochran (Bloomington: Indiana University Press, 1993).

Ford, Ford Madox, *The English Novel* (Manchester: Carcanet Press, 1997).

Ford, Ford Madox, *Selected Poems*, ed. Max Saunders (Manchester: Carcanet Press, 1997).

Ford, Ford Madox, *The Fifth Queen* (London: Penguin, 1999).

Ford, Ford Madox, *Return to Yesterday*, ed. Bill Hutchings (Manchester: Carcanet Press, 1999).

Ford, Ford Madox, *War Prose*, ed. Max Saunders (Manchester: Carcanet Press, 1999).

Ford, Ford Madox, *No Enemy: A Tale of Reconstruction*, ed. Paul Skinner (Manchester: Carcanet Press, 2002).

Ford, Ford Madox, *Critical Essays*, ed. Max Saunders and Richard Stang (Manchester: Carcanet Press, 2002).

Ford, Ford Madox, *England and the English*, ed. Sara Haslam (Manchester: Carcanet Press, 2003).

Ford, Ford Madox, *It Was the Nightingale,* ed. John Coyle (Manchester: Carcanet Press, 2007).

Ford, Ford Madox, *Some Do Not . . .*, ed. Max Saunders (Manchester: Carcanet Press, 2010).

Ford, Ford Madox, *No More Parades*, ed. Joseph Wiesenfarth (Manchester: Carcanet Press, 2011).

Ford, Ford Madox, *A Man Could Stand Up –*, ed. Sara Haslam (Manchester: Carcanet Press, 2011).

Ford, Ford Madox, *Last Post*, ed. Paul Skinner (Manchester: Carcanet Press, 2011).

Ford, Ford Madox, *The Good Soldier*, second edition, ed. Martin Stannard (New York: Norton, 2012).

Forster, E.M., *Howards End* (London: Penguin, 2000).

Foster, R.F., *W.B. Yeats: A Life, I: The Apprentice Mage, 1865–1914* (Oxford: Oxford University Press, 1997).

Fowles, Anthony, *Ford Madox Ford: The Principal Fiction* (London: Greenwich Exchange, 2002).

Frayn, Andrew, '"*This* battle was not over": *Parade's End* as a Transitional Text in the Development of Disenchanted First World War Literature', in Andrzej Gąsiorek and Daniel Moore (eds), *Ford Madox Ford: Literary Networks and Cultural Transformations*, International Ford Madox Ford Studies 7 (Amsterdam: Rodopi, 2008), pp. 201–16.

Garnett, Edward, 'Review of *Joseph Conrad: A Personal Remembrance*', *Nation and Athenaeum,* 36 (6 Dec. 1924), 366, 368.

Garnett, Edward, 'Review of *Joseph Conrad: A Personal Remembrance*', *Weekly Westminster* (14 Feb. 1925), 473.

Gąsiorek, Andrzej, 'The Politics of Cultural Nostalgia: History and Tradition in Ford Madox Ford's *Parade's End*', *Literature and History*, 3rd series, 11.2 (2002), 52–77.

Gąsiorek, Andrzej, '"Content to be Superseded?": Ford in the Great London Vortex', in Andrzej Gąsiorek and Daniel Moore (eds), *Ford Madox Ford: Literary Networks and Cultural Transformations*, International Ford Madox Ford Studies 7 (Amsterdam: Rodopi, 2008), pp. 81–104.

Giddens, Anthony, *The Consequences of Modernity* (Cambridge: Polity Press, 1990).

Ginner, Charles, 'Neo-Realism', *New Age*, 14.9 (1 Jan. 1914), 271–2.

Goldring, Douglas, *The Last Pre-Raphaelite: A Record of the Life and Writings of Ford Madox Ford* (London: Macdonald, 1948).

Goodheart, Eugene, 'What Dowell Knew: A Reading of *The Good Soldier*', *Antaeus*, 56 (1986), 70–80; reprinted in Ford Madox Ford, *The Good Soldier*, second edition, ed. Martin Stannard (New York: Norton, 2012), pp. 382–91.

Gorman, Herbert, [Untitled], *New York Herald Tribune Books* (29 Dec. 1929), 5.

Gose, Elliott B. Jr., 'Reality to Romance: A Study of Ford's *Parade's End*', *College English*, 17.8 (May 1956), 447.

Green, Robert, *Ford Madox Ford: Prose and Politics* (Cambridge: Cambridge University Press, 1981).

Greene, Graham, Introduction, in Ford Madox Ford, *The Bodley Head Ford Madox Ford*, 5 vols (London: Bodley Head, 1962–71), I, pp. 7–12.

Gregory, Adrian, *The Silence of Memory: Armistice Day, 1919–1946* (Oxford: Berg, 1994).

Gupta, Suman, and David Johnson (eds), *A Twentieth-Century Literature Reader: Texts and Debates* (Abingdon: Routledge, 2005).

Hale, Dorothy J., 'Henry James and the Invention of Novel Theory', in Jonathan Freedman (ed.), *The Cambridge Companion to Henry James* (Cambridge: Cambridge University Press, 1998), pp. 79–101.

Hampson, Robert, 'Travellers, Dreamers and Visitors: Ford and Fantasy', in Robert Hampson and Tony Davenport (eds), *Ford Madox Ford: A Reappraisal*, International Ford Madox Ford Studies 1 (Amsterdam: Rodopi, 2002), pp. 31–57.

Hampson, Robert, and Tony Davenport (eds), *Ford Madox Ford: A Reappraisal*, International Ford Madox Ford Studies 1 (Amsterdam: Rodopi, 2002).

Harding, Jason (ed.), *Ford Madox Ford, Modernist Magazines and Editing*, International Ford Madox Ford Studies 9 (Amsterdam: Rodopi, 2010).

Harvey, David Dow, *Ford Madox Ford: 1873–1939: A Bibliography of Works and Criticism* (Princeton: Princeton University Press, 1962).

Haslam, Sara, *Fragmenting Modernism: Ford Madox Ford, the Novel and the Great War* (Manchester: Manchester University Press, 2002).

Haslam, Sara, Introduction, in Ford Madox Ford, *England and the English* (Manchester: Carcanet, 2003), pp. xiii–xxvii.

Haslam, Sara, 'The Rash Act and Henry for Hugh: A Fordian History of Self-Construction', in Joseph Wiesenfarth (ed.), *History and Representation in Ford Madox Ford's Writings*, International Ford Madox Ford Studies 3 (Amsterdam: Rodopi, 2004), pp. 121–34.

Haslam, Sara, 'Making a Text the Fordian Way: *Between St. Dennis and St. George*, Propaganda and the First World War', in Mary Hammond and Shafquat Towheed (eds), *Publishing the First World War: Essays in Book History* (Basingstoke: Palgrave Macmillan, 2007), pp. 202–14.

Haslam, Sara, 'The Prophet and the Sceptic: George Eliot and Ford Madox Ford', in Paul Skinner (ed.), *Ford Madox Ford's Literary Contacts*, International Ford Madox Ford Studies 6 (Amsterdam: Rodopi, 2007), pp. 49–62.

Haslam, Sara, 'From Conversation to Humiliation: *Parade's End* and the Eighteenth Century', in Ashley Chantler and Rob Hawkes (eds), *Ford Madox Ford's Parade's End: The First World War, Culture, and Modernity*, International Ford Madox Ford Studies 13 (Amsterdam: Rodoi, 2014), pp. 37–51.

Haste, Cate, *Rules of Desire: Sex in Britain: World War 1 to the Present* (London: Pimlico, 1992).

Hawkes, Rob, 'Personalities of Paper: Characterisation in *A Call* and *The Good Soldier*', in Andrzej Gąsiorek and Daniel Moore (eds), *Ford Madox Ford: Literary Networks and Cultural Transformations*, International Ford Madox Ford Studies 7 (Amsterdam: Rodopi, 2008), pp. 43–60.

Hawkes, Rob, 'Visuality vs. Temporality: Plotting and Depiction in *The Fifth Queen* and *Ladies Whose Bright Eyes*', in Laura Colombino (ed.), *Ford Madox Ford and Visual Culture*, International Ford Madox Ford Studies 8 (Amsterdam: Rodopi, 2009), pp. 97–108.

Hawkes, Rob, 'Trusting in Provence: Financial Crisis in The Rash Act and Henry for Hugh', in Dominique Lemarchal and Claire Davison-Pégon (eds), *Ford Madox Ford and Provence*, International Ford Madox Ford Studies 10 (Amsterdam: Rodopi, 2011), pp. 229–42.

Hawkes, Rob, *Ford Madox Ford and the Misfit Moderns: Edwardian Fiction and the First World War* (Basingstoke: Palgrave Macmillan, 2012).

Heaney, Seamus, *North* (London: Faber and Faber, 1975).

Hemingway, Ernest, *A Farewell to Arms* (London: Arrow, 1994).

Hemingway, Ernest, *A Moveable Feast* (London: Arrow, 1996).

Henighan, T.J., '*The Desirable Alien*: A Source for Ford Madox Ford's *The Good Soldier*', *Twentieth Century Literature*, 11.1 (Apr. 1965), 25–9.

Henstra, Sarah, 'Ford and the Cost of Englishness: "Good Soldiering" as Performative Practice', *Studies in the Novel*, 39.2 (Summer 2007), 177–95.

Hibberd, Dominic, *Wilfred Owen: A New Biography* (London: Weidenfeld and Nicolson, 2002).

Hobsbawm, Eric, and Terence Ranger (eds), *The Invention of Tradition* (Cambridge: Cambridge University Press, 2007).

Hodges, Elizabeth, 'Sight and Scale in *Parade's End*', in Ashley Chantler and Rob Hawkes (eds), *Ford Madox Ford's Parade's End: The First World War, Culture, and Modernity*, International Ford Madox Ford Studies 13 (Amsterdam: Rodopi, 2014), pp. 107–18.

Hoffmann, Karen A., '"Am I no better than a eunuch?": Narrating Masculinity and Empire in Ford Madox Ford's *The Good Soldier*', *Journal of Modern Literature*, 27.3 (2004), 30–46; reprinted in Ford Madox Ford, *The Good Soldier*, second edition, ed. Martin Stannard (New York: Norton, 2012), pp. 404–12.

Hoffman, Michael J., and Patrick D. Murphy (eds), *Essentials of the Theory of Fiction* (Durham: Duke University Press, 1996).

Horne, Philip, 'Absent-Mindedness: Ford on the Phone', in Paul Skinner (ed.), *Ford Madox Ford's Literary Contacts*, International Ford Madox Ford Studies 6 (Amsterdam: Rodopi, 2007), pp. 17–34.

Hunt, Violet, *The Desirable Alien: At Home in Germany*, with preface and two additional chapters by Ford Madox Hueffer (London: Chatto and Windus, 1913).

Hunt, Violet, *The Flurried Years* (London: Hurst and Blackett, 1926).

Hunter, Jefferson, *Edwardian Fiction* (Cambridge, MA: Harvard University Press, 1982).

Hynes, Samuel, *Edwardian Occasions: Essays on English Writing in the Early Twentieth Century* (London: Routledge and Kegan Paul, 1972).

Hynes, Samuel, 'The Epistemology of *The Good Soldier*', *Sewanee Review*, 69.2 (1961), 225–35; reprinted in Ford Madox Ford, *The Good Soldier*, second edition, ed. Martin Stannard (New York: Norton, 2012), pp. 327–34.

Jain, Anurag, 'When Propaganda is Your Argument: Ford and First World War Propaganda', in Dennis Brown and Jenny Plastow (eds), *Ford Madox Ford and Englishness*, International Ford Madox Ford Studies 5 (Amsterdam: Rodopi, 2006), pp. 163–75.

Jacobs, Carol, 'The (too) Good Soldier: "a real story"', *Telling Time* (Baltimore: Johns Hopkins University Press, 1992), pp. 75–94; reprinted in Ford Madox Ford, *The Good Soldier*, second edition, ed. Martin Stannard (New York: Norton, 2012), pp. 354–61.

James, Henry, *The Art of Criticism: Henry James on the Theory and Practice of Fiction*, ed. William Veeder and Susan M. Griffin (Chicago: University of Chicago Press, 1986).

James, Henry, *The Tragic Muse* (Harmondsworth: Penguin, 1995).

Johnson, Lionel, *The Art of Thomas Hardy* (London: Bodley Head, 1923).

Jones, Peter (ed.), *Imagist Poetry* (Harmondsworth: Penguin, 1981).

Joyce, James, *Dubliners* (London: Penguin, 2000).

Judd, Alan, *Ford Madox Ford* (London: Collins, 1990).

Kaplan, Carola M., and Anne B. Simpson (eds), *Seeing Double: Revisioning Edwardian and Modernist Literature* (New York: St Martin's Press, 1996).

Karl, Frederick R., and Laurence Davies (eds), *The Collected Letters of Joseph Conrad: Volume 1, 1861–1897* (Cambridge: Cambridge University Press, 1983).

Karl, Frederick R., and Laurence Davies (eds), *The Collected Letters of Joseph Conrad: Volume 2, 1898–1902* (Cambridge: Cambridge University Press, 1986).

Karl, Frederick R., and Laurence Davies (eds), *The Collected Letters of Joseph Conrad: Volume 3, 1903–1907* (Cambridge: Cambridge University Press, 1988).

Kenner, Hugh, 'The Poetics of Speech', in Richard A. Cassell (ed.), *Ford Madox Ford: Modern Judgements* (London: Macmillan, 1972), pp. 169–81.

Kermode, Frank, 'Novels: Recognition and Deception', *Critical Inquiry*, 1.1 (1974), 103–21; reprinted in Ford Madox Ford, *The Good Soldier*, second edition, ed. Martin Stannard (New York: Norton, 2012), pp. 347–54.

Kolocotroni, Vassiliki, Jane Goldman and Olga Taxidoux (eds), *Modernism: An Anthology of Sources and Documents* (Edinburgh: Edinburgh University Press, 1998).

Kramer, Dale (ed.), *The Cambridge Companion to Thomas Hardy* (Cambridge: Cambridge University Press, 2003).

Kumar, Krishan, *The Making of English National Identity* (Cambridge: Cambridge University Press, 2003).

Levenson, Michael H., *A Genealogy of Modernism: A Study of English Literary Doctrine, 1908–1922* (Cambridge: Cambridge University Press, 1984).

Leed, Eric, *No Man's Land: Combat and Identity in World War 1* (Cambridge: Cambridge University Press, 1979).

Lindberg-Seyersted, Brita (ed.), *Pound/Ford: The Story of a Literary Friendship: The Correspondence Between Ezra Pound and Ford Madox Ford and Their Writings About Each Other* (New York: New Directions, 1982).

Lodge, David, *The Modes of Modern Writing: Metaphor, Metonymy, and the Typology of Modern Literature* (London: Edward Arnold, 1977).

Lowry, Bullitt, *Armistice 1918* (Kent: Kent State University Press, 1996)

MacShane, Frank, *The Life and Work of Ford Madox Ford* (London: Routledge and Kegan Paul, 1965).

MacShane, Frank (ed.), *Ford Madox Ford: The Critical Heritage* (London: Routledge and Kegan Paul, 1972).

Matthews, Stephen, 'Gender and Sexuality', in Stephen Matthews (ed.), *Modernism: A Sourcebook* (Basingstoke: Palgrave Macmillan, 2008), pp. 92–117.

Matz, Jesse, *The Modern Novel: A Short Introduction* (Oxford: Blackwell, 2004).

McCarthy, Jeffrey Mathes, '*The Good Soldier* and the War for British Modernism', *Modern Fiction Studies*, 45.2 (Summer 1999), 303–39.

McDonough, Robert E., '*Mister Bosphorus and the Muses*: History and Representation in Ford's Modern Poem', in Joseph Wiesenfarth (ed.), *History and Representation in Ford Madox Ford's Writings*, International Ford Madox Ford Studies 3 (Amsterdam: Rodopi, 2004), pp. 155–62.

Meixner, John A., *Ford Madox Ford's Novels: A Critical Study* (Minneapolis: University of Minnesota Press, 1962).

Mizener, Arthur, *The Saddest Story: A Biography of Ford Madox Ford* (London: Bodley Head, 1972).

Morris, Pam, *Realism* (London: Routledge, 2003).

Moser, Thomas C., *The Life in the Fiction of Ford Madox Ford* (Princeton: Princeton University Press, 1980).

Najder, Zdzisław, *Joseph Conrad: A Life* (Rochester, NY: Camden House, 2007).

Newbolt, Henry, *Collected Poems 1897–1907* (London: Thomas Nelson, 1910).

Nicholls, Peter, *Modernisms: A Literary Guide* (Berkeley: University of California Press, 1995).

Nicholls, Peter, 'The Poetics of Modernism', in Alex Davis and Lee M. Jenkins (eds), *The Cambridge Companion to Modernist Poetry* (Cambridge: Cambridge University Press, 2007), pp. 51–67.

North, Michael, *The Dialect of Modernism: Race, Language, and Twentieth-Century Literature* (Oxford: Oxford University Press, 1994).

Nünning, Vera, 'The Importance of Being English: European Perspectives on Englishness', *European Journal of English Studies*, 8.2 (2004), 145–58.

O'Malley, Seamus, *Making History New: Modernism and Historical Narrative* (New York: Oxford University Press, 2014).

Parrinder, Patrick, '"All that is solid melts into air": Ford and the Spirit of Edwardian England', in Joseph Wiesenfarth (ed.), *History and Representation in Ford Madox Ford's Writings*, International Ford Madox Ford Studies 3 (Amsterdam: Rodopi, 2004), pp. 5–17.

Pater, Walter, *The Renaissance: Studies in Art and Poetry* (Oxford: Oxford University Press 1998).

Pearson, Karl, from *National Life: From the Standpoint of Science*, in Mike Jay and Michael Neve (eds), *1900: A Fin-de-Siècle Reader* (Harmondsworth: Penguin, 1999), pp. 37–40.

Peters, John G., *Conrad and Impressionism* (Cambridge: Cambridge University Press, 2001).

Piette, Adam, 'War and Division in *Parade's End*', in Ashley Chantler and Rob Hawkes (eds), *Ford Madox Ford's Parade's End: The First World War, Culture, and Modernity*, International Ford Madox Ford Studies 13 (Amsterdam: Rodopi, 2014), pp. 141–52.

Plastow, Jenny, 'Englishness and Work', in Dennis Brown and Jenny Plastow (eds), *Ford Madox Ford and Englishness*, International Ford Madox Ford Studies 5 (Amsterdam: Rodopi, 2006), pp. 177–94.

Poli, Bernard J., *Ford Madox Ford and the Transatlantic Review* (Syracuse: Syracuse University Press, 1967).

Poole, Roger, 'The Real Plot-Line of Ford Madox Ford's *The Good Soldier*: An Essay in Applied Deconstruction', *Textual Practice*, 4.3 (1990), 391–427.

Poole, Roger, 'The Unknown Ford Madox Ford', in Robert Hampson and Max Saunders (eds), *Ford Madox Ford's Modernity*, International Ford Madox Ford Studies 2 (Amsterdam: Rodopi, 2003), pp. 117–36.

Pound, Ezra, *Literary Essays of Ezra Pound*, ed. T.S. Eliot (London: Faber and Faber, 1960).

Pound, Ezra, *Collected Shorter Poems*, second edition (London: Faber and Faber, 1968).

Pound, Ezra, *Selected Letters of Ezra Pound, 1907–1941*, ed. D.D. Paige (New Directions: New York, 1971).

Pound, Ezra, *Selected Prose 1909–1965*, ed. William Cookson (London: Faber and Faber, 1973).

Pound, Ezra, *The Cantos of Ezra Pound* (New York: New Directions, 1993).

Rademacher, Jörg W., 'Images of the First World War: Ford's "In October 1914" Read in the Context of Contemporary German Writers', in Paul Skinner (ed.), *Ford Madox Ford's Literary Contacts*, International Ford Madox Ford Studies 6 (Amsterdam: Rodopi, 2007), pp. 178–88.

Rainey, Lawrence (ed.), *Modernism: An Anthology* (Oxford: Blackwell, 2005).

Rau, Petra, *English Modernism, National Identity and the Germans, 1890–1950* (Farnham: Ashgate, 2009).

Reid, Fiona, *Broken Men: Shell Shock, Treatment and Recovery in Britan 1914–30* (London: Continuum, 2010).

Riede, Austin, 'The Decline of English Discourse and the American Invasion in *The Good Soldier* and *Parade's End*', in Dennis Brown and Jenny Plastow (eds), *Ford Madox Ford and Englishness*, International Ford Madox Ford Studies 5 (Amsterdam: Rodopi, 2006), pp. 211–24.

Reynolds, Stephen, 'Autobiografiction', *Speaker*, new series, 15.366 (6 Oct. 1906), 28, 30.

Ruskin, John, 'Of Kings' Treasuries', *Unto This Last and Other Writings*, ed. Clive Wilmer (Oxford: Oxford University Press, 1985), pp. 255–87.

Ruskin, John, from *Sesame and Lilies*, in Josephine M. Guy (ed.), *The Victorian Age: An Anthology of Sources and Documents* (London: Routledge, 1998), pp. 505–19.

Sackville-West, Vita, *The Edwardians* (London: Virago, 2003).

Sassoon, Siegfried, *Memoirs of a Fox-Hunting Man* (London: Faber and Gwyer, 1928).

Sassoon, Siegfried, *Collected Poems 1908–1956* (London: Faber and Faber, 1982).

Saunders, Max, *Ford Madox Ford: A Dual Life*, 2 vols (Oxford: Oxford University Press, 1996).

Saunders, Max, 'Ford Madox Ford: Further Bibliographies', *English Literature in Transition*, 43.2 (2000), 131–205.

Saunders, Max, 'Ford, the City, Impressionism and Modernism', in Sara Haslam (ed.), *Ford Madox Ford and the City*, International Ford Madox Ford Studies 4 (Amsterdam: Rodopi, 2005), pp. 67–80.

Saunders, Max, General Editor's Preface, in Dennis Brown and Jenny Plastow (eds), *Ford Madox Ford and Englishness*, International Ford Madox Ford Studies 5 (Amsterdam: Rodopi, 2006), pp. 9–11.

Saunders, Max, 'Ford Madox Ford and Nomadic Modernism', in Giovanni Cianci, Caroline Patey and Sara Sullam (eds), *Transits: The Nomadic Geographies of Anglo-American Modernism* (Bern: Peter Lang, 2010), pp. 77–100.

Saunders, Max, *Self Impression: Life-Writing, Autobiografiction and the Forms of Modern Literature* (Oxford: Oxford University Press, 2010).

Saunders, Max, 'Ford's Thought-Experiments: Impressionism, Place, History, and "the frame of mind that is Provence"', in Dominique Lemarchal and Claire Davison-Pégon (eds), *Ford Madox Ford, France and Provence*, International Ford Madox Ford Studies 10 (Amsterdam: Rodopi, 2011), pp. 259–76.

Saunders, Max, '"All these fellows are ourselves": Ford Madox Ford, Race and Europe', in Len Platt (ed.), *Modernism and Race* (Cambridge: Cambridge University Press, 2011), pp. 39–57.

Schorer, Mark, 'The Good Novelist in *The Good Soldier*', *Princeton University Library Chronicle*, 9 (1948), 128–33; revised in *Horizon* (1949), 132–8; reprinted in Ford Madox Ford, *The Good Soldier*, second edition, ed. Martin Stannard (New York: Norton, 2012), pp. 321–26.

Schwartz, Sanford, *The Matrix of Modernism: Pound, Eliot, and Early-Twentieth Century Thought* (Princeton: Princeton University Press, 1985).

Secor, Robert, and Marie Secor (eds), *The Return of the Good Soldier: Ford Madox Ford and Violet Hunt's 1917 Diary* (Victoria: English Literary Studies, University of Victoria, 1983).

Shakespeare, William, *Complete Works*, ed. Stanley Wells and Gary Taylor (Oxford: Clarendon Press, 1986).

Simmel, Georg, from 'The Metropolis and Mental Life', in Vassiliki Kolocotroni, Jane Goldman and Olga Taxidou (eds), *Modernism: An Anthology of Sources and Documents* (Edinburgh: Edinburgh University Press, 1998), pp. 51–9.

Sinfield, Alan, *The Wilde Century: Effeminacy, Oscar Wilde and the Queer Moment* (London: Cassell, 1994).

Skinner, Paul, 'Poor Dan Robin: Ford Madox Ford's Poetry', in Robert Hampson and Tony Davenport (eds), *Ford Madox Ford: A Reappraisal*, Ford Madox Ford Studies 1 (Amsterdam: Rodopi, 2002), pp. 79–103.

Skinner, Paul, 'The Painful Processes of Reconstruction: History in *No Enemy* and *Last Post*', in Joseph Weisenfarth (ed.), *History and Representation in Ford Madox Ford's Writings*, International Ford Madox Ford Studies 3 (Amsterdam: Rodopi, 2004), pp. 65–76.

Skinner, Paul (ed.), *Ford Madox Ford's Literary Contacts*, International Ford Madox Ford Studies 6 (Amsterdam: Rodopi, 2006).

Skinner, Paul, 'Tietjens Walking, Ford Talking', in Ashley Chantler and Rob Hawkes (eds), *Ford Madox Ford's Parade's End: The First World War, Culture, and Modernity*, International Ford Madox Ford Studies 13 (Amsterdam: Rodopi, 2014), pp. 129–40.

Sorum, Eve, 'Mourning and Moving On: Life After War in Ford Madox Ford's *The Last Post*', in Patricia Rae (ed.), *Modernism and Mourning* (Lewisburg: Bucknell University Press, 2007), pp. 154–67.

Snitow, Ann Barr, *Ford Madox Ford and the Voice of Uncertainty* (Baton Rouge: Louisiana State University Press, 1984).

Stanford, Derek, '"The Best Poem Yet written in the Twentieth-Century Fashion": A Discursive Note on Ford Madox Ford's "On Heaven"', *Agenda*, 27.4/28.1 (1989/1990), 110–19.

Stang, Sondra J., and Carl Smith, '"Music for a While": Ford's Compositions for Voice and Piano', *Contemporary Literature*, 30.2 (1989), 183–223.

Stannard, Martin, 'Cutting Remarks: What Went Missing From *The Good Soldier*', in Jason Harding (ed.), *Ford Madox Ford, Modernist Magazines and Editing*, International Ford Madox Ford Studies 9 (Amsterdam: Rodopi, 2010), pp. 229–42.

Stevenson, Randall, *Modernist Fiction*, revised edition (Hemel Hempstead: Prentice Hall, 1998).

Symons, Arthur, 'The Decadent Movement in Literature', *Harper's New Monthly Magazine*, 87 (1893), 858–67.

Tate, Trudi, *Modernism, History and the First World War* (Manchester: Manchester University Press, 1998).

Tennyson, Alfred, *The Major Works*, ed. Adam Roberts (Oxford: Oxford University Press, 2000).

Thirlwell, Angela, 'From Paint To Print – Grandfather's Legacy', in *Ford Madox Ford and Visual Culture*, ed. Laura Colombino, International Ford Madox Ford Studies 8 (Amsterdam: Rodopi, 2009), pp. 29–38.

Thirlwell, Angela, 'Ford's Provence: A Pre-Raphaelite Vision', in Dominique Lemarchal and Claire Davison-Pégon (eds), *Ford Madox Ford, France and Provence*, International Ford Madox Ford Studies 10 (Amsterdam: Rodopi, 2011), pp. 193–202.

Thomas, Edward, *Poet to Poet: Edward Thomas's Letters to Walter de la Mare*, ed. Judy Kendall (Bridgend: Seren, 2012).

Thornton, R.K.R. (ed.), *Poetry of the 'Nineties* (Harmondsworth: Penguin, 1970).

Tóibín, Colm, 'Outsiders in England and the Art of Being Found Out', in Andrzej Gąsiorek and Daniel Moore (eds), *Ford Madox Ford: Literary Networks and Cultural Transformations*, International Ford Madox Ford Studies 7 (Amsterdam: Rodopi, 2008), pp. 61–80.

Tonson, Jacob [Arnold Bennett], 'Books and Persons', *New Age*, 3.21 (1908), 412.

Tosh, John, 'What Should Historians Do with Masculinity? Reflections on Nineteenth-Century History', *History Workshop Journal*, 38 (1994), 179–202.

Turda, Marius, *Modernism and Eugenics* (Basingstoke: Palgrave Macmillan, 2010)

Vandevelde, Tom, '"Are You Going to Mind the Noise?": Mapping the Soundscape of *Parade's End*', in Ashley Chantler and Rob Hawkes (eds), *Ford Madox Ford's Parade's End: The First World War, Culture, and Modernity*, International Ford Madox Ford Studies 13 (Amsterdam: Rodopi, 2014), pp. 53–66.

Various, 'A Geography of Modernism', in Malcolm Bradbury and James McFarlane (eds), *Modernism: A Guide to European Literature 1890–1930* (London: Penguin, 1991), pp. 95–190.

Various, 'Modernity and the City', in Michael H. Whitworth (ed.), *Modernism* (Oxford: Blackwell, 2007), pp. 181–215.

Walder, Dennis (ed.), *The Realist Novel* (London: Routledge, 1995).

Watt, Ian, *Conrad in the Nineteenth Century* (Berkeley: University of California Press, 1979).

Watts, Cedric, *Joseph Conrad: A Literary Life* (Basingstoke: Macmillan, 1989).

Waugh, Patricia, *Metafiction: The Theory and Practice of Self-Conscious Fiction* (London: Routledge, 1996).

Wells, H.G., *What is Coming?: A Foretaste of Things After the War* (London: Cassell, 1916).

Wells, H.G., *Experiment in Autobiography*, 2 vols (London: Victor Gollancz and Cresset Press, 1934).

Wells, H.G., *Tono-Bungay* (London: Penguin, 2005).

West, Rebecca, 'Imagisme', *New Freewoman*, 1.5 (15 Aug. 1913), 86–7.

West, Rebecca, 'Mr. Hueffer's New Novel', *Daily News and Leader*, 2 Apr. 1915, 6; reprinted in Ford Madox Ford, *The Good Soldier*, second edition, ed. Martin Stannard (New York: Norton, 2012), pp. 236–8.

West, Rebecca, *1900* (London: Weidenfeld and Nicolson, 1982).

Wiesenfarth, Joseph, 'The Ash-Bucket at Dawn: Ford's Art of Poetry', *Contemporary Literature*, 30.2 (1989), 240–62.

Wiesenfarth, Joseph, 'Ford's *Joseph Conrad: A Personal Remembrance* as Metafiction: Or, How Conrad Became an Elizabethan Poet', *Renascence*, 53.1 (2000), 43–60.

Wiesenfarth, Joseph, 'Coda to the City', in Sara Haslam (ed.), *Ford Madox Ford and the City*, International Ford Madox Ford Studies 4 (Amsterdam: Rodopi, 2005), pp. 131–8.

Wiesenfarth, Joseph, 'Death in the Wasteland: Ford, Wells, and Waugh', in Ashley Chantler and Rob Hawkes (eds), *Ford Madox Ford's Parade's End: The First World War, Culture, and Modernity*, International Ford Madox Ford Studies 13 (Amsterdam: Rodopi, 2014), pp. 197–206.

Wollaeger, Mark, *Modernism, Media, and Propaganda: British Narrative from 1900 to 1945* (Princeton: Princeton University Press, 2006).

Woolf, Virginia, *Collected Essays*, 4 vols (London: Hogarth Press, 1966–67).

Woolf, Virginia, *Mrs Dalloway*, ed. David Bradshaw (Oxford: Oxford University Press, 2009).

Index